THE POLITICS OF RESPONSIBILITY

THE POLITICS OF RESPONSIBILITY

CHAD LAVIN

THE UNIVERSITY OF ILLINOIS PRESS
URBANA AND CHICAGO

⊗ This book is printed on acid-free paper.

Library of Congress Cataloging-in-Publication Data
Lavin, Chad
The politics of responsibility / Chad Lavin.
p. cm.
Includes bibliographical references and index.
ISBN-13 978-0-252-03297-4 (cloth : alk. paper)
ISBN-10 0-252-03297-7 (cloth : alk. paper)
1. Responsibility. 2. Political science—Philosophy.
I. Title.
BJ1451.L38   2008
320.01'1—dc22   2007044598

Contents

Acknowledgments

I am not responsible for this. Asma Abbas, Frank Baumgartner, George Davis, Jeremy Packer, Will Roberts, Chris Russill, Hasana Sharp, Steve Smith, Heike Schotten, Holloway Sparks, John Stuhr, Iris Young, numerous copanelists, and two anonymous reviewers carefully read parts (and in some cases all) of this book and generously helped improve it. David Clinton, Nancy Maveety, Jo Ellen Miller, and Martyn Thompson found me a place to work and helped keep me there, while Ariana French, Pableaux Johnson, Edie Wolfe, and Justin Wolfe made me glad I stayed. William L. Weiss, Josephine B. Weiss, and Naomi Fischer provided tremendous financial support while I was writing. John Christman (my favorite liberal) and Nancy Love (the world's greatest advisor) contributed as much as anybody to this book; my work begins with them. And I still blame my parents for just about everything I've ever done. I met Elizabeth Mazzolini just around the time I started working on this project, and it has been a thrill responding to her ever since. Thank you all.

An earlier version of chapter 2, "Postliberal Agency in the *Brumaire*" appeared in *Rethinking Marxism* 17.3 (July 2005): 439–54 (www.tandf.co.uk/journals/titles/08935696).

Preface: Responsibility after Liberalism

These are fertile times in the study of responsibility. Recent years have brought high-profile debates over the locus of responsibility for a rash of schoolyard shootings, manifold highly publicized cases of police misconduct, unprecedented acts of international terrorism, notable increases in teen obesity and diabetes, and the unexpected meltdown of some of the world's most admired corporations. In the summer of 2004, when confronted with photographs of the tortures at the U.S. military prison at Abu Ghraib, virtually every American wanted to talk about responsibility. Unfortunately, both professional and pedestrian analyses of this affair betray not only the polemic and vitriol endemic to U.S. political discourse but also the striking poverty of a hegemonic but historically specific theory of responsibility.

Largely because of such atrocities as the Holocaust and the massacre at the Vietnamese village of My Lai, the middle of the twentieth century saw the emergence of popular, legal, and academic cottage industries in studies of responsibility. With these tragedies as their touchstones, the most visible explorations and applications of responsibility have focused on particular types of situations (discrete events) to the neglect of others (impersonal and enduring conditions of deprivation). Limited thus to discussions of events, responsibility today functions almost entirely on the terrain defined by Anglo-American criminal law, in which responsibility stems from a competent agent's willed causality: we are responsible for what we cause (with specific and notable exceptions). Even though it proves immensely difficult to assign responsibility for such striking military offenses as My Lai and Abu Ghraib, philosophers, pundits, and policy makers are at least equipped with conceptual tools that help us understand what could make somebody responsible for them. These thinkers are significantly less well equipped to assign responsibility for recalcitrant social problems that lack such visible and tangible touchstones. Determining responsibility for poverty, for instance, seems a much more unwieldy project. Thus, despite the proliferation of philosophical and political literatures on responsibility in recent decades, debates over the concept seem stagnated.

The recent debates over Abu Ghraib offer a compelling picture of this stagnation. These debates repeated almost to a letter those surrounding My Lai three decades earlier, with government and military officials unequivocally declaring that a handful of deviant soldiers (Lynndie England and a few others in the 372d Military Police Company) were responsible for the affair, while critics indicted commanding officers (especially Donald Rumsfeld) for sanctioning and perhaps even ordering the abuses. The structural similarity of these two approaches troubles the conventional wisdom that U.S. politics and culture are defined by a cleavage between those believing in personal responsibility and those emphasizing systemic coercion. Here, both ostensibly antagonistic camps ultimately reduced the issue to one of individual blame that derives from voluntary, contributory fault. The parties disagreed only with regard to the identity of the individual. Apparently, the only possible reaction to this disgraceful affair was to hold somebody—some individual or individuals—responsible.

Of course, there were other, less-audible approaches. Voices on the margins diagnosed military torture as an unfortunate but not entirely unpredictable product of a popular culture saturated with normalized violence, sadistic imagery, and American exceptionalism. Perhaps most notably, Susan Sontag (2004) argued in a much-discussed article in the New York Times Magazine that the photographs of Abu Ghraib reflected the punitive and vengeful character of the American popular spirit; "the photographs," she brusquely proclaimed, "are us." From this perspective, torture is standard operating procedure in U.S. military installations and domestic prisons; only the photographs make Abu Ghraib extraordinary. But this argument is not easily reducible to familiar understandings of what makes for responsibility and where it might lie. Is Sontag really suggesting that we—you and I—are responsible? Pointing to the deeper roots of particular instances of state brutality, and neglecting to indict anybody for the tortures, Sontag ultimately displaces rather than answers the question of responsibility. Given the pivotal role that responsibility plays in contemporary political analysis, a story like Sontag's was destined to find little resonance. This refusal to speak in the fashionable idiom all but ensured her marginalization.

Conventional discourses of responsibility might provide tidy narratives of heroes and villains (e.g., England and Rumsfeld) that can provide satisfying insights into particular events, but they offer scant resources for navigating enduring social conditions without such causes and characters. Sontag's intervention suggests that the tortures endemic to U.S. penal institutions are easy to ignore precisely because they lack the punctuations and characters that tend to inhabit the familiar narratives of responsibility. The stakes of Sontag's argument lie well beyond understanding Abu Ghraib. Her essay points to one of the great shortcomings in contemporary political discourse: the incommensurability of dominant conceptions of responsibility and enduring political urgencies.

• • •

The Politics of Responsibility is an attempt to address this shortcoming by exploring and expanding the limits of responsibility. Clearly one of the most contentious concepts in historical and contemporary political thought, responsibility inhabits familiar debates as broad as that over free will versus determinism and as narrow as that over criminal liability for military torture. Insofar as it enables us to reward or punish actors for their behaviors, it seems indispensable to any practical ordering of human affairs. But insofar as it trades in a politically and ontologically dubious theory of individual autonomy, it seems deeply problematic. This book exploits both these dimensions of responsibility—its indispensability and its inadequacy—in moving toward a more capacious and progressive theory of responsibility.

Responsibility is much more than an innocent marker of a political virtue. Ascriptions of responsibility reflect an ontology of beings in a physical universe, ideas about the structure of the human agent, and political preferences for the allocation of punishments and rewards. It has consequently been argued that my claim about the indispensability of responsibility is thoroughly modernist. Responsibility, the claim goes, becomes central in political discourse only with the rise of modern individualism and widespread belief in individual agency; many argue that it had no (or significantly less) purchase in the classical world (see, e.g., Adkins 1960, 1970). This claim that responsibility is a modern (or even liberal) concept that is disingenuously or naively read into premodern cultures has a ready complement in the charge that the postmodern turn marks an abandonment of responsibility. I argue that this modernist exceptionalism is mistaken, that responsibility is endemic to both premodern and postmodern thought and merely takes different forms in the two.

The individuated subject of modern liberalism certainly provides clear narratives of causality and responsibility that contribute to relatively straightforward management of myriad political concerns about punishment and reward. In fact, Richard Flathman (1992) argues that liberalism's overwhelming popularity today arises precisely from its seductive and deceptively clear management of these concerns with reference to an autonomous individual will. A liberal theory of agency provides a procedural theory of distributive justice via voluntary contracts, a coherent vision of criminal liability via contributory fault, and a reliable model of democratic governance via representation. Using individual agency to gratifyingly and formally navigate these unavoidable political concerns, liberalism promises clear and intuitive responses to each of the perennial concerns of political life.

But the drive to liberalism is also coerced. Because the liberal model of the willing individual is widely (if usually only implicitly) presumed to have a monopoly on the concept of agency, challenges to this model are often disciplined for sacrificing the sort of individual responsibility required for organizing and justifying our familiar political institutions. Indeed, this position asserts that liberalism has a monopoly not just on agency but on viable interventions into constitutional politics. Challenges to the autonomy of the liberal subject are freely condemned not for their lack of metaphysical or ontological rigor but for their failure to provide a compelling theory of responsibility that could provide and justify manageable principles for rewarding or punishing citizens. Consider, for instance, the disquiet with which Arendt's (1963) refusal to hold Eichmann responsible for the Holocaust was received. Refusing to indict an individual yet lacking a ready alternative, Arendt's focus on bureaucratic plodding and administrative conformity does not lend itself to any comfortable ascription of responsibility. Such a displacement of the question of responsibility is as unwelcome today as it was then—not because it is unjustified but because it is intolerable.

John Rawls (1993) evidences this intolerability when he defends liberalism not with admittedly contentious ontological claims to individual autonomy but instead with a set of political preferences for basic rights and liberties. This is, he claims, a political, not metaphysical, liberalism that is (and will continue to be) endorsed for the political results it brings. But Rawls disingenuously denies an undeniable truth: these avowed political foundations of basic rights and liberties achieve almost universal support precisely *because* of their consonance with the putatively superfluous ontological commitments. Individual rights, representative government, private property, and criminal liability are coveted and nearly universally endorsed political institutions precisely because they conform to the liberal presumptions of bounded and autonomous subjects encountering discrete objects and expressing their autonomous wills in voluntary contracts. Liberals admit this when pressed; even Rawls concedes that political liberalism rests on "everyday conceptions of persons as the basic units of thought, deliberation, and responsibility" (1993:18). As I will show, thought about responsibility typically rests upon such commonsense notions of individual autonomy—notions that Rawls calls "political, not metaphysical" but that William Connolly (1995) more properly calls "ontopolitical." Connolly's cast reveals the circularity at work in Rawlsian liberalism: though Rawls roots liberal autonomy in a political commitment to individual responsibility, this responsibility is itself rooted in an unstated commitment to individual autonomy.

Exposing the circularity inherent in liberal responsibility might allow me to score points in a theoretical brawl (or to make enemies of many erstwhile allies), but my primary stakes lie elsewhere. I aim to show not merely liberal responsibility's conceptual flaws but also its political dangers. As well, I will show how challenges to liberalism do not necessarily abandon the concept of responsibility. Alternatives to liberalism—marxism, psychoanalysis, communitarianism, feminism, and postmodernism, for example—are all too often dismissed as apolitical (or even antipolitical) for collapsing public and private in a manner that jettisons any notion of individual agency upon which to justify punishment or reward. According to this anxious liberal rejection, alternatives fail to provide any incentive to political action; they leave us in a world of utter contingency, resignation, and impotence. I argue, however, that liberalism's presumed monopoly on responsibility reflects an unfortunate restriction imposed on the concept, a restriction that both limits the domains in which the term will be useful and also renders quite viable alternatives difficult to hear.

This book makes an argument for what I call *postliberal responsibility*—a conceptual marker of a broader philosophical movement linking marxism and postmodernism, a movement I will not merely describe but use. Postliberalism begins by challenging the supposed autonomy of subjects and objects, troubling the division between phenomena that liberalism reifies; it announces the porosity of the boundaries between subject and object, structure and agent, private and public, and examines these phenomena as relations rather than self-standing entities. While such a critique certainly might inspire a nihilistic abandonment of responsibility, this seems far from inevitable. As I will show, postliberals have often endeavored to articulate a theory of responsibility free of any reified subject considered sovereign over its actions and desires. Indeed, a major goal of this book is to show how, despite explosive charges to the contrary, the postliberal subject can also be a responsible subject.

• • •

The narratives of Abu Ghraib discussed previously, remarkable in their details but utterly mundane in their contours, reflect the hegemony of liberal responsibility. Suturing responsibility to willing individuals coheres with a

theory of history as the product of heroes and villains, but it all but eliminates the concept from a story like Sontag's. As a result, Sontag is politically
marginalized for failing to organize her analysis around this coveted political concept, and political analysis narrows to focus on situations that are
compatible with the tenets of liberal responsibility. Indeed, though various
determinisms have achieved currency in both the recent and not-so-recent
past, political debates today—both academic and popular—are almost entirely cast in the terms of liberal responsibility. These debates thus carry a
prejudice *for* examining distinct events and *against* social phenomena that
lack clear causal agents. Ultimately, this prejudice provides both the source
of and fuel for liberal hegemony over responsibility, since critics of the discrete and bounded subject of philosophical liberalism relinquish any claim
to this indispensable political resource.

Responsibility thus does more than identify causality or offer justifications for punishment or reward. It both draws upon and reinscribes deeply
entrenched views of the self, and of the relationship between individuals
and institutions, in a manner that solidifies a political culture and directs
political agendas. Mary Douglas (1992) has argued that shared conceptions of
responsibility form and reinforce the bonds of social membership, expressing
as they do fundamental convictions about the possibilities of human action
and freedom and the expectations and obligations of a society's members.
This, indeed, is the overlapping consensus upon which Rawls builds and
that marks us as a liberal society, as Rawls safely defines it. But responsibility
does more than just provide a foundation for representative government,
criminal liability, and property rights. It also mediates our phenomenal experience by providing the vocabulary and grammar through which we will
comprehend and navigate our daily lives. Rawls's everyday conception of the
willing individual provides common understandings of causality, marking
perhaps the broadest contours of a liberal society intent on understanding
history as the product of human initiative instead of, say, divine power, a
phenomenology of Spirit, or a micropolitics of desire. The conception thus
focuses public attention, ideologically framing history as a sequence of events
caused by individual actors. Politically speaking, it establishes the limits of
possible and appropriate targets for political attention.

I argue that marxist and postmodern critics of liberal autonomy tend to
fuel this criticism—and thus marginalize themselves in a liberalizing culture—by avoiding explicit discussions of responsibility, treating the concept
as tainted goods. This is not to blame these critics (whom I group together as
postliberals) for their marginalization but to emphasize a profound ideologi-

cal obstacle standing between postliberal political thought and a thoroughly liberal culture. I do not claim to chart out new territory so much as to tease out themes of existing literature in order to outline this renewed theory of responsibility. Focusing on the fallacy of voluntary actions, the question for postliberalism has always been how to retain any prescriptive or normative approach to human behavior. Again, this remains a question because few contributors to this tradition even attempt to discuss this seemingly oh-so-liberal concept.

This book will examine several exceptions to this postliberal tendency. Perhaps the most notable of these exceptions today is Judith Butler, who, after a decade enduring a reputation as the poster child for critical disengagement, has emerged with a set of works on interpersonal ethics, hate speech, and political violence that explicitly—if subtly—address the question of responsibility. See, for example, her treatment of the political imperative to straightforwardly hold somebody responsible for 9/11 (2004: ch. 1). Butler bases this imperative in an ontopolitical sensibility that favors individual causality and immediate criminal punishment. By contrast, postliberal attempts to focus attention on the production of anti-American, terroristic sentiments among particular sects of Islamic fundamentalists not only displace the question of legal or moral responsibility but ask difficult questions about what makes for causality and what constitutes an event. Such displacements suggest that the causes of 9/11 were many and varied, some locatable on that calendar date, but others reaching back years into the history of Islam and the politics of the Middle East. Butler's point is that such *explanations* of an event are typically heard as so many *exonerations* of the offenders and that this translation of explanation to exoneration is facilitated—indeed, mandated—by the reduction of discourses of responsibility to tales of individuals and "their" actions. Butler argues that these explanations do not abandon the project of assigning responsibility; rather, they ask us to consider how responsibility might be rethought without the dubious narratives of heroes and villains conjuring events out of thin air. This rethinking distributes rather than disperses responsibility, emphasizing not individual martyrs and their causal actions but rather the ability to respond that is afforded to socially constituted agents.

Another critic currently working with a postliberal theory of responsibility is Iris Young.[1] Young has recently argued that contemporary anti-sweatshop movements are already working with a postliberal approach to economic responsibility. In this "rather novel" approach, she argues, "agents are responsible for injustice by virtue of their structural connection to it, even though they are not to *blame* for it" (2003:40). By protesting in front of the Gap, by appealing to consumers rather than merely to factory owners, by drawing attention to the structural relations of international trade instead of individual labor contracts, this movement resists ascribing responsibility for exploitation to any particular actors and, at its best, decouples responsibility from individual causality. It thus expands the meaning of responsibility so that it can speak to situations that lack clear causal agents or identifiable starting points. Young sees great promise in this move, abandoning the demands for contributory fault that she identifies with what she calls a "blame model" of responsibility because this model cannot deal with complicated and enduring conditions of injustice such as exploitation and homelessness. Her critique is thus a political one in that she indicts liberal responsibility for arbitrarily limiting attention on situations that conform to its presumptions and for being unable to question the background conditions against which discussions of responsibility arise.

These commentaries, each of which I will be discussing at length in coming chapters, suggest both means and reasons to challenge the liberal suturing of responsibility to causality. Butler reveals the dubious ontological presumptions that underlie claims to identify individual causality, while Young focuses more directly on the insidious political consequences of restricting political attention to issues with identifiable causal agents. Together, they demonstrate the ontopolitical inadequacies of liberal responsibility. Throughout this book, I aim to demonstrate not only the political benefits of decoupling responsibility from causality but also the way in which the very determination of causality depends upon an ideological commitment to a problematic liberal ontology. So, while Young, for example, identifies the political shortcomings of liberal responsibility by positing a distinction between responsibility and blame, I endeavor to take a further leap of challenging the notion of blame as well.

Crucially, I am interested less in debunking liberal responsibility than in demystifying it. This parallels somewhat unorthodox marxisms that resist reducing Marx's critique of ideology to an argument about "false consciousness" and instead endeavor to explain the material roots and appeals of particular modes of consciousness. In other words, when Marx criticizes Christianity, Hegelianism, and commodity fetishism as ideologies, he declares not that they are *false* but rather that they are appropriate to a particular material situation. In a sense, his critique is not that ideology is wrong but that it is entirely too right. My argument about liberal responsibility is similar; my claim that it is inadequate should not be confused with a statement that it is false. Rather, my position follows historical work that roots liberal ideology in a market society in which individuals' selves and capacities are understood as property (see MacPherson 1962). More recently, Fredric Jameson (1991) and Michael Hardt and Antonio Negri (2000, 2004) have situated postmodern challenges to the liberal individual in the movements of global capital that upset the conventional narratives of national sovereignty. That is, while a material reality organized around sovereign states and capitalist markets provides conditions conducive to the spread of possessive individualism and liberal responsibility, a global order that challenges the established institutions of representation and sovereignty similarly poses a threat to the concepts of individual will and personal responsibility. Liberal concepts become decreasingly helpful for navigating a postliberal world.

I argue that the inadequacies of liberal responsibility are threefold. First, it trades in a dubious theory of causality that arbitrarily wrests actors and events from the historical contexts that enable them. Second, it perniciously limits the range of issues that call for a response. Third, it limits the range of possible responses to those issues. I argue that as each of these inadequacies has become more visible, postliberal alternatives have begun to find wider expression. That is, as liberal responsibility proves itself incapable of dealing with myriad and urgent social issues, and as transformations in global power begin to unseat institutions of sovereignty and autonomy developed through the seventeenth century, a crisis in liberal responsibility itself has emerged. *The Politics of Responsibility* is an attempt to trace the contours of this crisis in hopes of accelerating a transformation toward a more satisfying theory of responsibility.

• • •

The book is divided into two parts. In part 1 I engage liberal and postliberal approaches to agency in order to develop a vocabulary adequate to a postliberal theory of responsibility. I show that while critics of liberalism tend to avoid overt discussions of responsibility, the fashionable focus on agency covers the same ground without the overt ideological baggage.

Chapter 1, "Responsible Subjects," situates existing approaches to responsibility within a broader debate about political agency, causality, and subjectivity. Here I demonstrate how disparate theories of subjectivity inform particular approaches to responsibility and how debates over responsibility are overtly political manifestations of ontological commitments. I show how the coherent and autonomous individual of liberalism leads quite straightforwardly to a model of a responsible subject, and I reveal the dubious ontological assumptions that underlie it as well as the problematic political positions that arise from it.

Chapter 2, "Making Marx Effective," explores one particular contribution to a postliberal theory of responsibility: that of Karl Marx. While dominant strains of marxism have tended to dismiss responsibility as a fundamentally bourgeois concept, I read Marx as struggling to articulate a theory of responsibility for which he does not have an adequate vocabulary. In a reading of *The Eighteenth Brumaire of Louis Bonaparte*, I reveal a Marx seeking to avoid both the Scylla of liberalism and the Charybdis of structuralism. Through an exaggerated use of metonymy, Marx displays the reductive nature of the process of identifying coherent and autonomous subjects. He thus displays a desire to refashion the available concepts by exploring and testing their limits; Marx tinkers with linguistic convention as a means to open the possibility to think and write beyond liberal categories.

In Chapter 3, "Judith Butler's Responsible Performance," I demonstrate how the conceptual provocation identified in chapter 2 is performed in the literature of poststructuralism. Identifying Butler's significant and largely unacknowledged debt to Marx, I argue that her work on agency and performativity complements Marx's *Brumaire*, intensifying a postliberal approach to responsibility. Butler subordinates the liberal subject to forces that precede and exceed it, but she also calls attention to the way these forces endure though ritualistic performance. Butler thus tacitly but no less strenuously emphasizes that questions of agency are *always* questions of responsibility. Because she presents a theory of agency that moves beyond liberal subjectivity, she writes on the front line of political and philosophical debates over responsibility.

Part 2 exploits the theoretical developments of part 1 to demonstrate how established theories of agency restrict not only the available range of responses to social problems but even the particular issues that will receive attention. This half of the book engages popular and academic discourses of responsibility as they surround three highly divisive issues in contemporary politics: globalization, police brutality, and abortion. Part 2 thus demonstrates how to retain a commitment to economic, legal, and ethical responsibility while avoiding the problems of its previous iterations.

In chapter 4, "Who Responds to Global Capital?" I challenge traditional marxisms for failing to present a defensible theory of responsibility. Whereas liberal economics is predicated on the sanctity of voluntary contracts, marxist critiques of contract tend merely to replace the liberal subject with a similarly reified authentic expression of economic antagonism (the proletariat).

Consequently, liberals reduce responsibility to a question of contractual obligations, whereas marxists abandon the concept entirely. By contrast, I argue that the repeated responses of myriad individual and collective agents to global capital both produce and reproduce economic relations. Thus, while the liberal subject reflects the demands of capitalist exchange and the marxist subject reflects an abstract and similarly limited alternative, the postliberal subject is formed in its responses to the injustices provoked by the demands of global capital.

Chapter 5, "Postliberal Responsibility and the Death of Amadou Diallo," turns attention away from economic power and the shortcomings of a traditionally marxist theory of agency and toward the power of the state and the inadequacies of liberalism. I argue that political and journalistic approaches to the 1999 shooting of Amadou Diallo by New York City police officers was mediated by common assumptions about responsibility for the casualties of law enforcement. Explanations of the event were restricted by the limited explanatory potential of the hegemonic notion that agency stems only from individuals. While a belief in an autonomous subject informs a political preference for aggressive and punitive approaches to crime, I show how a postliberal approach highlights the event's causal overdetermination and encourages a response that will make similar events less likely in the future.

Chapter 6, "Conceptions of Responsibility," further explores the rhetoric and implications of liberal responsibility by examining its contributions to one of the more polarizing debates in U.S. politics: abortion. Troubling both pro-life and pro-choice arguments for their reification of individual subjects (the fetus in the former case and individual women in the latter), I follow a postliberal approach that locates responsibility for abortion in the collective actors capable of responding to the situation of unwanted pregnancy. While liberal autonomy certainly constitutes a great leap forward for women, postliberal subjectivity goes further, highlighting how the liberal model of the autonomous individual places women in the impossible position of being responsible for their condition. Worse, it ultimately legitimates severe restrictions on reproductive freedom.

The conclusion explores how postliberalism reconfigures the familiar responses to political tragedies: compensation, retribution, and forgiveness. Here I show how each of these responses is predicated upon what I call liberalism's "episodic prejudice," which seeks to explain individual vulnerability as an exception rather than the rule. As a result, they reinforce an essentially antidemocratic and ahistorical model of the autonomous individual, offering palatable ways to deal with exceptional violations while continuing to deny how prosaic violations of individual autonomy form the very possibility of democratic engagement and interpersonal responsibility.

• • •

Because this project aims to highlight the untenability of established sites of responsibility, it participates in an enduring political philosophical movement that challenges the notions of individual authorship legitimating such indispensable institutions as individual rights, criminal punishment, representative government, and private property. Clearly, it would be difficult to overstate the resilience of these institutions; a theoretical challenge to the individual subject is not going to immediately discredit American commitments to private property and the imprisonment of serial killers. But this book does not aim to be a heretical or heroic reveille. Rather, it is an attempt to chart out political philosophical tendencies that themselves reflect transformation in the material groundings of these institutions. The sovereignty of the individual subject, the philosophical foundation for each of these liberal institutions, is itself today under fire not merely from postliberal political theorists but from tectonic shifts in material production and global governance. The increased importance of immaterial commodities such as computer code and customer service presents a profound challenge to the notion of autonomous individual production more appropriate to yeoman farming. Thus, the tendencies of postliberal theory are already evident in, for example, the open-source movement, calling for a revised approach to property rights in the light of the necessarily collaborative nature of intellectual production.

This book, in other words, seeks to exploit tendencies, already evident in global culture and political theory, that question the tenability of particularly fetishistic approaches to individual responsibility. In addition to renewing attention to the justification of property rights, it asks salient questions about the possibilities of global democratic governance, criminal justice, and health care by recommending more defendable metrics for understanding issues such as political representation, street and white-collar crime, and public health and illness. Insofar as liberal responsibility continues to recommend the systematic neglect of these politically urgent issues, the question might be not whether we can afford to challenge their hegemony but how much longer we can afford not to.

PART ONE

Theories of Response

ONE

Responsible Subjects

Responsibility is something of an ideological barometer in contemporary American politics. Debates over economic inequality, crime, obesity, and unplanned pregnancy are largely debates over the extent to which actors can or should be held responsible for events in and conditions of their lives. More broadly, dominant philosophical traditions struggle to articulate the stakes, possibilities, and appropriate applications of responsibility. In this chapter I chart out the contours of hegemonic approaches to responsibility by describing what I call *liberal responsibility*, revealing its dubious assumptions as well as its problematic implications. Liberal responsibility, I argue, restricts our ability to perceive problems and then suggests ways to respond to those events that receive recognition; it directs attention toward social events and conditions that conform with its suppositions while casting into a discursive neverland those conditions and events that do not.

Responsibility is often held to be an essentially liberal concept, fastened as it is to the willing individual. This territorial claim fuels ongoing culture wars and represents a significant limitation on contemporary political discourse. Although critics of liberal individualism are often held to have abandoned the concept of responsibility, thus retaining an at best questionable attachment to political action, I show how the restriction of responsibility to a liberal conception is both myopic and pernicious. Responsibility may be an indispensable concept to ordering human affairs, but its liberal form proves inadequate on both theoretical and practical grounds.

Cause and Response

Responsibility undoubtedly means many things to many people. In its simplest and most obvious sense, the term intimates causality; agents bear causal responsibility for that which they make happen. Although questions of responsibility are rarely reduced entirely to causality, and philosophers admit to any number of difficulties in answering the litany of even the most basic questions of *moral* responsibility, causality does serve as something of a bedrock for more sophisticated notions of responsibility. Approaches to responsibility tend to correspond to the retrospective presumption of causality, as responsibility typically describes a relationship to an event that has happened. As well, the causal focus on individual agents tends to translate freely into conceptions of responsibility, for individual agents hold relatively unambiguous relationships to these past events.

The question of causality is ultimately one of agency. As Samuel Scheffler (2001: ch. 2) discusses it, causal responsibility is rooted in a hegemonic "phenomenology of agency" that posits individuals as relatively free actors capable of both the will and the action necessary to exert causal force. Scheffler is in steady company with this claim, as it underlies both professional and pedestrian analyses of causality. To take just a few representative examples, H. L. A. Hart (1968) and John Fischer and Mark Ravizza (1998) each invoke causal responsibility to explain how corporeally distinct, autonomous humans act to change the world. This ability of actors to cause events, they assert, is evident through the most mundane empirical observations, a familiar claim that trades on a commonsense notion of causality that few find interest in challenging.

But like much so-called common sense, this approach falters under scrutiny. Inviting as this retrospective and exclusive approach might be, Arthur Ripstein (1999) demonstrates how each of these presumptions is viable only given an arbitrarily restricted political disposition. For any given event, he convincingly argues, there are any number of causes; from a strictly causal perspective, the victim of an assault is just as responsible as the aggressor, since *one* of the causes of the crime was the victim's being where the attack happened. There are "indefinitely many actions that led up to the harm in question," Ripstein asserts; "Why isolate one as 'the' cause?" (37). Ripstein's answer to this question is, simply, politics. He explains that what counts as a cause is contested territory, settled by convention but rarely by unanimity and perhaps never by any deeper "actual" responsibility. In this example, the attacker appears responsible because of a general objection to street violence. But this ascription of responsibility says more about preferences for individual safety and the prevention of crime than it does about actual causality. In other words, the commonsense approach to causal responsibility is political from the get-go.

Identifying "the" cause of an event requires positing a transparent link between subjectivity and responsibility and disregards the complicated network of actions and conditions that give rise to any event. Putatively descriptive or diagnostic, such an approach to causal responsibility endorses a very short term (indeed, snapshot) vision of history in which each moment is isolated from history—a perspective that results from a belief in individual autonomy and the clear separation of subject and object. This is all of a piece with Samuel Scheffler's "phenomenology of agency," in which history is the product of individual action.

Ripstein is refreshingly open about this bias, and true to his Rawlsian roots, he defends holding individuals responsible for "their" actions not on metaphysical but on political grounds. That is, he endorses holding individuals (such as the previously mentioned mugger) responsible *not* because we can faithfully fault individuals on purely causal grounds but because doing so promotes individual rights, political representation, criminal punishment, and distributive justice (1999: chs. 1, 5). Scheffler (2001: ch. 2) does the same. In other words, they admit to the tenuous metaphysical grounds for the model (and maybe the essentially contentious nature of any such grounds in this postmetaphysical world) and appeal instead to a political sensibility that is, they presume perhaps rightly, relatively uncontentious.

Nevertheless, this admission belies their denial that this model appeals to a set of widely entertained (though perhaps rarely explicitly invoked) presumptions about individual autonomy. While its philosophical defenders maintain that the model is based in political rather than metaphysical commitments, these political commitments have widespread support precisely because they appear to be grounded in empirically verifiable distinctions between individual beings. Indeed, Scheffler admits that this approach is widely received because it resonates with a set of ontological beliefs. Though champions of this model overtly eschew the dubious ontological commitments and anchor themselves instead with political commitments, these political commitments are themselves grounded in the suspect ontological territory. They are precisely, in William Connolly's (1995) word, "ontopolitical." So the dubiousness of these ontological commitments remains even as discourses of responsibility are significantly complicated.

Liberal Responsibility

Causal responsibility is not only ontologically dubious, it is often difficult to justify on political grounds as well. Structures of punishment and reward are typically grounded in causality, but this relationship is usually mediated in one of two ways: either by identifying causality without responsibility or by ascribing responsibility without causality. In the first case, a wide range of generally accepted excuses can effectively release agents from responsibility for what they cause; infants, victims of a seizures, and cats, for example, are not typically held responsible for damage they cause surroundings (see Hart 1968: ch. 2). In the second, we often hold actors responsible for things they did not directly cause; insurance companies are held responsible for replacing stolen cars, parents are held responsible for the actions of their children, and waiters are blamed for undercooked filets. These widely entertained exceptions are rarely seen as challenges to the ontological presumptions of liberal responsibility. Instead, they are typically cast as political objections. As such, they retain the same faulty concepts and make similar missteps.

The admission of excuses reaches back at least to Aristotle's claim that actions are not voluntary if they are undertaken out of ignorance or force (1962:1109b30–11b5). It presumes that a viable theory of responsibility must recognize the significantly more knotty questions of motivation and ability. Aristotle's identification of ignorance and force as excusing conditions still carries great weight, not primarily for correctly identifying the two conditions under which an actor can be justly excused from responsibility, but for tying responsibility more closely to will than to causality. Aristotle forwards the position that individual responsibility lies beyond any easily identifiable and verifiable causal actions, demanding examination of the murky and opaque realm of individual intention. Because individuals might at times be little more than tools for enacting the will or plan of another, or they might not understand what they are doing, Aristotle endorses a more robust model of individual action rooted in an autonomous will.

This subordination of individual action to the operations of an autonomous will informs the centrality of intent and competence (i.e., *mens rea*) in Anglo-American criminal law and forms the core of what we might call *liberal responsibility*. It is most clearly articulated by Locke (1975: bk. 2, ch. 27), who claims that consciousness and memory provide a consistency in personhood, which legitimates blame and praise, punishment and reward. Responsibility, as Locke explains it, depends on diachronic personhood and individual sovereignty over actions and desires.[1] This shift to a self-contained individual proves crucial, for, as Balibar (1996) explains, Aristotle holds that we are essentially social animals who receive responsibilities by virtue of our social relations, whereas Locke paints us as essentially individuals with a contractual, propriety relationship to ourselves, our actions, and our relations. Locke, enacting a shift that "concerns both ontology and politics" (Balibar 1996:234), replaces the Aristotelian description of humans as social animals with an account of persons as defined by continuity in consciousness. As MacPherson puts this, Locke forwards a "conception of the individual . . . as an owner of himself" (1962:3)—a political philosophy of "possessive individualism" that underlies the principles of the liberal democratic state. Possessive individualism provides the ontopolitical ground for individual autonomy and thus responsibility.

Within the fields of analytical philosophy and applied ethics, this "Lockean criterion" is for the most part taken as a given.[2] It is the foundation for the models of causality discussed previously; Fischer and Ravizza's (1993, 1998) model depends upon it, Ripstein openly declares that he has no intention of questioning it (1999:14), and Scheffler warns that abandoning it threatens to undermine any notion of responsibility whatsoever (2001:45–46). Though liberal responsibility is regularly defended for its political effects rather than its metaphysical presumptions, it is an acceptance of this autonomous, coherent, contracting individual subject that makes the political virtues of liberal responsibility (fair markets, criminal prosecution, and political representation) attractive. That is, the political allure of liberal responsibility is rooted in an ontological commitment to individual autonomy.

While many pass casually over this commitment or leave it implicit, others explicitly defend it. Peter Strawson (1974) does so when he famously asserts that finding individuals responsible for events is a natural characteristic of human interaction. In one sense, Strawson provides a creative and provocative argument that we do not respond in particular ways because we find people responsible; rather, we find people responsible because we find ourselves experiencing the "natural human reactions" of resentment and praise (10). Dismissing the alternatives, which "overintellectualize the facts" (23), Strawson argues that the innate structure of human consciousness and interaction compels particular emotional reactions that lead us to hold actors responsible. This reversal of the presumed causal relationship between response and attribution—the assertion that notions of responsibility arise out of (rather than condition) our response—suggests a vibrant rethinking of what it means to be responsible: response-able.

But Strawson quickly curtails this rethinking, naturalizing the categories of liberalism with an inviolable theory of individual responsibility. Betraying a strong Kantian influence, he puts responsibility on an inescapable par with space, time, and causality. Strawson's subject is not merely responsibility, however—it's *individual* responsibility. In leaping from a claim about the naturalness of responsibility to a claim that responsibility inheres in individual action, Strawson betrays a commitment to a particular and historical worldview in which events are caused by individual forces, in which subjects and objects are clearly and impermeably distinct, in which objects and events themselves are defined by their uncomplicated singular identity rather than their interrelatedness and multiplicity. For Strawson, we identify individual causes of events not because we have inherited a grammar and an ideology of individualism through which we experience the world or even because it provides agreeable political results, but because such identification of singularity is an essential component of the natural workings of human consciousness.[3]

In basing liberal responsibility on an ahistorical individualism, Strawson is a somewhat exceptional case. His unflinching commitment to the individual clearly does not inform the putatively political liberal approaches. But even the more cautious approaches depend upon the Lockean presumption of individual autonomy and possessive causal force. While Strawson's rhetoric may be idiosyncratic, his resolve is not. He is one member of a sizable chorus avowing that while causality is inadequate for determining responsibility, attention to individual will allows us to meaningfully and justly ascribe responsibility to actors.

From Many to One

This reliance upon the will to shore up a notion of autonomy has a corollary. Recognizing that events result from multiple causes and that proximate causes are often only politically presumed to be acting autonomously, many assign responsibility to the instigating will rather than the causal agent. This gives rise to familiar notions of vicarious responsibility and strict liability endemic to the literatures on collective responsibility.[4] Complementing the vast applied ethics literature that focuses almost exclusively on pedestrian tragedies (broken vases) and the fallacies of radical voluntarism (frequently through redundant thought experiments involving aliens and subcutaneous microchips), discussions of collective responsibility focus on situations irreducible to individual experience. Recognizing the nonindividuality of causes and the nonidentity of cause and intent, these approaches demonstrate how an exclusive focus on individuals neglects the operations of modern institutions (e.g., markets and governments) irreducible to the power of isolated individuals. Atrocities such as My Lai and the Holocaust (and, more generally, the rise of corporate control and bureaucratic rationality) render questions of collective responsibility unavoidable.

The move to collective responsibility, however, facilitated through the concepts of strict liability and vicarious responsibility, does not necessarily mark a break with liberal responsibility. After all, the institutions of liberal democracy—especially representative government and a free press—are primarily mechanisms for consolidating aggregates of individuals into autonomous and coherent collective agents with the same characteristics as Locke ascribes to individuals. Encouraging informed participation in transparent and representative institutions, liberal governance enables distributing responsibility for state action to its constituents. Indeed, representative government promises to determine public will and thereby distribute responsibility; we, as citizens, are ultimately responsible for what our state does because we *consent* to its rule. Liberal responsibility can be reconciled with collective responsibility quite easily.

Yet the notion of collective responsibility is anything but uncontroversial. Karl Popper (1945) formed the vanguard in highlighting the dangers of depersonalizing responsibility, tying any inclinations toward collectivization to the history of totalitarianism. In only slightly less absolute terms, H. D. Lewis (1984) argues in his influential essay on My Lai that though judicial feasibility may legitimate finding some groups responsible, it would be a catastrophic error to think this can be justified on moral grounds. Responsibility, he immediately declares, "belongs essentially to the individual"; failure to recognize this threatens to lead to that "barbarous notion of collective or group responsibility" in which responsibility disappears "into a morass of hypostatized abstractions" (167, 183).

In a landmark essay on collective responsibility, Joel Feinberg (1968) offers a slightly more qualified and pragmatic argument that, except in rare instances, it is both unfeasible and unjustifiable to hold groups responsible for actions taken by members. Building on a recognizable notion of personal integrity, Feinberg suggests that most attempts to hold groups responsible (especially though not exclusively criminally responsible) constitute an intolerable violation of the private sphere; collective responsibility is an "extreme" measure that is "likely to offend our modern sensibilities" and is thus applicable only in "desperate times," such as international war (67–69). In other words, Feinberg (and I think he is representative here) argues that, more often than not, we *must* be methodological individualists when assessing responsibility, even when dealing with issues in which individual causality (contributory fault) is either weak or absent.[5]

But many recognize that the exclusive focus on individual behaviors cannot adequately theorize responsibility in the light of institutional power and group psychology. Peter French has written and edited multiple volumes attempting to develop a palatable approach to holding collectivities responsible. Beginning from the hardly contentious realization, evidenced by any supervisor/supervisee relationship, that intention and causality are often distributed across subjects, he holds that methodological individualism is helpful for understanding what he takes to be the uninteresting issue of *causal* responsibility but insufficient to address more complicated questions of *moral* responsibility (1984:6–7). He claims that while a focus on individuals is attractive for its emphasis on the apparent site of intention, motivations are anything but transparent to individual actors or others. While individualism claims to offer access to the necessary realm of intention, it fails to live up to this promise.

French therefore argues for the moral responsibility of at least some types of collectivities. He points specifically to those that are intentional, autonomous, and coherent (1984:10–14). His prime example of this is a business corporation because it has an internal decision-making apparatus and a fixed division of labor. Amorphous and accidental aggregates such as crowds and nations, he argues, may or may not share these features. French thus takes the method of individualism and applies it to groups; collectivities can be responsible when they operate as individuals. By showing the unity and intentionality of some groups, and even noting how a paper trail might render a corporation more transparent than an individual, French evokes Locke's depiction of the autonomous and coherent individual and then develops a theory of collective responsibility that operates with the same standards as more conventional forms of liberal responsibility. In this analysis, Lockean hegemony is not threatened by—but rather accommodates to—the rise of corporate control and bureaucratic rationality.

Though excuses allow us to identify causality without responsibility, concepts such as vicarious responsibility and strict liability attempt to reconcile this politically cherished model of the autonomous subject with the frequent difficulty of identifying causal responsibility. Both approaches constitute attempts to deal with causality's obvious inadequacy for establishing responsibility by prioritizing particular vehicles that we can presume to be the meaningful authors of particular events. In other words, while shifting attention to the commanding officer or the executive board changes the name of the subject that bears responsibility, it maintains the presumption of autonomy and leaves the concept of responsibility itself essentially undisturbed. Each of these approaches places a premium on the autonomous will of social agents and attributes responsibility retrospectively for the events they author(ize). While these complications of the causal model strive to provide a more defensible model of autonomy by recognizing the complicated social and political relations within which actors are situated, they too stand or fall on a presumption of the autonomy and coherence of (individual or collective) subjects—a presumption that today remains anything but unproblematic.

Against Autonomy

Rooted in the autonomous and coherent subject that voluntarily chooses actions, liberal responsibility is hegemonic in both academic and popular convention. Ontopolitical commitment to individual sovereignty marks the primary cleavage separating liberals from both preliberals (ancients) and postliberals (marxists and postmoderns). This division informs the well-rehearsed claim that only liberals can provide a coherent theory of responsibility.[6] While liberals supplement the clearly inadequate foundation of causality with reference to individual will, postliberals find this addition of will no less problematic than the presumption of independent causality. But what happens to our notions of responsibility when the individual—the stable locus of action and choice—dissolves into the structural or disciplinary institutions into which it is born? Are liberals correct to maintain that when individual sovereignty is called into question, the notion of responsibility suffers fatal collateral damage?

While liberal responsibility satisfies some of the more immediate political demands by allowing us to punish or reward actors for their actions (and also to excuse and transfer responsibility in difficult cases), its stock-in-trade—the sovereign individual—appears today increasingly threatened by revelations of the degree to which individual bodies and wills are permeated and formed by external conditions. The liberal emphasis on autonomy, postliberals claim, reifies subjective desire, distracting from systemic coercions and disciplinary mechanisms that lead to events that we arbitrarily attribute to individual actors.

Locke's theory of a consistent and autonomous individual offers seductive clarity on the issue, but liberal responsibility is only one particular approach to responsibility and does not exhaust the concept's possibilities. Bernard Williams (1993) finds in Homeric texts, for example, an alternative approach to responsibility that does not depend upon an autonomous will. Situating liberal responsibility in the historical specificity of modern subjectivity, Williams shows how liberalism did not produce a novel concept but instead transformed an existing one by tying it to the sovereign individual. Preliberals, he argues, had a robust sense of responsibility that differed from the liberal one only in the relative weight placed on individual intent.[7] While he acknowledges that this emphasis on intent often serves the purposes of justice, he denies that it is "supported at some deeper level by a basic idea of what it is to be 'really' responsible"; the idea of voluntary action is, he claims, "essentially superficial" (67). Addressing the claim that responsibility is essentially liberal, Williams demonstrates how preliberal subjects were responsible subjects.

Perhaps, then, postliberal challenges to the integrity of the individual subject similarly need not abandon responsibility. They might instead provoke its refashioning. Challenging the autonomy of mind and body, postliberals upset both the empirical foundations for a liberal theory of autonomy and the "superficial" notion of voluntary action to which Williams points. Karl Marx's historical materialism and Judith Butler's theory of performativity, for example, both begin with the proposition that desires and abilities arise not from any essential self but from cultural and disciplinary inputs that form subjects; the individual is not the cause but rather the effect of social life. Seeing the body as a site of social inscription rather than a boundary to or container of the autonomous self, they reject the myth of the sovereign subject, the grounding myth of liberal responsibility. While liberal responsibility is defended on political grounds often bolstered by implicit if disavowed ontological claims, postliberal responsibility historicizes both these liberal foundations and establishes ontopolitical grounds for a vibrantly rethought notion of responsibility.

In coming chapters I will discuss how particular postliberals (i.e., Marx and Butler) suggest we refashion responsibility, but this maneuver is evident in significantly less radical challenges to the individual. For example, though Bernard Williams (1973) shows utter commitment to a theory of identity based in individual corporeality, he nevertheless emphasizes how subjectivity is formed through the internalization of external conditions, raising significant questions about any notions of autonomy. Our understandings of human action and responsibility, he argues, arise not from notions of causation of or responsibility for an event but rather a complicated convergence of inherited ethical institutions and embodied social relations. Therefore, even as he seems to offer priority to the individual will when he attributes to actions no "external reasons" but only "internal" ones, he is also arguing that the relationship between internal and external is conventional, variable, and anything but apolitical (see 1995: ch. 3, 1981: ch. 8).

To the extent that liberal responsibility depends upon an autonomous will, responsibility is best understood as something possessed by subjects; as sovereign and autonomous beings, we *have* responsibility (see MacPherson 1962). This does not necessarily commit liberals to the libertarian conception that we choose our responsibilities voluntarily (most concede that responsibility may be ascribed to us), but it does invoke a contract model of responsibility in which we (tacitly or explicitly) enter into reciprocal relations that lead us to adopt an obligation toward particular (types of) behaviors. In other words, this is a chronological model in which we are first subjects and then take on responsibility. Liberal responsibility mimics liberal property, presuming the individual sovereignty it purports to explain.

Others have explained this contract model of responsibility as expressing the requirements of a society increasingly defined by needs of capitalist markets (see MacPherson 1962; Balibar 1996). And discourses of responsibility today raise important questions: Can this contract model of responsibility survive in a world in which complex bureaucratic institutions constitute the dominant decision-making apparatus? Do not unreconstructed notions of private property and individual reward seem perverse in a world in which resources are almost entirely controlled by the operations of a global corporate network? Are not condemnations of individualized violence grotesque when broad issues of social brutalization go relatively unnoticed? In affording primacy to the individual, the contract model appeals to anachronistic notions of individual sovereignty and simplifies social life to a function of individual choice.

Looking Forward

Liberal responsibility, then, suffers from two significant theoretical deficiencies. First, it is essentially retrospective, isolating events from their historical contexts and arbitrarily fixing points of causality to explain the origins of events. Second, it depends upon a dubious model of individual will. These shortcomings are undoubtedly implicated in the recent movement to defend liberalism on political rather than ontological grounds. However, examining liberal responsibility as a political doctrine presents its own set of problems.

Indeed, speaking strictly politically, liberal responsibility has at least two significant shortcomings.

First, and as Young (2003) and Feinberg (1970:129–37) show, what I am calling liberal responsibility is much better suited to discussing events than conditions. Largely because of the previously identified theoretical limitations, liberal responsibility focuses on disruptions to established procedure and neglects conditions that have no immediate cause. To take Young's example, it makes sense to ask who is responsible for a particularly egregious instance of sweatshop labor, but liberal responsibility offers little or no assistance for understanding exploitation in general. In situations that lack any particular causal will or even any particular event to identify as having been caused, the grammar of liberal responsibility offers few if any resources for making sense of this issue. Liberal responsibility, that is, speaks to specific injury but not to more general injustice. It thus all but proscribes the possibility that political phenomena do not result from the acts of individual agents or that politics depends upon unwilled and superbly complicated institutional arrangements embodied in bureaucracies, markets, and traditions. To the extent that this immediately satisfying notion of responsibility functions as the organizing concept of political analysis, we neglect issues in which it might not be particularly helpful.

Second, because liberal responsibility focuses on providing particular indictments, it simultaneously provides general exonerations (Young 2003). With its roots in causality and will, liberal responsibility endeavors to isolate *the* responsible party, to determine who is *ultimately* responsible, and to release from responsibility all others. So, for example, when Lt. William Calley was deemed responsible for My Lai, all other soldiers and the military hierarchy itself were exonerated of wrongdoing. In this sense, liberal responsibility seems tailor made to immediate and absolute conclusions, even though situations admit to multiple and complicated sources.

Liberal responsibility thus directs attention toward events with identifiable causal agents to the neglect of those without them. Liberal responsibility encourages us to ask who caused the untimely death of Amadou Diallo precisely because we are prepared with (admittedly conflicting) answers. But what does it do to help us to understand the unfathomable incarceration rates and prosaic brutalities in our nation's domestic prisons? Who is responsible for the decreased availability of living-wage jobs in the United States, the widespread lack of health insurance, or declining literacy rates? Where does responsibility lie for our national desire for vengeance or the "epidemic" of obesity currently plaguing America's youth? It is hard to make sense of these questions within the presumptions of causal responsibility. It is awkward even to ask them.[8]

In the coming chapters, I will argue two primary points. First, I will argue that contemporary U.S. political discourse is severely restricted by the presumptions of liberal responsibility. That is, the issues receiving attention *and* the positions taken on them almost always conform to the tenets of liberal responsibility. Second, and more contentiously, I argue that though postliberals rarely discuss it directly, they contribute to a significant rethinking of the concept of responsibility that avoids the shortcomings of the liberal version. Despite the common refrain about forfeiting any purchase on responsibility, I aim to show that postliberal critiques of the ontologically untenable and political dubious reification of the individual challenge not responsibility as such but only a particular model of responsibility that has been viewed as the sole possibility. A definite threat to liberal responsibility, postliberalism opens the possibility of talking about responsibility not contractually but as a feature of established social relations; postliberal responsibility does not presume that responsibility is a possession under our control but views it instead as something we embody by virtue of our positions in those relations.

Williams (1993) provokes such an approach when he demonstrates how the very meaning of responsibility, and not just its particular determinations, is a function of a rich set of social relations. Because what it means to be a subject derives from the institutions of social and political life, Williams suggests that we understand responsibility as an institutional arrangement through which subjects emerge instead of a feature or quality of subjects themselves. For Williams, this alternative offers the politically satisfying possibility of avoiding the rhetoric of individual guilt and moving toward one of shame, such that ascriptions of responsibility do not depend upon actors autonomously causing events but instead point to ways in which events and conditions emerge without such causality or will. This is satisfying for Williams because it allows responsibility to be more freely distributed, as it does not incline recipients to adopt the defensive posture that typically accompanies guilt. It also seeks to reorient the notion of responsibility in a manner that addresses each of the concerns raised previously, for it is not tied to causal agents or focused on identifying a single responsible party.

Williams thus suggests thinking about responsibility as a variable historical institution that precedes and shapes our actions rather than something that we, as rights-bearing and sovereign individuals, choose to take up or reject. One need not strain his rhetoric to see this as a critique of Lockean possessive individualism. Similarly, and parallel to Foucault's thinking about power, William Connolly (1993) recommends seeing ourselves not as possessing responsibility but rather as constituted by it. Rethinking both power and responsibility given the rise of disciplinarity and governmentality and the decline in traditional sovereignty, Connolly asks how we might "move from consideration of individual relations of power, agency, and responsibility to those involving collectivities such as organizations, classes, ethnic groups, and regions," which might not have the same relationship to power or responsibility as a sovereign individual would (219). Connolly argues that conventional understandings of, for example, CEOs wielding power are anachronistic for failing to recognize how market imperatives coerce their positions and behaviors. Rather than "stretch the language to say that power is exercised without being able to identify agents who exercise it," he suggests acknowledging that understanding *power as a possession* might have outlived its relevance (219). Pointing to a "lag between inherited terms of discourse and changing constellations of social life" (220), Connolly indicates why responsibility needs to be refigured: its old (liberal) form is inadequate to social life today.[9]

Approaching responsibility in this way is quite distinct from simply extending liberal responsibility to groups. Williams (1995: ch. 2) emphasizes that current institutions and conceptions of responsibility and justice are tailored to individual enforcement. He is thus left to wonder whether established political institutions could apply a postliberal theory of responsibility. This likely incompatibility of new ideas with old institutions surely informs Isaiah Berlin's and Scheffler's warnings against such experimentation, with the two men predicting that any attempt to update the notion of responsibility will lead to its catastrophic loss. Indeed, this is likely the seat of the resistance to postliberal responsibility: suggesting an approach that does not correspond to the established institutions and mechanisms of justice, postliberal responsibility *does* present a significant challenge to the practice and application of responsibility.

The potential payoffs of such a transformation, however, are promising. One key benefit is a way to talk about responsibility not retrospectively, in terms of punishment and reward for past actions, but instead proactively, encouraging meaningful political participation in determinations of collective action. Such a notion of responsibility might well jettison a narrow focus on dessert for a broad concern with justice. Further, while the liberal emphasis on the autonomy and consistency in personhood informs a *moral* or *political* argument for responsibility, postliberals describe the individual as a site of response, thus presenting an *ontological* argument for it. When the body becomes not the instrument of an autonomous self but a site of response, identity becomes not an expression of individual authenticity but a series of responses. This perspective does not provide an Enlightenment-based notion of tolerance in which individuals *should be* responsible; rather, it underpins a claim that response-ability is rooted in the very nature of our being. In other words, this approach promises to promote a responsibility that is not a possession but rather a component of the relations into which we are born and that constitute our very beings. It suggests thinking not about who caused an event or even who should respond but about what institutions bring attention to—and thus might encourage—response to particular types of situations.

Again, while the move into modernity can be characterized as the rise of the sovereign individual, the move into postmodernity might be characterized as its decline; the very institutions created to provide individual freedom, agency, and responsibility (states, markets, and sciences) are themselves transforming into impediments to freedom, agency, and responsibility. Indeed, as current trends in globalization research herald a decline in the sovereignty of individual states by focusing on the permeability of borders, the inevitability of international dependence, and the political power of international finance organizations and global trade agreements, one wonders whether the notion of sovereignty itself can remain viable much longer. If challenges to the paradigmatically sovereign institution might upset all other presumptions of sovereignty, the discourse that presents responsibility as a commodity that individuals possess might render us incapable of dealing with postmodern problems.

What would it look like if we saw ourselves as composed by responsibility instead of possessing it like an object or attribute? If we understood responsibility not as a contract but as an existential condition? Ideally, this is the dialectical ethics of recognition and responsibility that drives social thought from Hegel through Butler, where responsibility does not come and go as we please but forms our desires and abilities. This refiguring of responsibility renders subjects as being composed by their ability to respond, opening the self to a new understanding in which it not merely should be (in some moralistic sense) but essentially is respons*ive*. This approach does more than just avoid the theoretical problems of liberal responsibility by refusing to reify the individual subject; it also provides a more satisfying political comportment by helping us to perceive a greater range of problems—something that must precede the formulation of adequate responses.

Postliberal, Not Illiberal

Invested with Locke's theory of sovereignty, responsibility today appears to be incompatible with postliberal critiques of the individual, which have thus often been branded as abandoning this indispensable political concept. This branding is due in part to anxious liberal polemics but also to postliberals' relative silence about a viable alternative. In a passage cited earlier, William Connolly suggests that it might be time to admit that the anachronistic liberal notion of sovereignty has been "superseded" by "structural determination" (1993:219). If this is the case, if structural determination is the alternative to liberal responsibility, then the imperative of ensuring political order by holding individuals to standards may well demand that we defend liberal responsibility.

But what if Connolly has spoken too quickly or too eagerly? What if challenging the ontopolitical commitments of liberal responsibility does not lead to a fatalist or nihilist embrace of structural determination? What would a postliberal, instead of merely an illiberal, alternative look like? Liberal blackmail and postliberal reticence render these questions only infrequently asked. In coming chapters, I will discuss some of the rare and strenuous explorations of these questions, explorations that are neglected or criticized for their unwillingness to conform to the linguistic conventions that are more appropriate to liberalism. But these explorations are promising for their contributions to forward-looking rather than merely retrospective assessments of justice, for their ability to transcend the superficial priority given to the liberal individual, and for their ability to theorize a greater range of political issues. As increases in global trade, bureaucratic control, and technological manipulation continue to render our political world more dense and complex, political life becomes even less adequately reducible to the causal action of agents. To the extent that we remain beholden to a theory of responsibility rooted in this suspect territory, political thought grows decreasingly adequate to deal with the situations of global politics. As the conditions of globalization intensify, a theory of responsibility beyond the contract model of autonomous agents seems particular urgent.

TWO

Making Marx Effective:
Postliberal Agency in the *Brumaire*

Despite the deficiencies of liberal responsibility discussed in chapter 1, liberalism maintains a virtual monopoly on the concept of responsibility mainly because of a lack of alternatives. Again, this monopoly is typically enforced with the assertion that rejecting liberalism means relinquishing any claim to a theory of responsibility—an assertion sure to politically discredit alternatives. The archetype of this supposed relinquishment is surely Marx and the assorted theorists and movements loosely assembled under the banner of marxism. Defenders of liberal responsibility argue that a marxist focus on structural forces rather than individual subjects renders responsibility an essentially bourgeois ideal, much like consumer choice and limited government. In this chapter, I pursue another understanding of Marx's project. Abandoning the familiar essentialist tendencies within marxism for an approach I call "effective marxism," I explore how Marx navigates the pitfalls of liberalism and provides a positive and valuable contribution to a postliberal theory of responsibility.

While this approach is visible in the general contours of Marx's overall project, it is most manifest in *The Eighteenth Brumaire of Louis Bonaparte*. The form and content of this journalistic account of Napoléon III's coup d'état reveal Marx trying to avoid both the liberal ideology of individual sovereignty and the structural alternative bereft of agency. Marx thus painstakingly troubles the presumptions of liberalism while simultaneously maintaining the imperative for political action.

Marx shows how identifying individual agents as causing events entails reducing complex convergences of historical forces to unified actors. This practice finds rhetorical manifestation in the metonymic process of naming, and Marx's abundant use of metonymy in the *Brumaire* indicates a recognition of the inadequacy and the indispensability of liberal concepts we prosaically employ to register and make sense of the world. The *Brumaire* engages two rival approaches to agency (liberal voluntarism and structural determinism), exploits their weaknesses, and emerges with a sketch of a collective, postliberal theory of agency. Marx's writing betrays a frustration with the adequacy of the available concepts, and his provocations contribute to their refashioning.

Liberal, Structural, and Postliberal Agency

Political thought of the past two centuries exhibits a seductive dichotomy. On the one hand, various liberalisms posit the autonomy of subjects and the voluntary character of individual action. On the other, assorted structuralisms assert the construction, coercion, and even determination of these ostensibly autonomous subjects by macrolevel social forces. These antithetical positions carry obvious implications for determining the value of individualism as political philosophy, but they also inform no less serious positions on the more fundamental question of whether subjects can act in a manner undetermined and unintended by the conditions in which they exist.[1] For present purposes, the debate is relevant for its immediate and profound effects on our ability to hold actors responsible for events and our ability to diagnose and prescribe resolutions for undesirable situations.

Fred Dallmayr (1981) has discussed this dichotomy, identifying voluntarisms and their complementary individualist politics as arising from possessive individualism (from Hobbes to Nozick) and transcendental humanism (Descartes through Sartre). Forming the boundaries of modern liberalism, each of these approaches is committed to the notion that individuals have both the capacity and the right to act freely in the world; they both explain historical events with reference to individual actors, maintaining that we can generally presume individuals to author "their" actions. Over the last two centuries, the most visible alternative to this position has come from a series of theoretical attempts to disrupt this notion of autonomy. Starting in the middle of the nineteenth century with Marx and Weber and continuing through the various social and linguistic constructivisms of the twentieth and twenty-first centuries, these assertions of the primacy of impersonal structures have waxed as historical liberalisms have waned.

This dichotomy is often painfully obvious in individual thinkers, as, for example, in Will Kymlicka's (1991) claim that subjects exhibit "autonomy" as long as they are not absolutely determined by some monolithic force. Superficially compelling, this claim ignores the possibility that subjects might be *overdetermined* (in Althusser's sense of the term) by a litany of discordant forces and that resistance to a dominant cultural structure might express rival cultural forces instead of an insufficiently colonized self. More than anything else, Kymlicka's claim reveals an all-too-common belief that the poles of the dichotomy exhaust the possibilities.

While liberalism offers us a language that lets agency stem only from individuals, however, and structuralism tends to discard the baby (agency) with the bathwater (the liberal individual), various philosophies have attempted to work beyond this dichotomy by wresting the concept of agency from the presumptions of liberalism. Dallmayr identifies Althusser, Heidegger, Merleau-Ponty, Adorno, Foucault, and Derrida as the principal contributors to this tradition, which he takes to show the bankruptcy of the other two. Neither liberal nor structural, troubling the premises of individual autonomy without succumbing to the competing tendency to deny agency, and attempting to release the concept of agency from liberal voluntarism's grip, these philosophies might be labeled postliberal.[2]

While Marx is nominally absent from Dallmayr's list, one would be hard-pressed not to notice his influence throughout it. Conceivably, Dallmayr excludes Marx because he sees the contribution of these theorists to lie in their working *beyond* Marx's relatively straightforward abandonment of the subject. (Of those he does discuss, Dallmayr finds Althusser to be the least valuable, since he remains closest to Marx in his attempt to completely erase the subject from history.) However tempting and historically popular it is to read Marx as effacing the subject, and however dominant this reading has been in the construction of many marxisms, I argue that this interpretation does a disservice to his complicated approach to subjectivity.

In the coming sections I will discuss what happens when Marx endeavors to produce a theory of agency that threads a course between voluntarism and structuralism. Marx's account of Louis Bonaparte's coup d'état contributes to such a postliberal theory of agency, showing the hegemonic categories of liberalism to be inadequate to our phenomenal experience. Marx thus suggests a rethinking of these categories and gestures toward another possibility.

A Responsible Ontology

The Marx Dallmayr implies is no less essentializing than are the most committed practitioners of possessive individualism. Of course, Marx *does* identify the individual as a historical production consonant with the operations of modern capitalism, and he certainly attacks liberalism for denying this relationship.[3] It is less clear, however, that Marx's prescribed alternative is to replace one essentialism with another—to trade the autonomous individual for the economy, or for a universal subject that is the uncomplicated expression of the economy. This reading of Marx arises, typically, from the ubiquitous (and overemphasized) metaphor of a base and superstructure, in which economic arrangements immediately and unidirectionally determine law, politics, and ideology.[4] While Marx argued at length about the subordination of historical ideas to material contexts, his philosophy was one of revolution, not faith or resignation. Clearly committed to a position that emphasizes the historical production of subjectivity, he is no less emphatic of the active, productive capacities of subjects. It takes a certain amount of committed effort to reduce Marx to either of the established dichotomous options.

I use the term *effective* marxism to distinguish my approach from these essentialist marxisms that rely upon the strict division of realms presumed by the base/superstructure metaphor, which Marx used on remarkably rare occasions. I borrow the term *effective* from Foucault (1977b:152–57), who, drawing upon Nietzsche's *"wirkliche Historie,"* describes his method of investigation/intervention (genealogy) as "effective history."[5] Foucault here explains that genealogy, committed to unsettling the supposed bases and origins of social life and its categories and practices, "places within a process of development everything considered immortal in man," thus working in direct opposition to any form of essentialism. Effective marxism is predicated upon the idea that subjects are neither the unmediated expression of existing conditions nor atomistic autonomous beings independent from their conditions; instead, they are consolidations of historical force that are afforded capacities to act by virtue of a complex interchange of historical institutions. And, as Foucault emphasizes, *one* of these institutions is a belief in and articulation of the shape of the subject. What counts as a subject and what counts as action are neither predetermined nor *a priori* but are instead historically variable and determined through political struggle. Marx himself recognizes this capacity of discourse, as he variously describes his *Wissenschaft* (science) and his *Geschichte* (history) as *wirkliche* (see, e.g., Marx and Engels 1947:14–15).

The effectivity of marxism can be further clarified with reference to another German term, *Bildung,* that figures prominently in Marx and works in consonance with *wirklich.* Marx regularly uses this term to describe the production or formation of active subjects. For example: "Where, then, is the positive possibility of German emancipation? Our answer: in the formation [*Bildung*] of a class with radical chains" (Marx 1970a:141); "The immediate aim of the Communists is . . . the formation [*Bildung*] of the proletariat into a class" (Marx and Engels 1973:80). In these passages, "formation" translates *Bildung* quite faithfully. But the term can also mean "education," "shaping," or even "culture"; it refers to the forces through which subjects become capable, competent actors, as in *Bildungsroman. Bildung* is *not* a cognate for "building"; think cultivation, not construction.

I will discuss this term at greater length in chapter 3, but for now note that Hegel uses it to capture the dialectical process of becoming a subject; it is, for Hegel, both the world from which individuated subjects are alienated and the reconciliation of the individual with that universal (see Hegel 1952: §187, 1977: preface and ch. 6, B). This ambivalent term thus conveys what Gyorgy Markus (1986) calls Hegel's "double bind," in which human freedom can be attained only through subjection to the acculturating forces of Spirit; we make ourselves through our own labor, but only by internalizing the social forces that confront us. Subjects, as Hegel puts it, do not precede their predicates (1977: §23).

The ambiguity of *Bildung* also captures Marx's understanding of agency. Marx is no liberal, but he finds himself historically situated in such a manner as to find the reliance upon liberal concepts inescapable. As such, he attempts to retain a notion of agency while simultaneously challenging the notion of unified or autonomous selves that precede their constitutive environments: we act, but only after internalizing desires and abilities. The concept of *Bildung* is particularly useful for indicating this dilemma because it emphasizes liberalism's political value while challenging its ontological commitments. Marx's theory of agency arises from a recognition of the (current) inescapability of this ambivalence; with the concept of *Bildung,* Marx invokes the humanist subject and its capacities while simultaneously alluding to its social and historical production.

Marx's critique of Hegel seems premised on the belief that Hegel is insufficiently attuned to this bind: the problem with idealism is that it starts with an abstraction (Spirit or the State) and then proceeds to reduce actuality to its categories, whereas Marx (and, he says, democracy) operates in precisely the opposite direction, moving from the concrete to the abstract or "from earth to heaven" (Marx 1970a:29–30; Marx and Engels 1947:13–14). That is, Marx's Hegel pays insufficient attention to the internal processes of subject formation, wherein subjects are the products of external relations rather than a dialectical exchange between internal and external (or an overcoming of the dichotomy entirely). Marx, in other words, finds in Hegel a perfection that remains, in marxism and democracy, perpetually deferred—not through failure but through necessity.[6]

While this might seem a circuitous route toward a theory of responsibility, it is central to a theory of the production of agents capable of historical transformation. For Marx, the ambivalence of *Bildung* captures the complexity of the process. If we avoid this ambivalence, however, as the base/ superstructure metaphor suggests, we cannot help but issue primacy to one side of the established dichotomy at the cost of the other; we presume either individual sovereignty or structural determination. But Marx explicitly rejects the liberal approach and implicitly refuses the structural model. He suggests rethinking the concept of responsibility in such a manner that subjects are themselves composed in response and that distinct historical epochs provide different abilities to respond. As I will show, Marx at times finds himself focusing at length on the institutions and arrangements that render response possible.

Making a Hero

Writing for the *New York Daily Tribune* early in 1852, Marx produced a series of seven articles charting Napoléon III's coup d'état of the previous December. Collected, these articles form *The Eighteenth Brumaire of Louis Bonaparte,* the central essay in a trilogy often identified as Marx's clearest demonstration of historical materialism's value for interpreting current events.[7] Tellingly, Marx's writing in this supposedly exemplary essay is decidedly more playful than one might expect. The essay's title puckishly evokes the family connection between Napoléon III (born Louis Bonaparte) and Napoléon I (his uncle), as it was Napoléon I who put an end to the first French Republic by seizing power on 18 Brumaire 1799.[8] And the essay's famous opening sentences similarly suggest that the events being chronicled both are and are not historically new: "Hegel remarks somewhere that all the great events and characters of world history occur, so to speak, twice. He forgot to add: the first time as tragedy, the second as farce" (1973:146). These locutions signal the dilemma at the heart of the essay: How does one narrate historical events without reinscribing the problematic categories of individualism through which events are conventionally told and comprehended?

In a preface to the second edition of the *Brumaire*, Marx explains this dilemma as he distinguishes his narrative from two other notable representations of the coup: Victor Hugo's *Napoléon le petit* and Pierre-Joseph Proudhon's *La Révolution sociale demontrée par le coup d'état du 2 décembre*. According to Marx, Hugo "confines himself to bitter and witty invective" and "sees in [the coup] only a single individual's act of violence," while Proudhon "seeks to portray the coup as the result of the preceding historical development" and thus presents but "a historical apology for its hero" (1973:144). Marx rejects Hugo for being too liberal and Proudhon for being too structural. Marx thus sets for himself and the reader the task of telling history in a manner that avoids the seductive dichotomy in which previous accounts are caught.

Marx, in other words, seeks to tell this story without using the dominant and inadequate theories of agency. When Marx declares, in the essay's second paragraph, that people "make their own history, but not of their own free will [*aus freien Stücken*]; not under circumstances they themselves have chosen, but under the given and inherited circumstances with which they are directly confronted" (1973:146), he rejects both ostensibly viable alternatives. Subsequently, as Marx guides the reader through Bonaparte's election to the presidency of the "bourgeois republic" in December 1848 and the establishment of his "bourgeois monarchy" in December 1851, he talks of a long procession of class alliances, insurgencies, and counterinsurgencies in a manner that emphasizes how individual and collective subjects embody relations that allow their actions to become historically significant. The essay is, in short, an examination of the formation (*Bildung*) of subjectivity via the consolidation of political forces in unified beings that can act seemingly autonomously.

Rejecting Hugo's individualist and Proudhon's structural accounts of the coup, which reify, respectively, Bonaparte's will and historical circumstance, Marx announces that he aims to show "how the *class struggle* in France created circumstances and relations which allowed a mediocre and grotesque individual to play the hero's role" (1973:144; emphasis in original, translation modified). For Marx, the practices to which we are subjected (through which we are subjectified) provide the very conditions that render agency possible;

agency is not transcendence or avoidance of the conditions with which we find ourselves confronted but rather their preservation, cancellation, and sublation (*Aufhebung*). Agency comes not from an autonomy from structures but from a vulnerability to them. Rejecting the presumptions of both liberalism and structuralism, the essay conveys first of all how structural forces (the class struggle) provide the possibilities of agency (heroism). Though the inevitable failure to achieve the liberal model of autonomy might inspire resentment, Marx recommends embracing a more situated and attainable model of dependent subjectivity.

This statement from Marx merits closer attention. What does it mean to "play the hero's role"? In a philosophy wholly critical of the presumption of an autonomous and unified self, could *playing the hero's role* be the same as *being the hero*? Or does it suggest that individual heroism is something that we, as good liberal subjects, look for and actually demand from political figures? That we inhabit a historical condition that compels us to identify individuated actors as the authors of historical events? That we prefer stories with strong leading men? As I read this statement, it implies that the class struggle produced not only a moment of historical possibility on which Bonaparte was able to capitalize but also a set of concepts through which subjects of nineteenth-century France were obliged to grasp their world; the ideology of liberal agency directed them to talk about events as the willed product of individuals. Bonaparte, after all, did not create the hero's role; he merely played a role that was there to be played. This understanding of history allows Bonaparte to become a revolutionary agent; liberalism's model of the subject provides the interpretive categories that mediate our experience, allowing and even compelling heroes to emerge in the popular consciousness.[9]

The concept of heroism itself reduces the complex movement of history to the voluntary actions of extraordinary individuals and thus trades in the alienated and autonomous subject that Marx eschews. But while heroes are particularly effective subjects, Marx demonstrates how *all* subjects are produced by consciously or unconsciously consolidating a panoply of inputs into a coherent and autonomous space. Such cognitive shortcuts seem unavoidable in any attempt to make sense of our experiences, and Marx mischievously exposes this largely unconscious process through his use of metonymy: the reduction of complex and multiplicitous subjects (e.g., the political-military apparatus) to mere parts ("the sword"). Throughout the *Brumaire,* subjects are constituted by historically imposed categories wherein a single locus of identity is afforded the ostensible autonomy of a "whole." This is, I aim to show, much more than mere rhetorical free-play.

Since liberal autonomy is a historically produced myth (since a name is a manufactured label for an artificially and ideologically fixed subject position; since subjects are political constructions), a discussion of Bonaparte's rise to power and a focus on "his" agency remains, by definition, a simplification of the historical process via metonymic consolidation of multiple forces under a single banner: "Bonaparte." The present case offers a particularly strong example of this, since Bonaparte really did affect a name (that of his uncle, "Napoleon") as a means of invoking a historical legacy and thus bestowing upon himself a complex narrative of personal will and heroic ability. (Reportedly, Marx complained when the first edition erroneously carried the title *The Eighteenth Brumaire of Louis Napoleon*.) Marx shows how liberal ideology and the trope of heroism constitute a curtain behind which this process of consolidation hides.

In Marx's version of the coup, agency consistently stems from artificially stabilized subject positions: a "mediocre and grotesque individual" stands in for the products of class struggle (1973:144, 170–71); bestowing the title "president" upon Bonaparte creates a new subject who, legitimized as an institution, embodies an entire political apparatus (162); "puffed up into a statesman," the bourgeois "becomes a higher being" able to engage in all manner of practices previously inconceivable (205–6); a multiplicity of aggregates identify themselves as unified subjects, consolidate varied manifestations of historical force under a banner with a single voice, and thereby become new historical agents—classes (1973: passim, but esp. 239). Marx presents numerous other condensation points—themselves direct products of labor—as having capacities for agency, showing how this capacity inheres not in autonomy but in its absence. He attributes agency to historical coagulations in the form of memories, interests, and industries (146, 148, 149, 160, 223); to revolutions and other events (150, 163, 171, 182); and even to inanimate objects such as weapons and articles of clothing (162–63, 168, 175, 183). Marx consistently demonstrates how identifying subjects is an inherently metonymic operation, and he does it all very playfully, as if to mock this apparently unavoidable linguistic convention.

Hayden White (1973) similarly points to Marx's use of metonymy as demonstrating his ambivalent relationship to the liberal subject. White seems to miss Marx's playfulness, however, and so remains committed to the thesis that Marx reduces the complex processes of history to a manageable mechanicism. White thus retains the dichotomy that Marx tries to avoid; because Marx is clearly not Hugo, White casts him as Proudhon (1973:315). White passes over the absurdity, the utter laughability, in what Marx is saying, and so the joke, alas, is on White. Despite this, White's discussion of metonymy as a reductionist mode of narration is quite helpful. Marx is not mechanistic, but he is committed to writing reductively (metonymically), indicating and illustrating a recognition that metonymy is the only way to talk about subjects with capacities for agency; positing a coherent subject position from which to act *requires* denying or ignoring the unstable multiplicity of historical forces that form it. In other words, White misses how Marx's metonymy troubles the dichotomy and mocks (rather than rebels against) liberal ideology. Marx does displace the individual subject, but White stops his analysis here, whereas this displacement is only half the story Marx tells.[10]

Marx certainly does test the limits and adequacy of a logic of heroism as he disturbs the ostensible hero's putative autonomy by explaining him as an assemblage of historical forces, constituted, bound, and enabled by historical consciousness and material conditions just like the rest of us utterly nonheroic tourists. But, maddening as this may be, he avoids any simple implication of this displacement. Bonaparte is not merely an unwilling pawn in the power game of emergent capitalism. Quite the contrary. This game invested this grotesque mediocrity with a political power—it enabled him to play a key role in the production of history. The ideological categories of liberalism are essential to the form of political institution that Bonaparte would come to embody. The metonymic categories of liberalism actually contribute to the possibility of novel and historically productive forms and sources of agency; the reductionist project of understanding history as the product of individual will not only allows the illusion of Bonaparte as a hero but actually increases his capacities for agency. Metonymy is productive in-deed.

This argument that subjects are metonyms can be found in various other sources. We see it, for example, when Guy Debord claims that JFK was able to eulogize himself (1977: §61). Because the administrative machinery that produced the figure of the president (especially the speechwriters who produced his public countenance) remained largely intact after his death, the political agent that was Kennedy continued to speak after the somatic organism that was Kennedy died. As Debord puts it, the "agent of the spectacle placed on stage as a star is the opposite of the individual." So, for example, Janet Jackson is not an individual agent but rather a multimedia conglomerate that embodies the total labors of songwriters, producers, musicians, choreographers, stylists, trainers, marketers, and, of course, surgeons. Added to these factors are the constitutive discourses of race and gender; a celebrated genealogy; and technological and social powers of production, distribution, and consumption of sounds and images. Taking all these elements together makes it increasingly clear that the identification of Ms. Jackson as an autonomous or coherent subject conceals at least as much as it reveals. In other words, this identification satisfies the demands of liberal individualism and its narratives of individual achievement, but it tells us little about the operations of fame and entertainment media.

For other examples, consider Anne McClintock's claim that embodiments of Victorian womanhood (with all its class connotations) were made possible by the unseen labor of various members of the female working class, particularly in making, fitting, and installing clothing (1995:95–98). Note Holloway Sparks's (1997) and Lisa Disch's (1999) rejections of the typical narrative of Rosa Parks single-handedly setting into motion the Montgomery bus boycott; Sparks and Disch emphasize instead the collective labors of "various oppositional counterpublics" that planned and executed the protest simplistically attributed to Parks. In fact, I noticed this listening to a friend's radio show. Amazed at the vast quantities of knowledge she wielded over the air, it was only later when I learned that "her" knowledge—and the position of authority she was able to convey over the air, her on-air subject position—comes in the form of a format book that collects artist history and trivia drawn from the amassed knowledge of the entire radio station staff and label-supplied publicity materials. The DJ, like the movie critic who uses promotional literature provided by studios to write impressively knowledgeable reviews, produces authority and the capacity to act by obscuring the collaborative project that is their existence. The individual DJ, like the author and every other producer in an age of widespread cooperation, exists by virtue of reification.[11]

Marx uses metonymy to announce this reification, to illuminate how the concepts we use to grasp our phenomenal experience fall short and how identifying subjects means (perhaps consciously, but usually unconsciously) ignoring their production. Whether we posit an autonomous subject acting upon an object or an object (e.g., economic structure) acting upon subjects, we run the risk of undialectical reification—the risk of being either Hugo or Proudhon. But given the categories available to us for understanding historical causality, given the ideological constraints endemic to our historical conditions, how can this double threat be avoided? Marx does not create new categories to sidestep this dilemma. Rather, with his exaggerated use of metonymy, he ridicules the established categories to demonstrate how they are both inadequate and unavoidable. He proliferates reified sites of agency so as to highlight our constant compulsion to do so, the way in which our ability to grasp historical events and forces depends upon such reductions and reifications.[12]

As Marx uses metonymy throughout the *Brumaire* to demonstrate the production and reification of subjects, he simultaneously presents us with an unrelenting barrage of literary, dramatic, mythological, and historical allusions. This sets the stage for several undertakings. First, he meticulously situates his own work within a fertile context and challenges to the humanist self by invoking the multiplicity of inputs embodied in the liberal figure so easily characterized as an autonomous and unified subject (e.g., Marx himself). In addition, he emphasizes how knowledge and interpretation mediate our experience of the world, and he reveals the complicated role of an author in a world in which resignification constitutes a political contestation (Bové 1992:82–83). Beyond all that, Marx generously uses irony to demonstrate the productive power of language and the inadequacy of the concepts available to him. Signaling that "straight" discourse is inadequate to convey his intentions, Marx's irony indicates an inability to transparently communicate his ideas (Seery 1988). Only ironically can Marx even begin to articulate a theory of agency that transcends the language of liberal individuality available to him. Marx uses literary position and irony, in other words, to highlight his metonymy.

All this raises a pressing question for marxism: does even a putatively marxist invocation of Marx as individuated subject problematize Marx's project by reifying the category whose disruption stands at the center of marxism? Unless we recognize that *naming is always metonymy,* we risk believing in the appellations we assign to concentrations of historical force; unless we pay specific attention to the processes of subjectivation, we remain blind to ideology. By regularly conflating particulars with the collective forces they embody, Marx points out how subject positions are both produced and contingent, artificial and temporary. This provides us with a way to talk about "Marx"—and to hold on to something we might call marxism, despite Marx's own fears of the label (as he famously declared, *"je ne suis pas Marxiste"*)—while simultaneously foregrounding the elusive and illusive character of attempts to fix a subject under the marker. A metonymic discussion of agency facilitates and supports an explanation of Marx as a collection of forces with a historical effectivity, far from independent of the relations that form them.

Marx is an overdetermined rather than autonomous being, a postliberal subject individuated by virtue of liberalism's hegemony rather than his innate abilities or achievements. Neither a mere cog in the mechanical processes of History nor an individuated subject transcending his sociohistoric context, Marx becomes a revolutionary political icon whose marks have been and are subject to a multiplicity of contradictory interpretations and representations (humanist, scientist, philosopher, revolutionary, demagogue . . .).[13] These are the effective Marxes that have achieved historical significance, though they all work under the metonymic banner of "Marx."

Marx thus presents a theory of agency in terms that would interfere with its transparent and unobstructed reception. When we identify Marx as the author of the *Brumaire,* we are encouraged to recognize not only the typical reduction of Marx and Engels to "Marx" but also the reduction of the entire constellation of forces embodied in Marx (and Engels) to an individual, coherent, and autonomous subject. Illuminating this reduction's ideological marks of liberalism, the *Brumaire* suggests how agency might occur as a deployment of desires and abilities that preserve, cancel, and sublate the subjects to which it will be attributed. This is how Marx surpasses his corporeal status as individuated subject without forfeiting the promise of transformative political agency. "Marx" exists to the extent that "he" contributes to the production of the world as we know and experience it. Reading Marx as an autonomous subject engaged in philosophically or theoretically "pure" thinking, accepting the metonymy as anything less than the effective category it is, means alienating Marx from his object of study and the products of his labors. It means denying the social nature of existence and the constituent forces of culture. It means conceding to the purifying presumptions of liberalism. It also means alienating ourselves from texts and practices that inform *our* wills, abilities, and enduring possibilities of existence.

By inviting the reader into the processes through which meaning is produced, the *Brumaire* highlights the productive nature of texts and directs us to consider how interpretive categories are constructed and maintained. It thus draws our attention to our own capacities for agency. It is emblematic of Jameson's (1981) argument that encounters with texts are never pure but are always contaminated by historical baggage different from that of the author, and also of Barthes's (1977) claim that reading involves overcoming the supposed privilege of the text. The essay demonstrates the effective power of texts by suggesting an examination of the ideological categories used to read and interpret them (with texts defined most broadly). By articulating the ideological and rhetorical bases of supposedly stable subjects and subject positions, it contributes to their disruption and emphasizes our own role in—our responsibility for—their preservation or contestation.

Challenging liberal ideology from within liberalism's hegemonic codes, Marx shows how subjects are always produced. With a preemptive strike against opponents worried about the possibility or desirability of remaking humanity, Marx declares that we already do this every day—liberals no more or less than anybody else. The *Brumaire* does not abandon the subject but rather identifies *any* subject as the product of political labor; it thereby contributes to the *self-conscious* production of subjects. It recommends that though we may be compelled to use liberalism's reductive concepts, we should be careful of the tendency to assign to them any sort of ontological weight.

Postliberal Performance

The logic of metonymy in the essay demonstrates Marx's commitment to a logic not of voluntarism or of determinism but of overdetermination (Althusser 1970). In this model, the forces of subjectivation are many and historically variable. Resisting the enticement to pick a determinate institution, Marx regularly discusses how political institutions such as representative government and capitalist markets enable particular types of agency. Even the Napoleonic army, Marx declares, transforms peasants into heroes (1973:244). In addition to these obvious political institutions, ideological categories also contribute to this overdetermination. Mediating experience, liberal ideology encourages subjects to see history as arising from the willed actions of individuals and inspires a belief in the capacities of subjects to act. We act, that is to say, in part because we embody a historical location in which the dominating logic is one of individual action. The categories of liberal individualism have a performative character, making possible that which they purport to describe.[14]

This is not to say that I can today declare myself Napoleon and thereby enact such a transformation in my subject positions; it is to say that subjects are produced through the repeated performance of social conventions.[15] Neither a liberal voluntarism nor a structural determinism, this is a postliberal approach to subjectivity that situates human agency in a social project of subject formation (*Bildung*). Agency, in other words, is ripped from the grip of liberal individualism and inserted into a postliberal theory of the subject as rooted in a set of conditions that both constrain and enable.

Marx evokes the performative basis of identity with a dramaturgical rhetoric that runs throughout the *Brumaire*. Nearly every page of the essay describes events as a staged performance complete with actors, roles, costumes, scenes, curtains, stages, and extras. The coup is a "farce" and "a parody" of an earlier program: the empire of Napoléon I (1973:146, 234). And both of the text's openings—the prefatory criticism of Hugo and Proudhon as well as the opening declaration that we make our own history under inherited conditions—suggest that human action is a process of preservation, cancellation, and sublation of numerous institutional arrangements. This positioning of subjects certainly problematizes conventional notions of sovereignty. But Marx obviously does not believe that this entails rejecting the agency of that displaced subject—we *do* make our own history.

This, then, is not a simple, structural decentering that reduces the subject to an expression of its constitutive forces. It is, rather, a politically enabling suggestion of the transformative power of subversive performance. For Marx, our continual (re)constitution through engagement in social and historical practices actually allows subjects to engage in the production and reproduction of those very practices. In particular, while liberalism throws us into sometimes paralyzing conditions of isolation and alienation, it also suggests the possibility of individual heroism (like Bonaparte's) that can be conducive to political engagement. As Marx puts it, even an ideology of heroism can inform a democratically enabling notion of subjectivity: despite its obvious restrictions, the army is "the peasant himself transformed into a hero" (1973:244). The theme of heroism that permeates nearly every page of the *Brumaire* reflects the ambivalence of *Bildung;* it represents both a possibility of transformative political action and a barrier to a postliberal politics.

Marx announces the glorifying logic of heroism as the definitive moment of metonymy. Nonetheless, while his postliberal approach troubles the inclination to ascribe such agency to ostensible heroes, he does not deny the ability to act. He circumscribes this ability by demonstrating how we cannot be held to be the authors of our desires and abilities, while he simultaneously highlights how social orders (e.g., liberal capitalism) often produce subjects with desires and abilities to act and provides resources (i.e., ideology) through which to experience and interpret events. He refuses the dichotomy of liberalism and structuralism, the former for exaggerating agency and the latter for denying it. Instead, he forges new territory by attending to the truncated though crucial capacities that are brought together through metonymic processes of liberalism, and he provides the capacity to challenge a hegemonic order through seditious performance and rearticulation of one's role.

In allowing Bonaparte to play the hero's role, Marx tests (in an attempt to expand) the limits of the political language in which he operates. He thus highlights how our concepts are inadequate for understanding and thematizing our phenomenal experience, appealing to us to recognize and attend to this inadequacy and strive for the production of new concepts that exceed the limits of liberalism and structuralism. The little man behind the curtain is no wizard (1973:151, 248) but rather a farcical assemblage of historical factors with access to a vast set of inherited mechanisms with which to satisfy the audience demand for illusions of superhuman strength. Bonaparte appears a hero because liberal ideology conceals the operations of history and encourages the individualization of political drama. Demonstrating how theories of agency mediate our experience of history, Marx draws the reader's attention to the production of historical-political agency. He thereby shows how we are always engaged in the production and reproduction of modes of subjectivity and also introduces a role for human (and particularly intellectual) agency in the political struggle of history.

What Is an Intellectual?

Just as Marx's theory of agency rejects the established dichotomy of liberalism and structuralism, his writing is similarly difficult to squeeze into the established categories of intellectual work. Dominick LaCapra (1983) argues that this dual status of subjects as producers and products is reflected in Marx's "double voicing," which is both "positivistic" and a "critical problematization."[16] The *Brumaire*, as both description and intervention, refuses the consonant dichotomy of intellectual work. In testing the limits of these categories with the form and content of his writing, Marx not only presents a theory of agency but performs a particular type of agency, that of intellectual workers.

The form and content of the *Brumaire* suggest that for Marx, the role of intellectual workers is not, contra Lenin, to guide myopic masses through the obstacles of history toward earthly salvation. Lenin's theory of the vanguard, placing Party operatives in a privileged (alienated) position with access to a pure knowledge of history, is markedly more essentialist than effective. It clashes directly with the earlier discussion of *Bildung*, a clash that informs the traditional association of marxism with authoritarianism and that mirrors the adoption of liberal heroism by Bonaparte's monarchy.[17] Rather, as Gramsci grasped, the political value of intellectual agency lies in the possibility of contributing to the production of subjects willing and able to engage critically in the material practices of everyday life. That is, critical intellectuals engage the ontological and political categories through which the world is grasped, produce alternative understandings, and thereby produce novel possibilities for agency. Marx writes from within the division of mental and manual labor that characterizes the modern age—a division of labor that he roots in industrial society's separation of rural from urban life and that he identifies as Hegel's undoing.[18] He writes *against* this division, and the liberal language that grounds it, in an effort to reconcile the mental with the manual, the ideal with the material. With the metonymic and ironic rhetoric that guards against its passive reception, the *Brumaire* does not provide readers with conclusions so much as it announces the inadequacy of established categories. Marx, as an "initiator of discursive practices" (Foucault 1977c), shaping the way in which we grasp the conditions of our lives, points toward new, postliberal categories through which we can experience the world—categories that can contribute to the increasingly democratic shape of society. Just as Barthes (1977:48) declares that "the birth of the reader must be at the cost of the death of the Author," John Coombes (1978:20) reads the *Brumaire* as a contract on the life of the author, working against the vanguard theory of intellectuals by showing how "only the questioning of [texts] is radical." Whereas Lenin seeks to concentrate responsibility for the revolution in a privileged authorial population, Barthes and Coombes call upon the political agency of readers—thereby democratizing responsibility.

Where the content of the *Brumaire* articulates the dangers and potentials of a logic of heroism, its form demonstrates the role of intellectuals in a period of historical crisis. It draws our attention to the restrictive forms of agency we reify and depend upon for self- and social awareness while suggesting possibilities for their overcoming. Articulating the possibilities for historical agency through the example of Bonaparte and those subjected to his rule (who remain anything but passive throughout the document), Marx performs this possibility not merely through telling an account of French politics that might incite dissent but by suggesting that the categories used for apprehending the events, essentially bound with the present order, may be inadequate for guiding genuine transformation. Indeed, the *Brumaire* suggests the political value of contesting our interpretive categories and alludes to the possibility of alternative formations to facilitate and navigate a transformed sociopolitical terrain. It is an exemplary effective text.

Democratic Responsibility

From the opening of the *Brumaire,* Marx alerts us that he is working with a theory of agency that avoids the seductive dichotomy of liberalism and structuralism. His narrative challenges the presumptions of both these dominant modes of understanding the human condition. Highlighting how subjects are produced through the metonymic process of naming, he encourages us to recognize that we are neither autonomous from nor reducible to the relations that confront and form us. Stressing the production and proliferation of subjects, the essay highlights the revolutionary potential of intellectuals who engage the social relations of existence, exploiting the evident inadequacies of hegemonic ideologies that mediate our experience and inform conservative politics.

In other words, Marx rhetorically engages the structure of our thought because he recognizes how the categories we are historically obliged to employ mediate our experience and action in the world. Because these categories (indeed, any categories) constitute a reductive approach to represent phenomenal experience in thought, Marx demonstrates this process of reduction so as to denaturalize and politicize it. Crucially, Marx does not argue that these categories are mistaken but focuses on revealing their effects. He thus illustrates the limited capacities of both liberalism and structuralism, inviting us into his essay to demonstrate how agency is not something we find in a text but something we bring to and might take from it. Against critics who see no responsibility in Marx, I see here a democratization of responsibility. Revealing how an ideology of heroism informs and legitimates antiliberal politics, Marx suggests how the relations of production we embody are carried in the performative adherence to a set of codes, investing the reader with a recognition that subjectivity is inherently contestable. Marx's willingness to engage these codes—to demonstrate and embrace the power of metonymy rather than avoid it—suggests his own recognition that while we cannot merely make new codes out of thin air, we can work to overcome those available.

We cannot think of the world as being otherwise and force its transformation. We can't, this reading of the *Brumaire* suggests, even adequately do the former. But the *Brumaire* also suggests how intellectual labors can test the limits of historically situated consciousness and expand beyond the categories of thought most consistent with (and therefore most amenable to) the contemporary division of labor and distribution of wealth. Illustrating the limits, implications, and manufacture of the liberal subject, Marx points toward the possibility of a postliberal politics. He also reorients our approach to responsibility, pointing toward a way to identify political imperatives without reifying subjective desires and abilities. Explaining subjects as conditioned and politically determined sites of agency instead of autonomous beings freely choosing actions, Marx provides not a moralistic claim that we *ought* to be responsible but rather an ontological claim that we are constituted by our responses.

THREE

Judith Butler's Responsible Performance

In chapter 2 I argued that Marx wrote from an unenviable position of being limited by the inadequacy of the available concepts. Though Marx navigates magnificently, his dilemma is anything but unique. Indeed, his navigation is compelling because of the familiarity of the dilemma. In this chapter I explore navigations from both before and after Marx, moving from Hegel to Judith Butler so as to better map the postliberal tradition. I focus on Hegel because of his obvious influence on both Marx and Butler; I focus on Butler not simply because she is currently visible but also because her work demonstrates a surprising and revealing resonance with Marx that helps to solidify this tradition. This connection is surprising because Butler is most commonly seen as a prominent figure in a tradition (poststructuralism) that emerged on the scene in large part as a rejection of marxism. It is revealing because, despite years of persistent criticism that she abandons the concerns and tactics of ordinary politics, her recent work has announced that she has always been concerned with refashioning (rather than abandoning) that deeply problematic yet indispensable concept: responsibility.[1]

I argue that though they draw on the same insights, Butler goes further than Marx in articulating a theory of responsibility. While Marx encounters the limits of his language and then playfully tests those limits to demonstrate their inadequacy, Butler, emboldened by the linguistic turn in Continental philosophy, debunks the common logic that some terms are exclusively liberal and suggests that heretofore liberal language might be reconfigured with postliberal meanings. She thus diagnoses the dilemma not as an inability to speak postliberal terms but as the tendency for postliberal ideas to be translated into liberal ideology. This inability to *hear* postliberalism is informed by and reinforces the illusion that, insofar as postliberalism is coherent, liberalism can and does contain it.

Working Response

The displacement of the individual will, the central commitment of what I'm calling postliberalism, perhaps owes more to Hegel than to any other philosopher.[2] Though he rejects the model of individual sovereignty that underlies most approaches to responsibility today, Hegel does not dismiss responsibility, as liberal critics such as Isaiah Berlin and Karl Popper would have it.[3] Rather, while his explanation of the way subjects arise though perpetual encounters with others certainly displaces the individual will and upsets the complementary logics of continuity and sovereignty, Hegel describes a subject that is composed by its responses. Against Locke's continuity, Hegel posits perpetual transformative attempts to overcome a lack; this is a dependent rather than an autonomous subject defined by its response rather than its identity, by its transformation rather that its continuity. While liberals talk of responsibility as a contract that subjects are assigned or willingly adopt, Hegel writes responsibility into the very fiber of the human body.

To describe this responsive subject, Hegel relies upon the same concept that Marx uses to describe the political formation of a class: *Bildung*. But the concept's rich history far exceeds Hegel's or even Marx's ambivalent usage. Tracing its transformations from fourteenth-century German mysticism through nineteenth-century German idealism, Klaus Vondung (1988) explains that since the term's verb form (*bilden*) is both transitive and reflexive, it can suggest conditioning either via an external force ("culture," "education," or "shaping" are all common translations) or through an internal process ("self-cultivation" is also typical). *Bildung* can be either a primal reconciliation or a historically progressive production. As such, the term has played a prominent role in both humanist and antihumanist projects, most notably in nationalist valorizations of the modern state (see Bruford 1975; Schmidt 1981).

In *The Limits of State Action* the Prussian education reformer Wilhelm von Humboldt (1969) provides a revealing liberal use of the term. Pursuing the best organization of a limited state so as to facilitate individual human development guided solely by the "eternal and immutable dictates of reason," von Humboldt explains *Bildung* as the fullest and richest development of the capacities of the individual, community, and race: "the highest and most harmonious development of [our] powers to a complete and consistent whole" (16). *Bildung* is thus the form of education liberals have always advocated: education that allows humans to grow into sovereign and responsible actors.

This type of education, however, has always been a point of tension for liberals, upsetting as it does the myth of autonomy by admitting the cooperative nature of individual development and thus the inevitability of coercion. Von Humboldt reacts to this tension with the familiar and arbitrary (or historical) distinction between public and private coercion. That is, he claims that development of individual powers is "spontaneous" when not restricted by the state, even as he admits that it is "determined by social lot and circumstance" (51). With this classically liberal division between determination by the state and determination by social forces (between coercion and *Bildung,* between public and private), von Humboldt promotes limited government and negative liberty while conceding the cooperative nature of development. He admits that this development according to "the dictates of reason" occurs only with the introduction of a cooperative division of labor and rich webs of social relations; *Bildung* thus stands as *species* development, even as von Humboldt characteristically solders it to a liberal individual. His *Bildung* operationalizes a fundamental tension in the history of liberalism, that between the desire for autonomy and the realization of the social production of said autonomy.[4]

In a substantially less subject-centered approach, Hans-Georg Gadamer (1995:9–19) explains *Bildung* as the reconciliation with that from which the humanist subject has been divorced; it is the process of making the alien (that which one encounters, e.g., language and custom) one's own. This usage clearly draws from Hegel, who in *The Phenomenology of Spirit* and *The Philosophy of Right* uses the term to refer to both the world of Spirit alienated from itself (i.e., culture) and the reconciliation of the liberal individual with the universal Spirit (i.e., education); *Bildung* is the encounter with the world through which we become both subjects and agents (Hegel 1952: §187, 1977: preface and ch. 6, B). In his lectures on Hegel, Alexandre Kojève (1969: ch. 1, esp. 52) explains *Bildung* as the labor through which subjects transform the world and through which they (we) are transformed, educated, realized. It is, for Hegel, the work through which we impose our (collective or individual) will on the world and also through which we attain the ability to do so. It is the internalization of the world with which we find ourselves confronted, the response enabled by that internalization, and the (self-)cultivation that these two moments describe. It is, in other words, the self-reflective expression of the world into itself. For Hegel, subjects are not autonomous and authentic selves but rather particular internalizations of the external world, perpetual and incomplete efforts to overcome alienation.

While liberals fret that such a decentering of the individual subject is incompatible with the established evaluative metrics of constitutional politics (especially blame), Hegel explains this not as an effacement of the subject but as a map of its production, its production in response. Though critics are quick to claim that such challenges to autonomy lead perniciously to a world of structural apologias and cultural relativism, one might read Hegel's work as actually intensifying individual responsibility, since the call for response is not ethical or political but ontological. In the *Phenomenology* subjectivity is produced through response; subjects are, in fact, a series of responses. Such a decentering does not release actors from responsibility; instead, it explains precisely why they are *always* responding.

Again, this position, that human freedom (the ability to act) is attained through acculturation—that we make ourselves through our own labor, but only by internalizing the world that confronts us—constitutes what Gyorgy Markus (1986) calls Hegel's "double bind." This is the same predicament that we saw Marx confront: the refusal of both apparent alternatives of liberal voluntarism and structural determinism with an attempt to emphasize that one is thinkable only in a dialectical couplet with the other. But Marx, of course, staged his philosophical coming out with a *critique* of Hegel, a critique that centers on Hegel's ultimate reconciliation of this tension by reducing the concrete particularity of real life to the abstracted essence of *Geist*, the individual to the state, the private to the public (Marx 1970a:29–30; see also Marx and Engels 1947:13–14). For Marx, this reveals Hegel's affinity for authoritarian rule over democracy and also the failure rather than the success of the Hegelian dialectic. Hegel, in other words, ultimately wriggles out of the double bind, whereas Marx's persistence in it establishes the perpetuity of antagonism that is the essence of democracy.[5]

On another reading, Hegel's struggle for recognition and individual identity mitigates Marx's critique. This is a more difficult interpretation to maintain, since Hegel's struggle for recognition is clearly a function of individual vulnerability and dependence. But readings of Hegel tend to emphasize one or the other of these options: Hegel is describing either a subordination of the subject to the culture (offering a philosophical defense for totalitarianism) or a politics of individual recognition (which manifests today as identity politics). The slide to these options is familiar enough, explaining the historical debates as to whether Hegel was a totalitarian (Popper) or a liberal (Kojève). Such appropriations of Hegel reflect attempts to ontologize these conditions, to essentialize rather than historicize Hegel's narrative, and to issue primacy to one side of Hegel's double bind at the cost of the other. The internal ambivalence of *Bildung,* however, posits the impossibility of either of these proposed reconciliations; liberal recognition is rooted essentially in the subject's dependence on the other, while *Geist* manifests only through the willed labors of individual subjects. Hegel's story thus posits its own impossibility, though liberals and totalitarians evade this difficulty and translate Hegel into a narrative of completion.

To the extent that theories do not evade this ambivalence, retaining both sides of the double bind, they trouble the liberal imperative to fix a subject who might be held responsible. As Charles Taylor puts it, however, this is a difficulty only insofar as we buy the liberal imperative; Hegel's double bind "only appear[s] mysterious because of the powerful hold on us of atomistic prejudices" (1975:380). Taylor argues that readings of Hegel all but demand that he correspond to one of the accepted categories, either an Enlighten- ment liberalism that endows natural rights or a premodern metaphysics that subordinates individual wills to a divine order. When Hegel refuses this dualism, the reader has two options: either call it contradictory and incom- prehensible (itself part of a historical worldview prejudiced against contradic- tion) or selectively manipulate it so that it conforms to familiar ideological possibilities: liberalism or statism, voluntarism or structuralism.

Though Marx ultimately indicts Hegel for failing to maintain both sides of the dialectic, he relies upon Hegel for a method of thought that does not reify subject or structure; at its best, Hegel's system shows subjects emerging through the internalization and transformation of the structures they encounter. Hegel describes the condition of agency and responsibility, and this condition is not autonomy but dependence; the possibility of meaningful action comes precisely from being shaped by the world. Agency is thus not avoidance of or autonomy from structures but vulnerability to them. This understanding of agency and work (*Bildung*) is coterminous with an ability to respond. It upsets liberal autonomy without forfeiting responsibility. It transcends the impoverishing contract model, in which responsibility is something to be acquired and worn or shorn; it is, rather, something we are.

Whereas Barthes (1977) promotes overcoming the supposed authority of author and text in a democratic birth of the reader, the *Phenomenology* challenges the sovereignty of either author or reader (as well as text). Hegel not only enacts the very transformations that the text ostensibly details, but, as Butler puts it, "the narrative strategy of the *Phenomenology* is to implicate the reader indirectly and systematically" (1987:20). Meaning here is produced by a dialectical relationship among reader, author, and text that upsets conventional notions of sovereignty and autonomy.[6]

Third Verse, Same as the First

Hegel certainly disrupts the coherent and sovereign individual. That this disruption leads him to an authoritarian politics is a familiar enough criticism; indeed, few democratic theorists today are interested in reviving Hegel. But this democratic interdiction against Hegel seems a mark more of liberalism's virtual monopoly on discourses of freedom than of totalitarian tendencies in Hegel. Perhaps his most visible defender today is Judith Butler, who arrived on the scene over a decade ago with the groundbreaking and still very contentious *Gender Trouble* (1990) and has come under persistent fire since then not so much for a lack of philosophical rigor as for her avowedly difficult prose and her putatively irresponsible politics. Nevertheless, Butler has recently focused on explaining how her Hegelian origins lead her to a refashioned and amplified commitment to responsibility.

For Butler, Hegel's most valuable if often unrecognized contribution to postliberal thought is a model of subjectivity that avoids the indefensible and ahistorical universalisms endemic to liberal and illiberal thought. Hegel, she argues, formulates a willing subject who "is not a self-identical subject who travels smugly from one ontological place to another" but rather "*is* its travels" (Butler 1987:8). For Butler, this is not a totalitarian collapse of the individual into the collective but instead an "optimistic" critique of the myth of liberal autonomy; each of the subject's encounters with otherness provides the occasion for the subject to "admit its interdependence, and thereby gain a more expanded and expansive identity" (1987:35). The Hegelian subject, in other words, is a perpetual work in progress—a subject perpetually formed and transformed by its responses to otherness.

This model of responsive subjectivity underlies Butler's defining contribution: the theory of performativity. This theory trades a liberal theory of an essential self for a notion of identity as the product of the repeated performance of cultural rituals. That is, identities are not something we *are* but something we *do*; we are, in a very real sense, the practices we inhabit. Performativity, she explains, denotes the compulsory citation of a set of norms that simultaneously reify both norms and subjects. Identity is, literally, work and response (*Bildung*): the productive expression of our (constructed) selves into the world.

Butler summarily claims that identity is "a reiteration of norms which precede, constrain, and exceed the performer and in that sense cannot be taken as the fabrication of the performer's 'will' or 'choice'" (1993a:234). This lack of a sovereign will distinguishes "performativity" ("the reiterative and citational practice by which discourse produces the effects it names") from what Butler merely calls "performance" ("a singular [and] deliberate 'act'") (1993a:2). Performance involves a willful agent's consciously embracing an assumed identity (as when an actor recites memorized lines on a movie set, or when a reveler dons a rooster suit on Mardi Gras), whereas performativity posits that the ostensibly choosing subject is itself constituted through ritualistic conduct (as when I teach a class in such a way as to assert and thus establish institutional authority over students or dress in such a manner as to conform to and thus produce conventions of masculinity). In performance a sovereign will chooses to read a script; in performativity the will and the script are mutually constitutive.

In claiming that regulatory norms provide the script through which identity is composed and enacted, Butler directs attention away from the congealed desires and abilities that seem to form a sovereign individual and toward the social institutions that condition and enable their formation. This is not an abandonment of the subject, however; like Hegel's, her focus on the production of the subject is anything but a claim of its fallaciousness or irrelevance. Quite the contrary. Performativity is Butler's way of navigating the same conceptual bind in which Hegel and Marx find themselves. Encouraged by political and linguistic convention to reify either structure or agent, she endeavors to trouble the presumptions of liberal voluntarism without embracing the fatalistic or messianic presumptions behind many constructivisms. In fact, she attacks the "linguistic monism" into which social constructivisms appear to slip (either because of their presentation or reception) and announces her project as a constructivism that resists the familiar seductions of a grammar that precludes a space for agency (1993a:8–9).

This attack has not inoculated Butler against persistent criticisms that she abandons the subject and thus any hopes for a responsible politics—criticisms that perhaps testify to liberal hegemony's anxious and precarious state.[7] She has spent the past decade refining and defending the ontological viability and political potential of her position. In her more recent works, specifically *The Psychic Life of Power* and *Excitable Speech,* she responds to her critics with the counterintuitive claim that her theory in fact retrieves and reconstructs that problematic but indispensable concept of political analysis: responsibility (1997a:27).[8] She argues that by highlighting the citational power of language, the way utterances achieve and maintain meaning through repeated use, she illuminates the conventional and unstable character of social norms. Grammars and vocabularies constitute identities and consciousness, but grammars and vocabularies are themselves maintained only through repetition; speaking subjects are, thus, not merely the products of language but complicit in maintaining it. Insofar as any particular language has positive or negative, emancipatory or oppressive effects, Butler argues, the theory of performativity assigns to speaking subjects responsibility for its use and transformation; "the citationality of discourse can work to enhance and intensify our sense of responsibility for it" (1997a:27). In other words, Butler responds to criticisms that her model of discourse reduces individuals to the material clay of language by emphasizing how language itself is maintained only through repetition. For Butler, the production and reproduction of language through a perpetual process of repetition renders speakers capable of upsetting conventional meanings and creating new ones. Focusing specifically on hate speech, an exceptional but not unique demonstration of the material force of language, Butler argues that when an element of speech injures others or interferes with democratic practices, speakers are "responsible . . . for reinvigorating" it (1997a:27).

The theory of performativity, Butler claims, establishes a relationship between institutions and individuals that does not revert to either of the conventional and prematurely reconciled theories of sovereignty, in which language is either a tool that individuals wield or a set of linguistic imperatives that individuals express but do not determine. It retains both sides of the Hegelian double bind by rejecting both of the familiar models of sovereignty, wherein either speakers control language or language controls them. Each of these positions requires reference to a static organism; conceptualizing either freedom (agency) or power (structure) in absence of the other requires, for Butler, a purified metaphysics inattentive to the processual nature of existence. Butler's phrase "subjects of power" concisely reflects this ambivalence; subjects are both subject to and constituted by power—the phrase "connotes both 'belonging to' and 'wielding'" power (1997b:14).

Butler thus offers something markedly different from the simple claim that "regulatory norms" prevent us from freely expressing the contents of our souls. This is precisely the deterministic and aresponsible model of the subject with which postliberals such as Butler have had to contend, since it casts subjects as the pawns of an impersonal and abstract "power" and universalizes one of Aristotle's excusing conditions (force). Further, this repressive model demands reference to an authentic subject untouched by power as well as a sequential model of history made up of discrete events rather than citational processes. Butler rejects both these propositions and argues that regulatory norms are in effect not merely at the time of repression—not merely negatively—but always and positively. The imposition of a fixed identity does not merely truncate processes of becoming; it also provides stabilizations that enable coherent agency and response. Identities, she argues, are essentially "sites of ambivalence"—not simply reifications that restrict the possibilities of becoming other but stabilizations that provide the pleasures, attachments, comforts, and wills absolutely necessary for the emergence and deployment of agency and continued social existence (Butler and Connolly 2000). These attachments and pleasures, certainly nothing to be taken lightly, will inform individual desire, collective political projects, and the notions of freedom that any society might pursue. This is again Hegel's double bind: freedom is available through the internalization of external forces—that is, through continual response and work.

This, then, is a theory of agency without the arrogant presumption to the sovereignty of agents. As Butler puts it, "I propose that agency begins where sovereignty wanes. The one who acts (who is not the same as the sovereign subject) acts precisely to the extent that he or she is constituted as an actor and, hence, operating within a linguistic field of enabling constraints from the outset" (1997a:16).[9] While the "I" is established through all manner of coercions, only a formed "I" can act. Subjectivity always arises from within a structured set of social and political relations, and agency—"the assumption of a purpose *unintended* by power" (1997b:15)—is response to the very conditions that produce events and agents. Subjectivity consists in "dependency on a discourse we never chose," but this discourse "provides the subject's continuing condition of possibility" (1997b:2, 8); "the subject who speaks is also constituted by the language that he or she speaks," so for all the restrictive and coercive impacts of language, it remains "the condition of possibility for the speaking subject" (1997a:28). We make the world through our labor, but the conditions under which we labor and the will that drives our labor are inherited from generations past. This criticism of a juridical model of power and self-sovereignty unsettles conventional, contract models of responsibility, in which individual wills are held clearly and causally responsible for events, yet it suggests an alternative model of responsibility that can get along without this unrealizable ideal. Rejecting "the sovereign conceit" (1997a:16) that informs liberal responsibility, Butler roots responsibility precisely in the absence of sovereignty.[10]

Butler clarifies the presumptions and implications of this approach in *Excitable Speech*. She borrows the term *excitable* from a legal parlance that accommodates the mitigating factors of force and ignorance discussed in chapter 1. Just as "excitable" acts are those performed under duress and for which we are therefore not wholly responsible, speech/behavior is "excitable" in that it is "always in some ways out of our control" (1997a:15). Speech acts are both compelled, since we do not get to choose the discourse we use, and beyond our control, since authors have little or no control over how their words will be received. Butler refuses the contract model of sovereignty, which roots the legitimacy of our acts in our willful and knowledgeable participation; that is, all acts are excitable. This position is precisely where liberals indict her for irresponsibility, suggesting that every act we engage in is subject to the standard excusing conditions of Anglo-American law and all theories of responsibility since Aristotle. Butler, however, does not move from the excitability of speech to excuse from responsibility; rather, she seeks to invoke responsibility for acts *because of* rather than *in spite of* their excitable nature. The responsibility for the performative use of language, according to Butler, arises not from the free choice of what to say but in the possibility of changing the use and meaning of words—in an ability to respond to the situation of language that we find.[11] A discourse is the condition of the speaking subject, but that discourse is not a fixed and stable system. It is instead a mutable and contingent set of practices dependent upon repeated performance for its endurance and inherently vulnerable to subversion. This is a postliberal articulation of responsibility without the authentic authorship presumed by a contract model of responsibility.

Again, such an attempt to retain this all-too-familiar tension tends to invite much criticism. And like others in her position (especially Marx and Hegel), Butler is frequently indicted for dismissing the subject as so much modernist claptrap and also for espousing a radical voluntarism that denies the materiality of real-life conditions; she apparently heralds the "death of the subject" by arguing that we are completely determined by an inescapable web of power yet also possess a revolutionary ability to change identity as we might change our socks. Critics charge Butler with providing us with both too much and not nearly enough agency—sometimes simultaneously. She is, in the terms of chapter 2, both Hugo and Proudhon.[12]

This schizophrenic reception stems from Butler's refusal of the liberal monopoly over responsibility. For Butler, responsibility lies not with the sovereign will voluntarily choosing and causing actions and events but instead with a series of citational practices with regard to which actors are not authors but participants. She responds to the critics who read performativity as denying agency or responsibility by claiming that it provides a model of responsibility that is both more realizable and more demanding. Butler does not call upon subjects to make their own history out of thin air (or through tugging at an inherited or purchased set of bootstraps), or to isolate events as pure acts of will, but to examine the ways in which their behaviors contribute to the production and reproduction of opportunities and possibilities for themselves and others. With the logic of performativity, subjects are themselves implicated in the production and reproduction of regulatory norms. Responsibility arises not from sovereignty and will but from the abilities ascribed to actors by virtue of the scripts they embody; not from their autonomy, but from their dependence.

Inside and Out

Though Butler tackles the twin threats of voluntarism and structuralism (and is often accused of failing on both fronts), her philosophical and political comportment leads her to be interested more in correcting (and defending herself against) the structuralist tendency to dissolve the individual into an abstract, depersonalized subject than in the liberal tendency to reify it. She is, in other words, more interested in recovering Foucault than in retaining Locke. No doubt because of the liberal subject's privileged position in contemporary philosophy, this recovery entails explaining how the decentering focus on regulatory norms does not sacrifice the political virtues of the liberal subject. Butler thus embarks on a quest to correct what she sees to be the structuralist missteps of philosophers to whom she has profound allegiance, most notably Louis Althusser.

Butler dedicates substantial portions of *Bodies That Matter* and *Excitable Speech* and an entire chapter of *The Psychic Life of Power* to Althusser's theory of interpellation, in which subjects are literally called into existence via their situation in the material practices of everyday life. Most famously, Althusser (1971) provides the example of the hail from a police officer—*Hey, you there!*—responding to which transforms mere pedestrians into subjects of the law. Invested in and indebted to this theory as she is,[13] Butler maintains that it lacks attention to the subject's "interior," wherein capacities for agency reside; that is, it is good at explaining how subjects are produced but less adept at talking about the capacities for response that are thereby created. At his worst, Althusser reduces the subject into an efflux of the (legal) structure, painting a totalizing and paralyzing portrait of subjectification.[14] With such exclusive attention to what we might clumsily label the "outside" of subjectivity—the social forces that go into the production of subjects— Althusser provides scant if any attention to the psychic resources (will, desire) that enable both submission and resistance to disciplinary authority. *Why*, Butler wants to know, do we turn around when hailed by the cop? Where is the enduring possibility of resisting that authority and becoming a "bad" subject?[15]

While Butler seems to overstate her case that Althusser's narrative makes "the possibility of becoming a 'bad' subject more remote and less incendiary than it might well be" and that his interpellating call is "a voice almost impossible to refuse" (1997b:109–10), she makes the more credible claim that Althusser is ultimately unable to address her project of finding ways "of being elsewhere or otherwise, without denying our complicity in the law that we oppose" (1997a:130). Although Althusser debunks the liberal presumption of autonomous or authentic subjectivity, he neglects the shape and desires of formed subjects and provides no theory of agency that would allow resisting the subjectifying forces to which we are *necessarily* tied. Althusser may give us an indignant ethical claim to resistance, but Butler wants to provide an understanding of response that is less episodic than perpetual, less ethical than ontological.

Again, Butler argues that this is the strength of her theory of performativity. Bringing speech-act theory to bear on the theory of interpellation, Butler emphasizes the "citational" character of practices and rituals and sees interpellations less as discrete events and more as ritualistic enactments of enduring cultural and material conventions. Her primary resource in this balancing act is J. L. Austin, whose landmark text *How to Do Things with Words* (1975) demonstrates how the meaning of an utterance is a function of its repeated use. Austin argues that meanings are produced through conventions, not out of any inherent definition of a term. For Butler, this implies that meanings are unstable and contestable, and the subjects who ritualistically deploy them are responsible for their perpetuation. This argument for the citational nature of speech informs Butler's argument for the conventional and unstable character of social norms, and thus our complicity in maintaining them.

Butler's problem with Austin, however, comes from his suggestion, evident in the title of his book, that subjects exercise sovereignty over language. For Butler, Austin thus plays Hugo to Althusser's Proudhon; "Austin assumes a subject who speaks, [whereas] Althusser ... postulates a voice that brings that subject into being" (1997a:25).[16] Butler thus aims to build a bridge between Althusser and Austin, placing her in the same bind as Hegel and Marx. To faithfully navigate this bind, she argues, "one would need to offer an account of how the subject constituted through the address of the Other then becomes a subject capable of addressing others. In such a case, the subject is neither a sovereign agent with a purely instrumental relation to language, nor a mere effect whose agency is pure complicity with the operations of power" (1997a:25–26).[17]

To offer this account, Butler turns to an unlikely place: psychoanalysis. I say unlikely because psychoanalysis has typically been associated with the sort of essentialized subjectivity that her work rejects. But her turn to psychoanalysis is mediated by the concerns already mentioned. Her interest in psychoanalysis stems not from such essentializing and heteronormative myths as the Oedipal crisis but rather from its understanding of the production of identity through identification, mourning, and melancholia (1990: ch. 2, 1997b: ch. 3, 2004: ch. 2). Though von Humboldt, for example, calls such development "spontaneous" and uses it as a marker of individual autonomy, Butler argues instead that these processes are social and demonstrate the porosity and "passionate attachments" that form subjects. Psychoanalysis tends to posit an essential inner core and then "reifies" this "interior psychic space," which in turn reifies the liberal notion of subjectivity (1990:66–68). Psychoanalytic narratives of mourning and identification, however, speak to the production of an interiority that postliberals such as Althusser often neglect (1997b:86–88). While the turn to psychoanalysis might appear to be a reversion to liberal categories that Butler claims to want to do without, she argues that this return through Althusser and Austin constitutes their transformation; the "interior" is no longer a space untouched by power but is instead a space created by power and invested with the ability to respond.[18]

Complementing Arthur Ripstein's claims about the political roots of responsibility (see chapter 1), Butler argues that liberal appropriations of psychoanalysis disavow constituent attachments with presumptions to "autonomy" because of a political imperative to assign blame to willing agents that can be held accountable for "their" actions and contracts (Butler 2005:14–15). The contract model of responsibility, she argues, artificially reifies and individualizes subjects so as to facilitate representative politics and criminal liability (Butler 1995). Her rival focus on subjects' formative "passionate attachments," however, does not abandon responsibility but replaces contractual with ontological responsibility. Whereas liberalism reduces responsibility to an ethical charge that we might refuse or avoid through excuse, postliberalism presents it as constitutive of our very identity, a charge that we cannot refuse.

Thus focusing on the enabling constraints of social conventions, Butler emphasizes that the subject constituted by power "is neither a ground nor a product, but a permanent possibility of a certain resignifying process" (1995:47). Such resignification, however, is difficult and dangerous business. It is difficult because becoming a "bad subject" and acting not in accord with the hegemonic practices of power means contesting the very forces the constitute our being. It is dangerous because such subversions are often not taken lightly by others cathected to these same institutions; "bad subjects," Butler warns, often find themselves in real physical jeopardy (1993a:133).[19] Yet Butler does not argue that we succumb to interpellation out of fear. Rather, she suggests that we respond to interpellating calls because we develop "passionate attachments" to these interpellating forces and ultimately come to seek our own subjection. Indeed, refusing them would ultimately mean abandoning our identities, jettisoning the established security and stability afforded by such conformity—a possibility that offers the very real threat of nonexistence (1997b:112–13). This, again, exhibits Butler's enduring debt to Hegel: in contrast to the various interpreters who read Hegel as positing the ontological primacy of the master-slave dialectic or the emergence of the modern state, Butler reads him historically and argues that particular modes of subjection will be more or less effective in another historical period (see 1987: ch. 2, 2000b, 2005:29). In other words, customs, laws, and ideologies become hegemonic not when they express more evolved sentiments but when they become capable of reinforcing one another. To the extent that rejecting one institution implies rejecting another, such rejections entail questioning the institutions of one's *Bildung*.

Rehearsing the Future

Butler's breaks with marxism are not difficult to deduce, and there is a certain unassailable logic in reading Butler in a tradition critical of marxian totalizing. Most bluntly, this involves a rejection of a marxist "grand narrative" that posits the primacy of economic antagonism.[20] Nevertheless, traditions are created, not found, and we can find a certain explanatory value to locating both Marx and Butler in a tradition of postliberalism, a tradition that begins with Hegel's displacement of the autonomous self and seems to bubble up whenever self-satisfied liberalism and structuralisms prove themselves inadequate to navigating historical conditions.[21]

Butler suggests that it is no accident that the French interest in Hegel reached its peak in the 1940s, when the collapse of the Third Republic and the German occupation reemphasized human action and responsibility as questions of paramount importance. Similar outbreaks occurred around the Bolshevik Revolution, as sympathizers attempted to reconcile the marxist critique of the willing subject with the imperative for revolutionary action. As evidence for the intractability of the postliberal sensibility, take V. N. Vološinov's groundbreaking study of linguistics in the early part of the twentieth century, *Marxism and the Philosophy of Language* (1973 [1929]). Vološinov identifies two primary strains of linguistic theory in his day, strains that map fairly precisely onto Butler's dueling antagonists. He calls the first strain "abstract objectivism" and explains that it holds to an idea of language as a system of "phonetic, grammatical, and lexical forms of language" that, he argues, eliminates any traces of agency (53). Exemplified in Saussurian structuralism, such theories present language only in its inert state, and history (specifically, but not necessarily, permutations in the language) appears as a series of accidents (73, 78). Resonance with Butler's late-twentieth-century example of Althusser (and Marx's nineteenth-century Hugo) is clear. The second strain, "individualistic subjectivism," holds that "the basis of language [is] the individual creative act of speech." This is a markedly subject-centered, voluntaristic ideology that Vološinov attaches to the work of Benedetto Croce (48, 52).[22] Later, this is Austin (Butler); earlier, Proudhon (Marx).

Marxism, Vološinov argues, does not look solely to structure or agent to determine the forces that drive history; rather, it considers their mutual and dialectical infection (1973:82). Vološinov argues that marxism attends to both the former ("abstract" or "systemic" or "structuralist") and the latter ("individualistic" or "psychologistic" or "biological") accounts. Marxism sees language as neither an objective system nor a series of isolated utterances but rather "the social event of verbal interaction implemented in an utterance or utterances" (94); language exists and therefore must be examined *in the interaction (and mutual reconstruction) between structure and agent*—a series of performative responses that forms the material process of history itself. For Vološinov, marxism's distinct contribution is its critique of possessive individualism, its refusal to forcibly remove individual agents (speakers) from their social situations.

Vološinov thus declines the essentialist's exclusive focus on either the capacities of the individual to make language (freedom, agency) or the alleged individual's determination by a language (necessity, structure). Instead, sounding quite Butlerian, he emphasizes the "dialectical coupling of necessity with freedom and with, so to speak, linguistic responsibility" (1973:81). For Butler, "The speaker assumes responsibility precisely through the citational character of speech" (1997a:39). For Vološinov, speakers are responsible for language because it is made not of "signals" with fixed, representational meanings but instead of malleable "signs" with which understanding is created (101). Subjects are responsible for their use of language because their language exists only in their use of it.

Ultimately evoking Marx more than Butler, Vološinov turns to typical and troubling metaphors—especially the architectural metaphor of base and superstructure—when he encounters the limits of his language. Criticizing voluntarist explanations of history by stating that individuals are "not the architect[s] of the ideological superstructure, but only . . . tenant[s] lodging in the social edifice of ideological signs" (1973:13), Vološinov gestures toward a pretty straightforward structuralism. He immediately upsets this metaphor, however, when he emphasizes that "every ideological sign is not only a reflection, a shadow, of reality but is also a material segment of that very reality" (11), or that these "ideological signs" are themselves "nothing but the materialization[s] of [social] communication" (13). Vološinov's metaphor sloppily allows speakers as tenants, landlords, and builders of the ideological edifice. This sloppiness is not atypical among marxisms; Raymond Williams shows how doctrinal marxisms have always had difficulty contending with the fact that prisons and schools, for example, are both base *and* superstructure (1977:75–100). Like Marx, Vološinov uses terms that are obviously inadequate to what he's trying to explain. Marx, however, uses these limits ironically, playfully, and productively, undermining the conventions to which he is beholden; this playfulness is absent from Vološinov's more straightforward frustration.

Writing in the 1920s, confronting the failures of both liberalism and structuralism to deal with the recent revolutionary change in eastern Europe, Vološinov optimistically forecasts a solution to this frustration in a decline in the popularity of individualisms and rise in the use of decentering phenomenologies (1973:32, 39). In retrospect, we now know that Vološinov was wrong; his century was dominated by psychologies (not phenomenologies) and liberalism (not dialectics). The twentieth century did witness persistent attempts to distinguish the autonomous biological creature ("natural specimen") from its social manifestations ("person") (34–35), as Vološinov predicts. As Dallmayr shows, however, these trends were largely responses to hegemonic liberalisms: marxism attained a certain historical vogue as psychoanalysis grew to dominate the field; postmodernism emerged just as liberals were heralding the end of history; Marx responds to a logic of heroism facilitating a classically authoritarian power grab; Butler writes in response to the preeminence of identity politics and the translation of liberal values into economic dogma.

Old habits die hard, and so the frustration endures. The postliberal refusal to reduce history to the play of wills and contracts is rarely welcome in a society habituated to representation and blame (as Arendt could well attest). A post–cold war, intensified global arena wherein "reality" television allegorizes human life as one big market; Auschwitz; the tragedies of eastern communism; May 1968; and the relative demise of both student and organized labor movements in the United States and Europe—these circumstances show critical theory to operate in a terrain where a reversion to structural determination at the cost of individual responsibility seems both unavoidable and disastrous. Decoupling responsibility from causality is read as forfeiting this seemingly indispensable concept, giving rise to the common judgment of postliberals as unwilling or unable to assign criminal responsibility to poor youth (structural inequalities!), wealthy CEOs (imperatives of capitalism!), or frightened cops (inadequate training!). At the same time, conventional reversions to individual will reveal themselves as increasingly inadequate to explaining movements of capital, populations, and ideologies. Liberalism has robbed Darwin of his dialectic (the one who doesn't study trivia is the weakest link) and rendered Weber the utmost theorist of resignation. Crisis looms.

The First Time as Tragedy

Pressed by vitriolic critiques and political urgency, Judith Butler has emerged in recent years as a visible and steadfast promoter of postliberal responsibility. Her recent works, especially her works on political and ethical violence (2004, 2005), have demonstrated both the shortcomings of liberal concepts and the concrete political purchase of putatively irresponsible and abstract theorizing. In the coming chapters, I will demonstrate how these criticisms not only miss the point but are themselves culpable for absolving subjects of responsibility. Presently, however, I want to show how Butler demonstrates advances in postliberal thought that were unavailable to Marx.

As I discussed in the previous chapter, Marx's postliberal subject is the class, a unified mass arising from a common economic situation with sufficient political organization to be able to represent itself (1973:239). Neither embodiments of material interests nor tools wielded by human agents, classes are for Marx collective and contingent capacities for response. Interpellating the proletariat through documents such as the *Manifesto* (Hey, you there! Workers of the world! Become an agent!), Marx's writings contribute to the *Bildung* of a revolutionary class. Nevertheless, postliberals of recent decades have consistently and fairly emphasized that because twentieth-century class politics prioritized only one dimension of social experience, it proved significantly less emancipatory than Marx had hoped.

In a transformed historical context, in the light of the sexism and racism inherent in a privileging of industrial labor, postliberal subjects today are fighting different battles and can be expected to take different shapes. Given recent history, it makes sense that when Butler advocates the postliberal production of new "I"s and "we"s, she expresses great concern that any such production is necessarily built on exclusion and therefore treads lightly when making positive statements about the size and shape of such subjects (Butler 1995, 1996, 2000c). She asks "what kinds of agency are foreclosed" by the demands of liberal identity (1990:144) but then hesitates to answer her own question, for doing so would signal the establishment of a novel subject potentially ill-attuned to its own exclusivity. Nonetheless, her embryonic discussion of the "new configuration of politics [that] would surely emerge" from a deconstruction of identity appears strikingly individualistic (1990:144–49, quotation on 144). Exploring the political potential of performativity, she seems to return to the categories she herself seeks to problematize by placing a premium on individual rights and *relatively* uncoerced choice. This move is perplexing given her criticism of the sovereign, choosing individual. It fuels the earlier-mentioned criticism that, insofar as this is a coherent argument, it is merely a warmed-over liberalism. But while Marx suggests getting beyond such ideologically bound concepts as individual choice, Butler instead pursues their transformation. Instead of abandoning the concepts used to frame freedom within liberalism, she refashions them to shed their dubious baggage. (This is why she is *post-* rather than *anti*liberal.) While choice today seems to evoke the free expression of an autonomous self, a recognition of the production of desire and identity through regulatory norms and passionate attachments suggests a model of choice that does not (as does psychoanalysis) reify the product of subjectivation into an authentic expression of will. Again, because Butler does not see any fixed meanings in terms, she endeavors to transform them.

As I discussed in chapter 1, the liberal imperative to tether responsibility to individual sovereignty convicts postliberals for abandoning one in challenging the other. And while challenging sovereignty might well resign one to a world without responsibility (e.g., a deterministic universe without agency or a purely contingent one in which there's no way to predict what will happen if I fall asleep behind the wheel), I'm not familiar with anybody who is interested in pursuing this possibility. Were anyone to do so, they would rightly be subject to damning criticism for failing to offer any viable recommendations for organizing social life. Instead, postliberals seek to tether responsibility to something other than the politically and ontologically dubious territory of the individual will. Butler's project is not to abandon the subject and the institutions of representation and liability that accompany it but to refashion the subject so as to admit—and thus mitigate—these institutions' exclusions.[23]

Take, for instance, Butler's (2004: ch. 1) commentary on 9/11—or more precisely, her commentary on the commentary. Butler convincingly argues that approaches to the event were encouraged to correspond to one of the familiar narrative tropes: the liberal narrative in which one or more individuals is causally responsible or the structural narrative in which nobody is. Narratives that refused these guidelines, she argues, were quickly reduced to one of the "legitimate options." Consequently, explanations of the conditions that give rise to the possibility for international terrorism are heard as so many exonerations of the actors involved. In other words, Butler diagnoses the discussions over 9/11 as being hamstrung by responsibility's ostensible need for causality; attempts to invoke a responsibility—an ability to respond—that is not immediately anchored to the hijackers or Osama bin Laden (or only slightly less immediately rooted in U.S. imperialism or an elaborate CIA conspiracy) are heard as abandoning the project of assigning responsibility. Unlike Marx, Butler does not argue that such postliberal narratives are unspeakable. In fact, she argues only that they are spoken fairly infrequently. (She points to Arundhati Roy as an exemplar). Such narratives do assign responsibility, Butler argues, but because they do it in an unfamiliar language, because they root responsibility not in willed causality but in an untidy matrix of overdetermined social forces, their positions get lost in the translation to the familiar liberal categories. While Marx asks (implicitly) what we can say, Butler asks (explicitly) what we can hear.

This restricted discourse of responsibility leads to a limited theorization of possible responses, evidenced by the predictably punitive and retributive war on the parties presumed responsible for 9/11. And the cycle continues.

With the ensuing war on terror itself restricted to causal narratives, President Bush is allowed to play either the hero's or the villain's role (as are the hijackers), with supporters invoking Bush's moral courage and critics chalking up the war to his revenge for Saddam Hussein's attempt to kill his dad (or Vice President Cheney's desire to enrich his Halliburton cronies). Attempts to situate the war by invoking the production of subjects through cold-war militarism, evangelical manicheanism, and American exceptionalism are heard as the only possible alternatives: exonerations in which nobody can be held responsible for the situation. Because this narrative will be reduced to the recognizable (if unacceptable) category of structural apologia, dissent takes a more familiar tack: Bush's personal vendetta stands in for this condition because of the iterability of the conventions of personal conflict.

The reduction of the central categories of political discourse—freedom, responsibility, choice—to their liberal meanings amounts to a liberal blackmail that one accept these definitions or surrender the political struggle over them. To the extent, however, that Butler's politics of performativity and resignification amounts to a contest over the meaning of these fundamental concepts, her occasional reliance upon them should be seen not as her failure (and concomitant admission that liberalism can contain her project) but rather as her recognition that the extension of these familiar concepts to unfamiliar terrains constitutes the political contestation par excellence. Indeed, her strategy of resignification here mimics (and refines) Marx's own strategy: testing the bounds of a language so as to test and ultimately shift the terrain of the possible.

Postliberal Response

If the critics are to be believed, refusing the liberal narrative of the sovereign and authentic individual entails abandoning the organizing political logics of our day. Without this subject, the argument goes, criminal liability, representative government, and meritorious distribution of resources is impossible. Postliberalism, in other words, surrenders each of the political resources that can realistically be used to organize social life. With her theory of performativity, Judith Butler responds directly to this familiar and ubiquitous criticism by emphasizing not only how a postliberal subject can be a responsible subject but also how postliberalism heightens and intensifies the call to political responsibility. By decoupling responsibility and causality, Butler shows how to apply the coveted rhetoric of responsibility on situations that lack individual causes. Indeed, though the liberal narrative affords clearly delineated subjects ample refuge from responsibility by limiting the transactions that one can be said to have willed or caused, the postliberal approach emphasizes the permanence of response—not to mitigate responsibility but to generalize it. While liberals talk of responsibility for events, Butler talks of responsibility for enduring conditions; whereas ascriptions of liberal responsibility are restricted to episodes and particular violations, Butler's postliberal responsibility attends to these situations and more.

One hundred fifty years after Marx encountered the unavailability of postliberal concepts, Butler finds in speech-act theory a possibility of contesting liberal hegemony through seditious performance and iteration. Such theorists as Althusser and Austin have contributed to a radically rethought understanding of the production of individual will and the ideological roots of the authentic subject, such that, Butler suggests, talking of the individual subject today might mean something different than it did in the nineteenth century. While the content of these floating signifiers (individual, choice, etc.) remains the subject of intense political contestation, Butler suggests that resources developed through the twentieth century have opened into the era of postliberalism, which has crippled the sovereign individual but not the drive to responsibility. Instead, responsibility is transformed from a discourse of causality to one of constitutive responses; from one of autonomy to one of dependence; and, finally, from one of contract to one of performativity. We are responsible not because we choose to be but because we cannot not be. Butler locates responsibility not in contractual relations and individual will but in the production and performance of subject positions through sustaining or seditious behaviors. In this postliberal approach, subjects do not have an ethical responsibility for particular events; they do, however, have an ontological ability to respond to the ever-present possibility of action.

The payoff of this struggle, as I will show more explicitly in the coming chapters, is a theory of responsibility that can attend to the manner in which our identities and capacities for agency remain in many ways beyond our control without contributing to a paralyzing constellation of concepts unable to laud or condemn particular situations. Postliberalism wrests crucial political assets away from free-market zealots and individual moralizers, transplanting responsibility away from phantasmagorically autonomous subjects and toward dependent contributors to existing states of affairs. In doing so, postliberalism actually intensifies political responsibility, taking the concept to areas in which its liberal variant cannot tread, such as unwilled economic injustices, prosaic and anonymous physical violations, and the unavailability of crucial forms of health care. Postliberal responsibility heightens both the possibility and urgency of political intervention by bringing the heretofore exclusively individualist (or corporate) concept of responsibility to bear on anonymous but no less injurious conditions of social and economic injustice.

PART TWO

Responses of Theory

FOUR

Who Responds to Global Capital?

With its commitment to the autonomous and sovereign will, liberal responsibility organizes economic concerns around the sanctity of voluntary contracts. Contracts both privatize and circumscribe responsibility, reducing questions of economic injustice to the direct violations of fraud, theft, and coercion. Though a focus on contracts allows for clear identification of individual responsibilities, it is incapable of ascribing responsibility for myriad economic situations irreducible to particular contracts. Marxists, of course, have relentlessly attacked this privatization of economics, arguing that contracts are merely the visible manifestations of impersonal material imperatives and that they justify holding individuals impossibly accountable for the economic environment in which they find themselves.

Though they emphasize that the primacy of contract is anything but politically neutral, these critics have been less clear about providing an alternative. Does a critique of contract exonerate, for instance, Enron's Ken Lay and other perpetrators of corporate fraud? What, liberals reply, happens to such indispensable political concepts as responsibility and dessert? So here is the familiar impasse: while liberals hold individuals impossibly responsible for their situations, marxists threaten to refrain from holding anybody responsible for anything; liberals legitimate contracts by presuming volition, and marxists deny them by emphasizing the ubiquity of coercion.

This chapter explores how postliberal economics avoids this dichotomy by avoiding both the liberal proceduralism that ignores consequences and the marxist totalizing that denies the agency of economic actors. My argument in this chapter is threefold. First, I trace the limitations of the familiar marxist and liberal approaches to economic analysis. Second, providing a parallel to the argument of chapter 2, I demonstrate the performative and metonymic character of the terms we use to characterize our economic order (*capitalism* and *globalization*). Third, I discuss postliberal attempts to theorize economic organizations that transcend the familiar markers of class endemic to twentieth-century marxism. I aim to show that, ironically enough, liberals preserve responsibility by neutralizing it. Promising to hold individuals responsible for particular economic transactions, liberals forfeit meaningful diagnosis of grander issues of economic opportunity and inequality.

Contracts, Ltd.

The shortcomings of the liberal right to contract stem primarily from its unrealized and unrealistic reification of the individual will. The logic of contract paints economic transactions as discrete, with identifiable beginnings and endings, removed from the historical conditions that enabled them. When I buy some khakis at the Gap, for instance, the transaction supposedly emerges spontaneously from my sovereign will and concludes when I hand over some money and walk out the door. This story, however, ignores the historical compulsions that led to the transaction (the establishment of factories producing khakis that needed to be sold and my fascination with the animated pants in those "Khakis Swing" commercials) and also the lingering effects of the exchange (the reinvestment of my consumer dollars as international capital and my interpellation as middlebrow fashion dupe by anarchists and hipsters alike). Such transactions appear as voluntary and discrete out of two ideological compulsions: first, to accept consumer choices as legitimate, and second, to restrict the scope of concerns that market participants must consider. The former stems from a liberal tolerance that refuses to judge individuals' preferences; the latter, from a liberal pragmatism that endorses limited liability.

Critiques of contract politicize each of these compulsions. Postliberals argue that liberal economics reifies individual desire, arbitrarily refusing to interrogate how the production of desire itself interferes with its legitimizing theory of individual autonomy. Indeed, the desire for khakis appears *mine* only because of the refusal to consider the material processes (interpellation, identification, and marketing) through which the desire was produced.[1]

Postliberals also politicize the presumed completion of the contract wi
the purchase of the good, highlighting how this is legitimated more by the
political protection of private property and corporate investment than by
any apolitical determination of the flow of resources. In other words, neither the origin nor the completion of the contract withstands scrutiny; the
former removes the contract from the history that makes it possible; the
latter, from the history that it makes.

But liberal economics has a bigger problem: by privileging contracts, it
ignores substantive outcomes. Because it refuses to judge individuals' preferences, liberal economics does not evaluate the results of contracts; they are
presumed just so long as the contracts were entered into voluntarily and
carried out faithfully. Liberalism thus not only lacks a normative theory
of distributive justice but also restricts itself to considering the visible and
procedural manifestations of economic relations (contracts). A focus on
contracts subjects particular events to evaluation but lacks the resources for
assessing the enduring conditions of existence; as Iris Young (2003) puts
this, liberals assign responsibility for changes to the state of affairs but not
for the state of affairs itself. This limitation is most obvious in the libertarian
trends within liberalism, but even welfare-state liberalism criticizes economic
inequality almost entirely on the grounds that it interferes with voluntary
contracts by giving participants unequal bargaining power. If responsibility
is a function of contracts, then nobody is responsible for situations such as
geographically concentrated poverty, systemic racism, or the unavailability
of affordable housing. These situations do not conform to the presumptions
of liberal responsibility and so are all too easily cast as misfortunes rather
than injustices; they might call for sympathy, but not for political remediation (see Shklar 1990).

Liberal responsibility thus limits possibilities for making claims of injury
by rendering the background conditions against which economic transactions take place irrelevant to discussions of justice. With this naturalization
of contract, the rights to recognition and fair-market participation stand as
the only bases for political plaint. Exit critique of the economic structure;
enter identity politics. This focus on political recognition, Wendy Brown
points out, "is partly dependent upon the demise of a critique of capitalism"
(1995:59). Seeking the protection of fair contract, identity politics is incapable
of addressing the injuries done by contract itself. With the depoliticization
of contract, race, gender, and sexuality are called upon to explain all social
injustices (Brown 1995:60). Within the contractarian logic of identity poli-

lf is depoliticized, as are the rules governing it and the
awn up; only one's disadvantaged place within the game
attention.[2]

alism pursues a world of truly voluntary contracts, postliber-
very notion of self-sovereignty that underlies this ideal. One
see the ubiquity of identity politics as a predictable outcome
of the ⌐ on's perpetual failure. For if, as Judith Butler argues, identity
politics is predicated on the notion that "identity must first be in place in
order for political interests to be elaborated" (1990:142), it will be perpetually frustrated by the inability to establish the individual sovereignty that
it pursues. Identity politics is the reactive attempt to safeguard an illusory
sovereignty; hence, even white American males are claiming violation of
their inalienable sovereignty (see Connolly 1995: ch. 4; Nealon 1998: ch. 7).
Crucially, identity politics' lock on claims to injustice threatens to render
postliberal discourse apolitical. If the fixed subject is the sine qua non of
politics and responsibility, troubling identity means abandoning both (Butler
1995:36).

The hegemonic suturing of politics and responsibility to the sovereign
individual explains the anxious and vitriolic liberal condemnations of postliberals.[3] Such anxiety certainly might justify reactive and nostalgic affirma-
tions of individual sovereignty, but another approach might be to retheorize
politics and responsibility in the light of postliberal problematics, for while
liberals purport to be preserving valuable political resources, this preservation
comes at the cost of their impoverishment. In other words, liberals promote
what they can explain best (willed causality) and then condemn alternatives as apolitical, necessarily neglecting those issues that they are less well
equipped to handle. Postliberal thought, by contrast, refuses to limit itself
to the evaluation of individual actors' causal responsibilities, seeking instead
to expand these concepts beyond their procedural limits and thus provide
more consequential evaluations. While such decoupling of responsibility
and causality may threaten to delegitimate the discourse of responsibility
entirely, taking the risk can pay off in a heightened and expanded approach
to economic responsibility, the ability to repoliticize conditions of economic
inequality that have been all too hastily depoliticized by liberalism.

One or Many Capitalisms

The critique of contract is nothing new, of course. Hell-bent on correcting
the liberal privatization of economics, marxists have tirelessly challenged

the integrity of supposedly discrete economic transactions by explaining contracts as visible punctuations in a dynamic and impersonal economic structure. Instead of seeing contracts as expressions of autonomous wills, marxists have sought to describe the totality of the economic system within which these transactions take place. Marxists thus depersonalize contracts as well as the movements of history, at their worst replacing the liberal conceit of sovereignty with a humbling model of subjectivity as the organic expression of established structures.

Casting contractual responsibility as a central legitimizing component of bourgeois ideology, many marxists have historically reacted to liberal economics by fetishizing the economy. Today, this is most evident in the World-System theory of Immanuel Wallerstein and Giovanni Arrighi. Arrighi's commanding work *The Long Twentieth Century* (1994) is so intent on illuminating the global command of capital that the author all but completely dismisses the radical differences among the historical capitalisms to which he himself points. From "state (monopoly) capitalism" intent on increasing territorial control to "cosmopolitan (finance) capitalism" intent on securing capital (systems that Arrighi at times describes as "antithetical"), from nineteenth-century British "imperialism" to twentieth-century U.S. "anti-imperialism" and beyond—it's all just capitalism manifesting itself with different faces. Such an economics is essentially apolitical; social transformations arise from technological developments, historical accidents, or (more commonly) the tautological imperatives of capitalism itself. With this fetishized, essentialist economics, capitalism precedes politics (ontologically, if not historically); it is eternal, omnipotent, essential, and autonomous. Subjectivity is nowhere in this picture, except as the paradigmatically bourgeois apologia.[4]

Arrighi thus presents an antiseptic structural account of history with no role for subjects in the production and reproduction, maintenance and transformation of capitalisms. Capitalism appears as an alien being descending from the heavens to command human life—precisely the sort of fetish that Marx himself attacks in his assorted critiques of Hegel, Christianity, Proudhon, Feuerbach, and capital itself.[5] As Arrighi's own analysis suggests, there are many capitalisms today, and there have been even more in the past. Post-Fordist and post-Keynesian downsizing in the United States, industrialization in India, emergent markets in the former Soviet Union, and a developing (sexual) service economy in Singapore, for example, are not easily reducible to a monolithic system. Further, despite the obviously symbiotic relationship between private property and the nuclear family, kinship remains irreducible to the dictates of capital (see Stevens 1999). Noncapitalist and anticapitalist practices—from interpersonal love to societies only nominally postfeudal to de facto slave institutions such as street prostitution and prison labor—are all pervasive today.[6]

The totalizing approach to economic thought is not merely inaccurate but politically paralyzing. Invoking capitalism as the economic force constructing the political world metonymically produces a historically effective subject (the market) with the totalizing spirit that precludes democracy; focusing exclusively on the interpellating powers of capital, this model fails to recognize the agency produced through interpellation. Produced and reproduced through ritualistic performance of its roles, capitalism not only behaves quite differently in different historical and geographical locations but also enables novel constructions of agency and desire. As is evidenced by Marx's discussions of *Bildung* and cooperation, as well as Butler's approach to psychoanalysis, regulatory norms produce not just docile bodies and private consumers but willing actors.

Such totalizing abandonments of agency, however, are not inevitable in the displacement of contract. Hardt and Negri (2000:237–39) recently criticized this facile model of anonymous and pristine capital operating seemingly independent of the subjects enacting its will; Negri (1991) has been making this argument for years, explaining that, for readers who spend more time with the *Grundrisse* and less with *Capital*, this move is evident in Marx himself.[7] More straightforwardly, Gibson-Graham (1993, 2007) argues that capitalism is not a discrete and autonomous economic system that unilaterally imposes its will on passive subjects; rather, it is the product of human labor and political contestation, subject to all the vicissitudes and variations of human activity. Not only has capitalism varied historically, but global capitalism today is marked by profound internal variegation, discord, and disarray.

These considerations raise an unsettling question: is there something we can innocently call "capitalism"? Or does this identification require the artificial reduction of a complex multiplicity of relations and practices to a coherent system? Is capitalism but another metonym? Further, does not this identification of a total economic system produce the very totalization that renders it a site of such vicious critique? Does not the refusal of subjectivity threaten to remove the very site of resistance and reorganization it purports to promote? Does not the performative articulation of capitalist hegemony contribute to the production of that very hegemony? Don't essentialist economic models reinforce the limitations on agency by convincing subjects that the power of the market is total?[8]

Doctrinal marxist assertions that the moments of disarray and anti-capitalism are internal to (are moments of) capitalism, that capitalism *is* antagonism, parallel the models of interpellation and domination that I criticized in chapter 3. That is, if everything—including anticapitalism—is capitalism, if the economic realm is somehow autonomous or "sutured," then even anticapitalist activists are merely the expression of structures, markers of an internal antagonism rather than agents enabled by its inter-pellations. This is precisely the subject-effacing move that postliberals have had to resist; it merely inverts the liberal assertion of individual autonomy with a straightforward denial. In this model, revolutionary movements are not products of human labor and political agency but rather expressions of capital's internal contradictions; revolutionaries lack agency and thus respon-sibility. The rhetoric of class warfare, so often presumed to be a catalyzing and enabling rhetoric of political transformation, here functions as quite the opposite, reducing political transformation to a spontaneous expression of the demands of the economic structure itself.

Such totalizing theories of capital, certainly attractive for promising the definitive statement of the present condition at the dawn of a new century, are on full display in the ubiquitous discussions of nearly everybody's favorite indeterminate buzzword: *globalization.* Often presumed to have its origins at Bretton Woods, its escalation in the U.S. abandonment of the gold standard in 1971, and its realization in the end of the cold war, globalization tends to refer to an economic order characterized by free flows of capital decreasingly bound by national or territorial allegiance. With technological advances raising the value of such immaterial commodities as computer code and access to data, capital is decreasingly tied to territories. Globalization, goes the refrain, poses a direct affront to the sovereignty of representative govern-ments since legitimacy now stems less from the consent of the territorially fixed populations and more from international finance organizations.

Nevertheless, although announcing the arrival of globalization has be-come something of a cottage industry within punditry and publishing, one wonders whether there really is something specific and new here. On the most obvious level, Arrighi demonstrates the existence of "deterritorial-ized" finance capital as far back as the sixteenth century; decades ago Ernest Mandel (1978) and Fredric Jameson (1991) noted this phenomenon, calling it "late" or "multinational" capitalism. At their worst, the pundits of novelty paint a picture of globalization arising *outside* history, with mobile capital unrestricted by national laws, unchecked in its pursuit of profit, either run-ning roughshod over individual and collective wills or liberating all that it touches. In either case, the market acts upon us, and globalization is Marx's pyrrhic victory, not only with the familiar landmarks Kojève (1969) and Fukuyama (1992) heralding the end of history, but also with the fashionable pundits Thomas Friedman (2000) and Fareed Zakaria (2003) resuscitating economic determinism by promoting industrial capitalism as the royal road to democracy.

This desire for coherence also manifests itself in attempts to explain the operations of labor in the so-called postindustrial economy, such as Robert Reich's (1991, 2001) focus on the "symbolic analyst" or the "creative worker" and Hardt and Negri's (2000, 2004) focus on "computerization" and "immaterial labor."[9] This is a peculiar and provincial trend, standing in stark contrast to the recent rash of books detailing the enduring alienation and exploitation endemic to familiar forms of wage labor (see, e.g., Schlosser 2001; Ehrenreich 2001; Cheever 2001; Fraser 2001; Ross 2002; and Levison 2002). The aggressive move to write the conventional proletariat out of the new economy represents an unreflective metonymic attempt to grasp the economic totality, echoing Marx's predictably Hegelian forecast of the homogenization of labor and capitalist society. Friedman's latest offering, *The World is Flat* (2005) is but the most recent and candid denial of the multiplicity of capital.[10]

This scramble for the unified theory of the economic scene, this persistent metonymic reduction of plural and mutually contradictory practices into a singular system, betrays a widespread discomfort with antagonism. This discomfort has been manifest in ungenerous readings of Hardt and Negri that paint them as declaring the death of the state in 2000, ironically just before the United States embarked on a series of relatively conventional military actions (see, e.g., Wood 2003). Responding to this common criticism, Hardt and Negri suggest that globalization debates have been hamstrung by purely quantitative assessments of state power, whereas it might be time to assess qualitative shifts. Instead of making yet another argument about rising or declining state power, Hardt and Negri argue that states remain important players in the political game but "are transformed by the emerging global power that they tend to increasingly serve" (2004:163). In other words, states are not disappearing or even losing power, but they are increasingly receiving their legitimacy from different sources. When national solvency requires accepting the prescriptions of the World Bank and the IMF, when localities surrender the right to regulate trade and arbitrate disputes to the WTO, and when capital mobility increases corporations' bargaining power over national governments—when such power shifts take place, government policy becomes increasingly mediated if not dictated by international banks and corporations rather than voting citizens. The question is not whether states are disappearing but only to what imperatives they must respond.

Hardt and Negri argue not that globalization anachronizes the nation-state but that it challenges the comforting liberal myths of national sovereignty and political representation by shifting its source of legitimacy. (Of course, concern that globalization unseats the sovereignty of nations works only from within a liberal conceit that national sovereignty resides in the faithful representation of citizens and not, for example, the effective enforcement of a ruling class's interests.) Globalization is not a question of more or less state; it is instead one of shifting sources of legitimacy and transformed capacities. Certainly one of the more hotly debated books in recent years, *Empire* (2000) may attract both its backers and its critics for just this reluctance to conform to the established options.

As a corollary to Hardt and Negri's view, I argue, the anxieties of globalization run deeper than particular challenges to familiar sites of responsibility. Globalization poses a challenge to the notion of responsibility itself. Threats to national sovereignty reverberate in challenges to other sites of sovereignty (e.g., individuals and corporations) by highlighting their mutual dependence on multiple sites of influence; the postliberal rupture of the individual subject reflects the collapse in the myth of national autonomy and univocity of rule. Whereas the ideology of self-ownership and liberal responsibility flourished under the conditions of a possessive market society and strong national governments (see MacPherson 1962), an increasingly globalized world that cannot ignore the porosity of borders and mutual dependence of institutions upsets the very notion of national and individual sovereignty underlying liberal responsibility. On this issue Hardt and Negri convey an optimism stemming from their conviction that structures of power do not merely coerce or erase subjects but form both collective and individual subjects with new capacities for political agency. Mimicking Marx's (1977: ch. 13) claim that the cooperative division of labor in industrial manufacture disturbs the ideology of individualism appropriate to the yeoman farmer and opens new capacities for collective political agency, Hardt and Negri see in the increasing visibility of the international division of labor new possibilities for international political organization. This potential perhaps explains the neoconservative emphasis on "nation building" in the Middle East and George W. Bush's promotion of an "ownership society" in 2004.

Each strategy attempts to rescue a concept threatened by the global crisis of sovereignty, and both suggest that the crisis spells not the end of politics but its renewal.

What Comes after the End of History?

Postliberals from Hegel through Butler have focused on the way subjects are formed in response to social conditions. Marx's discussion of the *Bildung* of a revolutionary class not only historicizes the equation of freedom with voluntary contracts but also points to the *political* production of alternatives (see chapter 2). Of course, Lenin hijacked this *Bildung* (the concept if not the term) and stripped it of its ambiguity, rendering class politics not entirely different from the heroic liberalism it was supposed to supersede. Gone was Marx's recognition that sovereignty is always fictional. Instead, Lenin merely transferred sovereignty from one metonymic production (the individual) to another (the class), ostensibly the unified and organic expression of a pure economic antagonism. Lenin replaced one reductionism with another, one immediacy with another, both of which ultimately provided limited and limiting understandings of economic responsibility. Lenin's reputation among democrats today is hardly any better than Hegel's,[11] but recent years have seen reconstructed marxisms working toward salvaging the economic focus of class politics without repeating the tragedies of Soviet Communism. Perhaps most notable in this movement are a pair of pairs, Ernesto Laclau and Chantal Mouffe, whose *Hegemony and Socialist Strategy* (1985) has consistently been both challenging and challenged since its publication twenty years ago, and Michael Hardt and Antonio Negri, whose *Empire* (2000) has been the most visible contribution to left-wing political theory so far in this century.

For Laclau and Mouffe, traditional narratives of class suffer from the same untenabilities as does liberal individualism: both trade in ideological theories of the immediacy, transparency, and unity of the subject, and both depend upon the identification of an authentic subject whose interests and emancipations can be envisioned (and perhaps realized) outside the field of discursive mediation that facilitates the notion of a subject. Laclau and Mouffe indict the history of class politics for its "monist aspiration" to reduce all social antagonisms to one: economics (1985:4). They thus call economics "the last redoubt of essentialism" (75–85) and point to new social movements (feminism, antiracism, and peace activism) as material manifestations of the plurality of social antagonisms.[12]

Laclau and Mouffe emphasize the insidious and antidemocratic reductionism inherent in establishing an ostensibly coherent political agent, be it the contracting individual or the revolutionary class. Too many political programs, they claim, deny how subjects are formed by a multiplicity of social antagonisms and instead presume *"a priori* agents of change" (1985:178). For Laclau and Mouffe, Leninism is the primary culprit in this mistake, "arbitrarily" grouping different antagonisms under the banner of a "universal class" with a privileged ontological and epistemological perspective (1985:167). Class, Laclau has argued on his own, is a part of the "dogmatic assertions" of "an insufficiently deconstructed traditional Marxism" (2000a:205); it does not avoid the insidious traps of the cult of heroism but only replicates them on a collective scale. This approach resonates with postliberal critiques of both liberalism and traditional marxism, for it parallels earlier statements concerning the multiplicity of capital as well as the critique of contract and sovereignty.

Laclau and Mouffe stumble, however, when they forward their postliberal critique under the banner of "radical democracy"—a seductive banner to be sure, but one that proves difficult to articulate.[13] Seeking an alternative to both Leninism and liberalism, each of which posits an organic unity of a sovereign subject, Laclau and Mouffe celebrate new social movements for admitting to the social and historical contingency of their emergent identities (1985:159–71). "Radical democracy," they argue, is "only possible . . . if we relinquish the category of 'subject' as a unified and unifying essence" (1985:181). But they do not explain why their criticism of unified subjectivity should apply only to identities that take themselves to be universal. Indeed, they seem to suggest that any assertion of identity (including the contingent identities of new social movements) threatens democracy.

Laclau and Mouffe dismantle the straw conception of the "universal class" to debunk economic analysis, but this leaves them implicitly endorsing two unsatisfying and incompatible positions. First, they explain new social movements as spontaneous expressions of existing social antagonisms, using the movements as evidence of the antagonisms. Though they report that their central concept—hegemony—refers explicitly to the situation in which everything is always politically contestable, they ultimately paint a political scene of movements as echoes of conditions without actors, precisely the apolitical scene they want to avoid. Second, while they politicize this scene by focusing on the struggle to articulate and rearticulate identities, they describe new social movements as "democratic" because they articulate the interests of the speaking subjects themselves. In other words, the authority of the sovereign speaker is used to establish the movements as democratic; Laclau and Mouffe thus rely upon reified individual preferences, effectively becoming liberals (1985:167, 184).[14] In short, Laclau and Mouffe promote democracy as dependent upon a relinquishment of the sovereign subject, but then they use this same subject to legitimate new social movements. They thus trade in the very categories they have been scrutinizing from the beginning, with scant if any attention to how their "rearticulation" avoids the pitfalls they have identified. Sleight of hand distracts from their post-liberalism's slide back into a warmed-over liberalism.

In setting out to elaborate the authoritarian foundations for class politics, Laclau eviscerates the subject in either guise, whether individual or collective, essential or contingent, liberal or postliberal. In contrast to Judith Butler, who endeavors to establish contingent, performative identities that can assume responsibility for their language and become "bad subjects," Laclau and Mouffe eschew such reconstructive work. They, like Butler's Althusser, fail to contribute to a reconstitution of the subject; they highlight how interpellation represses but ignore how it produces. As Laclau puts it: "We gain very little . . . by referring to [now deconstructed identities] through simple designations such as classes, ethnic groups, and so on, which are at best names for transient points of stabilization. The really important task is to understand the logics of their constitution and dissolution, as well as formal determinations of the spaces in which they interrelate" (Laclau 2000b:53). Though the little that "we" gain is in fact the possibility of collective political action, Laclau and Mouffe regularly dismiss such designations as authoritarian (often, and more polemically, totalitarian). Though they argue that radical democracy depends on renouncing "the category of the subject as a unitary, transparent, and sutured entity" (1985:166), they fail to clarify who or what might perform democracy. True, the stabilizations that Laclau and Mouffe trouble cannot capture the richness of diversity both among and within subjects, but they are nonetheless indispensable for any notion of political responsibility. Indeed, the radically democratic refusal of the false unity proposed by either liberal or collective identities is essentially a refusal of political institutions.[15] Because Laclau and Mouffe accept the choice between sovereignty and democracy, they choose the latter but fail to describe what subject might fill this emergent democratic space.

Encountering this same problem of sovereignty, Hardt and Negri offer a substantially more gratifying response. As they explain it, "The entire tradition of political theory seems to agree on one basic principle: only 'the one' can rule" (2004:328). In liberal legitimations of states, this principle is evident in the sovereignty of a crowd ("a people") that can be faithfully represented in governance; it is evident, too, in marxist refusals of the nation in favor of a class ("the proletariat") with a similar unity of interests (2004:328–31).[16] Indeed, it is this presumption of the self-identical subject that has legitimated social-contract theory since the seventeenth century, and expressed alternatives to liberal democracy have themselves maintained the legitimating foundation of representing the true interests of a unified collective subject. The crisis in political thought and institutions today, Hardt and Negri argue, is that this grounding myth of sovereignty is becoming less valuable as autonomous subjects become more difficult to find. They argue that because it threatens the most familiar site of sovereignty (the nation-state), globalization has created a crisis in the notion of sovereignty itself; echoing Jameson, they claim that the postmodern critique of individual sovereignty is an efflux of challenges to the most established manifestations of sovereignty (2000:142, 150–54). Their work responds to this crisis not by seeking to reestablish sovereignty but by reconstructing politics without it.[17]

Whereas Laclau and Mouffe smuggle sovereignty into their radical democracy, Hardt and Negri attempt to describe a political logic that is not beholden to it, and they call this logic "the multitude." The multitude, they argue, is the emergent postliberal subject composed of diverse populations and identities acting in concert but without centralized authority; it is both a product of and response to the decentering apparatuses of global capital. That is, in contrast to the unified subjects of "the people" or "the class," the multitude, enabled by the proliferation of information technologies and the international division of labor, never purports to achieve a singular identity but acts without it. Again, drawing from Marx's claim that the division of labor provides both the form and the content for the structure of subjectivity, Hardt and Negri argue that the dispersed mode of production corresponding to an increasingly deterritorialized network of finance capital and immaterial commodities informs a subjectivity that is dispersed and lacking in traditional sovereignty. This contrasts starkly with an earlier industrial age in which commerce took the form of buying and selling discrete material objects and units of labor power. It has become more and more difficult to believe the myth of self-ownership or to identify where the product of my labor ends and that of another worker begins.

This embryonic discussion of governance without sovereignty replicates Butler's claims about postliberal agency: the multitude's agency comes not from its autonomy from global capital but precisely from its position in it; the multitude does not seek to establish an identity so that it can act but instead creates itself in acting. This is not identity politics but performative politics, not possessive individualism but effective collectivism. The multitude refuses the representational and sovereign model of subjectivity. It announces the metonymic nature of subjectivity not as a liability but as an asset. Such political action, Hardt and Negri argue, was ephemerally realized in the antiglobalization protests materializing at the 1999 WTO meetings in Seattle, a moment they view as the model of cooperative political action independent of the traditional model of sovereignty and hierarchical organization. This was not, as Marx puts it in the *Brumaire*, the peasant playing the hero; it was instead a refusal of the logic of heroism that is tied to the cult of genius in capitalist markets (2004:336–40) or the vanguard in authoritarian socialism (219–27). While the logic of heroism is utterly consistent with aristocratic or emergent capitalist orders, it is inconsistent with the current state of global deterritorialized finance capital and so does not manifest in the organic effluxes of responsive subjectivity; political action today, they argue, is not heroic and sovereign but multiplicitous and anarchic.[18] Whereas Marx returned to the familiar logic of heroism and authenticity in the age of an emergent financial aristocracy, Hardt and Negri see a dislocated subject emerging in response to the decentering logic of global capital. Seattle, for Laclau, is ironic: thousands take to the streets to contest global capital right as he announces its impossibility. For Hardt and Negri, it is kismet, evidence of the multitude.[19]

The specifically economic implications of this transformation in subjectivity, Hardt and Negri note, include a direct threat to the centrality of private property, which has, at least since Locke, rested on a narrative of individual initiative and autonomous authorship. In a milieu of intensified communications networks that facilitate the increased importance of intellectual production, the open-source movement exemplifies the demise of individual authorship and proprietary ownership of the products. Hardt and Negri suggest that this movement, coordinating production and innovation through collaborative and collective efforts instead of individual initiative, can serve as the model for democratic governance without sovereignty; democracy of the multitude might be an "open source society" (2004:340). At present, however, they see us occupying a middle space between sovereignty and open source, a transition point that has recently become manifest in the debates over torture at U.S. military prisons. With the Bush administration claiming that the historically unprecedented nature of the "global war on terror" renders the government exempt from the protocols of the Geneva Convention, it becomes clear that there is no standing code or apparatus for regulating this novel situation. For Hardt and Negri, this signals the need for new agencies that might respond to the current state of affairs, which they describe as an interminable and global civil war of Empire (2004:4).

Though the multitude resists the facile causal narratives of individual or even collective responsibility arising from willed causality, it contains an implicit reformulation of responsibility without the baggage of sovereignty. Its contours upset the logic of contract and authorship that legitimate representative government and capitalist markets, but, as I show in the next section, it also refigures subjectivity as capacities for response to issues irreducible to contracts and representation. The multitude thus transcends the liberal proceduralism that condemns particular instances of fraud or theft but offers scant resources for understanding responsibility for situations that lie beyond any actor's causal will. This reconfiguration of subjectivity also provides an enhanced rather than diminished commitment to issues of economic justice, for it contains a vulnerability and dependence that ultimately informs an ethos of generosity unrestricted by the presumed autonomy of individual contractors.

Economic Revival

Though Hardt and Negri trace the possibilities of governance without sovereignty, they do not speak at length about the status of the concept of responsibility. Iris Young (2003, 2004, n.d.), however, has recently endeavored to articulate a theory of economic responsibility that transcends the liberal priority of contracts and can account for a postliberal responsibility for basic human resources such as food, housing, and education. Just as Hardt and Negri argue that the logic of the multitude is on display in protests confronting international trade conferences, Young argues that a postliberal theory of responsibility is already operating—if only implicitly—in the antisweatshop movement. In protesting outside the Gap or petitioning universities to restrict licensing agreements to apparel manufacturers certified sweatshop free, this movement pitches its claims not against actors causally responsible for gross exploitation but instead to actors institutionally invested with the ability to respond to economic injustices. According to Young, these protests "make little sense within [the] dominant conception of responsibility," which is rooted in contract, but make perfect sense from within an alternative theory (2004:366).

Insofar as liberalism arbitrarily ties responsibility to contractual obligations and causal wrongs, it is difficult to assign responsibility for structural inequalities and violations.[20] With regard to sweatshop labor, this diffi-culty arises not only because the causal agents (operators of sweatshops) are typically located in remote territories, rendering them largely invisible and politically inaccessible, but also because these operators are themselves merely jockeying for position in a cutthroat production market, structurally compelled to reduce costs or go out of business. They are, in other words, superficially responsible because they authorize particularly exploitative contracts but only ideologically held to be the authors of those conditions in which production happens. Indeed, exploiters are coerced into contracts just as the exploited are.

For Young, this realization threatens to lead to our familiar impasse, de-manding that sinister individuals be held accountable for deplorable working conditions or allowing the ubiquity of market coercion to displace the ques-tion of responsibility. Again, neither option is terribly attractive. The former promises to safeguard responsibility as an instrument of political analysis and prescription, but it does this by refusing to attend to the background conditions against which contracts happen. The latter highlights the theo-retical and political inadequacies of the logic of contract, but it undermines the conventional justifications for punishment or political remediation for particular injustices. Once again, displacing responsibility from individual actors to anonymous structures threatens to abandon the rhetoric of injus-tice, instead casting the situation entirely as an uncaused and accidental misfortune (Shklar 1990).

These are the familiar and unsatisfying alternatives that render respon-sibility so inadequate and so indispensable. According to Young, the anti-sweatshop movement attends to both these dimensions in its "rather novel" approach to responsibility, which targets not individuals or corporations who sign particularly offensive contracts but rather consumers and licensers who indirectly support such contracts via their own market transactions. As such, this movement lays responsibility for exploitation at the feet of those who benefit from it indirectly (and often ignorantly). Emphasizing how the results of contracts extend well beyond an agent's vision or intention, this activity challenges the foundations of limited liability in a way consonant with the porous and dependent nature of postliberal subjectivity. The move-ment does not target consumers merely because the sweatshop operators are abroad and inaccessible; rather, it exploits the arbitrary nature of an exclusive focus on proximate and seemingly causal agents. While liberal responsibility strains at its seams when trying to attribute deplorable working conditions to anything other than employers, this movement suggests that the requirements of liberal responsibility are inadequate to the situation of economic injustice through global trade. Young argues that the movement is not merely displacing responsibility from anonymous corporations onto individual consumers. Instead, it is transforming what makes for responsibility.

Young sees one advantage of this reworked theory of responsibility in the fact that unlike the contract model, it does not indict particular actors and thereby exonerate everybody else. Whereas liberal responsibility trades in presumptions of sovereignty and so focuses on finding *the* responsible agent or agents, postliberal responsibility instead focuses on identifying capacities for response, an operation that never promises to release all (or any) other actors from responsibility. This entails abandoning the rhetoric of guilt (which is exclusive), replacing it with something closer to shame (whose stock does not deplete in being assigned).[21] Further, the contract model focuses exclusively on events, on deviations from normal activity. As a result, it has nothing to say about responsibility for business as usual, even when business as usual involves widespread economic injustice. By decoupling responsibility from causality, however, the concept can continue to operate in absence of identifiable causal actions; responsibility can thus be rooted not in contributory fault but in the ability to respond. This expands our political vision, enabling the application of the effective rhetoric of responsibility to situations that heretofore lacked the requisite characteristics for political remediation. This ability to theorize novel situations might be the principal contribution of postliberal responsibility, since it is a prerequuisite to the formulation of adequate responses.

Individual, contractual responsibility is easy to manage and codify, whereas postliberalism disrupts the conventional markers of responsibility (such as the beginning and endings of particular exchanges) in a manner that threatens to render everybody responsible for everything. This threat is exacerbated, but not qualitatively altered, by the increasingly dense, multilayered, and geographically dispersed character of the market. While institutional borders circumscribe individuals and corporations so as to delimit and assign particular responsibilities, they also establish the limits of what situations will beckon a response. The metonymic construction of subjects goes a long way toward determining what will be an injustice and what merely a misfortune.

Young's readiness to describe sweatshop labor and global poverty as "structural injustices" (rather than, say, "economic misfortunes") already indicates a more capacious model of responsibility for global economic con-

cerns. Young attributes homelessness, for example, to "the normal operations of markets and institutions of planning, building, land use regulation,
investment, finance and exchange" (n.d.). But this does not stop her from
calling this an "injustice"; though the situation results not from any particular contracts but instead from "the actions of a large number of agents—
renters, home buyers, mortgage lenders, real estate brokers, developers, land
use regulators, transport planners, and so on" (n.d.)—she continues to see
this as a situation to which a rhetoric of responsibility is appropriate. This
is possible, however, only from a consequentialist rather than a procedural-
ist theory of responsibility, and Young marshals the language of injustice
because of the possibility of response.

Recognition of liberal responsibility's inability to engage economic injustice is certainly not restricted to the antisweatshop movement. Currents
of globalization and globalization theory have rekindled dialogues on responsibility for international aid. Tectonic shifts in global capital and international governance have inspired anxious attempts to argue for a renewed
responsibility for assisting the world's poor, and the vibrant debate on this
issue reveals perhaps as well as any other the conceptual limitations on liberal responsibility and its inadequacy to the contemporary global economy.
Some argue that responsibility for international aid stems from the fact that
the wealth of particular territories depends on the exploitation of others;
comfort and style in the United States, that is, depends upon the exploitation
of workers abroad (see, e.g., O'Neill 1985, 1996; Pogge 2002, 2004). Others,
however, argue that responsibility stems from a moral obligation to assist
the less fortunate (e.g., Singer 1972, 2004; Rawls 1999). While the former
argument trades in the conventional causal logic of guilt (extended to account for the density and distance of transactions in the global economy),
the latter reverts to a logic of shame (locating responsibility not in any
causal harm but in moral obligation to ease suffering). The former takes First
World residents to task and asks them to take responsibility for the effects of
their contracts—the same old liberal model that holds individuals accountable for their contracts. The latter model tends to abandon the rhetoric of
responsibility, speaking of abstract and utilitarian obligations but avoiding
any discussion of the way institutional arrangements systematically produce
poverty. A postliberal approach, by contrast, takes what is most valuable from
each of these approaches, situating a responsibility for global poverty in the
interpellating and performative institutions of global capital by explaining
both markets and desires as sites of perpetual response. Responsibility thus
inheres not in contributory fault nor in utilitarian cosmopolitanism but in

the opportunities for subversion and transformation bestowed upon subjects of global capital.[22]

A postliberal subject—the multitude, for example—provides such a transformed relationship to international economics and thereby responsibility. In Young's story, decent housing is difficult to see as a responsibility because the situation lacks a sovereign causal agent; even if we were to talk about the sovereignty of state, local, or national governments, consideration of architectural, environmental, industrial, and commercial interests reveals less a sovereign institution than a set of disparate agents converging at a legal apparatus. In this situation, highlighted by globalization's threat to national sovereignty, liberals are understandably anxious about the status of responsibility. But by abandoning the imperative to causal responsibility, and by working through the transient and nonsovereign points of stability opened up by the movements of global capital, postliberalism provides an alternative, more capacious and responsive, diagnosis of economic responsibility. For just as churches, families, and nations draw borders around assemblages of bodies so as to coordinate responses and obligations, the multitude creates a broader and less conceited subject, capable of responding to material conditions without presuming to be sovereign over them.

Economic growth and the transnational exchange of goods and services have removed the immediate and familiar checks on sweatshop labor: visibility to the consumer, federal worker safety regulations, unified ownership and control of corporations. In such a situation, liberal responsibility experiences its limits—not merely because it cannot deal with the situation but because while it proposes to enable, it actually paralyzes. A postliberal approach reveals how the conceit of sovereignty neutralizes the very concept it is intended to protect.

Young declines her own invitation to argue for the superiority of postliberal to liberal responsibility. Instead, she focuses on the limitations of each and suggests that the incapacity of liberal responsibility to attend fully to global inequalities makes it inadequate to guide reflection on economics and bureaucratic violations. Though her reluctance clearly stems from a desire to retain such liberal institutions as representative government and criminal liability, I would like to go slightly further than she does. For the inadequacies of liberal responsibility are not merely political; the notion is predicated on the dubious ontological presumptions I discussed in the first three chapters of this book.

Like Young, I appreciate the value of representative government and criminal liability; I am, again, postliberal, not illiberal. But these institutions rest on the sovereign conceit that is today under heavy fire, as Hardt and Negri demonstrate. The strain on these established institutions as they confront changed historical conditions is also evident from the renewed attention to campaign finance: when it is not merely votes that influence electoral success and thus state policy, the institution of representative government must attempt to reestablish its legitimacy by regulating other forms of political speech. Reconstruction of these institutions cannot legitimately stem from a political imperative to turn a blind eye to their current ideological justifications. Instead, the project must be to create institutions justifiable from within a postliberal ontology, in which the performative nature of subjectivity is not taken as a general threat to the health and interests of other beings but instead informs a generous reception of otherness in a manner that invokes a responsibility for the economic and material well-being of neighbors and collaborators in the project of human (and maybe nonhuman) history.[23] Indeed, abandoning the liberal logic of individual sovereignty for a postliberal recognition of the inevitable dependence of subjects on one another suggests seeing other actors not as competitors in history but as necessary complements of our own being.

Beyond Contract

The postliberal critique of individual autonomy poses a direct threat to the institution of private property and free contract. To respond to this threat with a reactive grasp at these concepts, however, threatens to reduce their application to instances that conform to the tenets of individual authorship. Marx noticed this one hundred and fifty years ago, arguing that the privatization of property ignores the public issues that interfere with its acquisition. When responsibility is privatized, and when responsibility functions as the organizing concept of economic activities, only private issues receive consideration. In other words, liberals protect responsibility by restricting its application to convenient and conservative situations.

Again, liberal commitment to sovereignty reduces economic responsibility to the fulfillment of voluntary contracts. In doing so, it trades in a model of agency increasingly frustrated not only by larger and more powerful social actors (large corporations and international finance organizations) but also by the background conditions against which economic transactions take place; the marketing of desires and the restriction of opportunities, both severe obstacles to autonomous choice, are difficult to accommodate within the vocabulary of contractual responsibilities. Political necessity, rather than ontological legitimacy, casts the visible movements of bodies and currencies as autonomous—fetishes, acting of their own accord.

A postliberal theory of responsibility that is rooted less in individual willed causality and more in the capacities for dealing with economic situations politicizes many heretofore private economic issues, such as poverty, exploitation, and inadequate housing. Because these are not products of any individual or collective actor's choice and are only legalized (but not caused) by individual contracts, they are entirely legitimate and justifiable from within a liberal, procedural approach to economic responsibility. They appear as misfortunes rather than injustices. Liberalism thus provides little by way of a concrete theory of distributive justice, whereas a postliberal challenge to the presumed autonomy of individuals opens the door for an ethical and generous encounter with others.

While a marxist economism abandons the problematic but indispensable concept of responsibility, a postliberal reworking of collective agency—such as that provided by Hardt and Negri—need not become the subjectless play of contingencies that it has been in the past. The multitude is not an autonomous actor with a will and sovereignty that can cause shifts in distributions of wealth and power. It is a metonymic construction produced by the condition of global capital that can respond to that situation. Its agency— and its responsibility—comes not from its autonomy but from its contingency. In a theory of interpellation that recognizes the productive rather than merely repressive power of naming, the multitude emerges as a subject ready to take responsibility for the economic texture of globalization. Such a postliberal concept does not offer a replacement for the increasingly threatened notion of sovereignty but rather suggests a way to distribute responsibility without it.

FIVE

Postliberal Responsibility
and the Death of Amadou Diallo

Preface

February 4, 1999. Four plainclothes officers of the New York City Police Department's Street Crimes Unit (SCU), assigned to aggressively and proactively patrol high crime-rate areas, approach a man for loitering and acting suspiciously in front of a Bronx apartment building. They suspect that the man may be participating (or preparing to participate) in a robbery, or he may resemble the description of a serial rapist preying on the neighborhood. The tension and fear that mark moments such as this one take over when the suspect reaches for his wallet, and the officers, thinking the shiny piece of leather to be a weapon, react. A few moments and pints of adrenaline later, the unarmed African immigrant Amadou Diallo lies dead of nineteen gunshot wounds (twenty-two other shots having missed their target). A year later, a jury declares the incident to be an honest though admittedly tragic mistake.

February 4, 1999. Four NYPD officers see a black man on the street and, as is typical for trigger-happy thugs with badges, decide to harass him. They approach the "suspect" without identifying themselves, point guns at him, and fire when he, in a panic (perhaps thinking that he was being robbed), reaches for his wallet. The officers and the NYPD later justify this twentieth-century lynching of Amadou Diallo with claims that, in the dark, a black piece of leather can appear to be a gun and that the suspect failed to remain still when ordered to do so. One year after the rabidly racist, uniformed savages fire forty-one shots at the unarmed man, an upstate jury far removed from and incapable of understanding the conditions of the Bronx finds the officers not guilty of all charges—even the least serious charge of reckless endangerment.

February 4, 1997. Responding to Mayor Rudolph Giuliani's promise to increase the size and scope of aggressive policing in high crime-rate areas and to the national sentiment favoring increased policing and surveillance, NYPD Chief Howard Safir announces a decision to triple the size of the high-pressure Street Crimes Unit. Many SCU members complain that this dramatic increase means less screening and training of applicants, leading to more volatile situations. Exactly two years later, as the media darling Giuliani is being praised for cleaning up many areas of the city and little dissent is heard locally or nationally about the more aggressive and arguably unconstitutional practices (e.g., "stop-and-search") being used to curtail crime, four officers who joined the SCU during its rapid expansion empty their weapons on the unarmed Amadou Diallo in the vestibule of his apartment building.

Question: Who is responsible for the death of Amadou Diallo? The officers? Chief Safir? Mayor Giuliani? Citizens who support more aggressive policing and punishment but not education, prevention, rehabilitation, and generally respectable living conditions? Intellectual workers who do not consistently challenge this support? Me?

• • •

Few images have been so prominent in the United States over the past few decades than that of the police. From the war on drugs to the Battle in Seattle to 9/11, from Dirty Harry to "Miami Vice" to scores of interracial buddy flicks to "Cops," from Rodney King to Mark Fuhrman to Amadou Diallo, we encounter police at every cultural and political corner. Cops, we hear, both protect us and attack us. They are superheroes and supervillains; they are the "thin blue line" that stands between us and total anarchy and the enforcement mechanism of a racist and oppressive state.

Each of the preceding representations of the Amadou Diallo case attributes responsibility for the same affair to a different site; each is informed by and visibly reproduces a particular theory of agency.[1] Narratives of the police, implicated as they are in cultural discourses of freedom and control, are a particularly productive site for examining how these theories mediate our experience of social and political events. Because attempts to explain events are inseparable from attributions of responsibility (the term *agency* asserts this affinity), their form and content condition not only our ability to theorize solutions but also the types of events we consider as worthy of our attention.

In this chapter I explore the language and concepts used to narrate and comprehend police misconduct in order to demonstrate the restricted explanatory power of the hegemonic ideology mediating our everyday lived experiences. I argue that liberal responsibility is inadequate for attending to the causes of events and that postliberal responsibility provides a more satisfying understanding of criminal justice and political violence.

Privatizing Agency

The first two narratives of the Diallo case trade in conventional theories of agency, in which events are the expressions of either determining, stable institutions or autonomous, voluntarist subjects. These options constrain discussions of practically every event that captures public attention, and they reproduce the ubiquitous dichotomy between structuralisms and liberalisms identified in previous chapters. The former approach focuses on the way historical conditions dictate behaviors, and the latter emphasizes how events arise from willed actions. Eschewing both, I aim to show that their inconsistent and politically convenient deployment demonstrates how they are both sutured to a liberal understanding of responsibility that recommends punitive and retributive responses to social ills.

I have already discussed many of the ontopolitical shortcomings of liberal responsibility. My project here is to apply this liberal understanding to the specific field of criminal justice. I demonstrate how the theory of agency it provides narrowly circumscribes which types of social conditions will receive attention. Coding events as the products of the actions and desires of individuals, it encourages us to examine historical events for which we can find an identifiable agent and proscribes discussions of events that cannot be identified as the product of individuated actors. By privatizing agency,[2] this approach suggests that socially meaningful action stems from individual actors, ignoring the structural and public resources necessary for and implicated in the production of history.

The Diallo narratives demonstrate this tendency. The first account (which ultimately carried the day in an Albany courtroom and in the court of public opinion) locates the essential cause of police brutality in ghetto crime. The horrifying conditions under which officers work render it predictable and justifiable (if still regrettable) that they will occasionally respond with over-zealous enforcement and tragic results; a violent culture mandates (*justifies*) particular behaviors on the parts of officers. This approach was most clearly demonstrated by John Podhoretz (1999, 2000) in the *Weekly Standard,* where he argued that neither police nor soldiers can be blamed for killing in the line of duty.[3] More generally, James Q. Wilson roots this approach in an overtly racial social Darwinism that offers a biological determinism peppered with a healthy dose of individual choice: though nonwhites are biologically inclined to criminal behavior (where "criminal behavior" is unjustifiably reduced to street violence), they ultimately *choose* to be criminals (see Wilson 1992; Wilson and Herrnstein 1985; cf. Dumm 1993). Though Podhoretz and Wilson both blame residents of low-income black neighborhoods for police brutality, their less immediate project is to argue that the causes of police brutality precede and exceed the actions and wills of offending officers.

By contrast, the second story places responsibility for the event squarely in the lap of individuals, claiming that officers beat and shoot civilians and suspects because they are racist thugs. From this position, evident in academia, the media, and the streets, little or no attention is paid to cultural inputs or structural incentives to police violence. Witness the astounding hostility toward the police during the so-called antiglobalization protests of recent years, de rigueur slogans such as "Cops Are Not People" and "Shoot Cops in the Face" suggesting no discomfort with identifying officers as monsters. See also the polemics that regularly emerge in progressive organs such as *The Nation,* which present cops as nothing other than glorified class traitors exaggerating professional dangers to justify habitual and unprovoked violence (e.g., Cockburn 2000a, 2000b). Similarly, Human Rights Watch (1998) issued a report that holds individual officers almost exclusively responsible for incidents of excessive force.

These approaches to police brutality are particular manifestations of general presumptions about causality and responsibility. One approach reduces street crime to the systematic violations to which poor and nonwhite populations are subject (poverty, racism, lack of opportunity), and the other, to individual defect. Similarly, corporate malfeasance is the predictable expression of a culture of avarice or arises from a few rotten apples in an otherwise wholesome Wall Street barrel. The divide was particularly noticeable around another event from the spring of 1999: the Columbine High School massacre. Did Dylan Klebold and Eric Harris attack their classmates because of personal defects—psychological disorders or inadequate parenting? Or is the event best explained with reference to a set of structural conditions—a classist jock culture, alienation, and access to weaponry? In contrast to "the pinstriped Mafiosi of the culture wars, from Gary Bauer to Trent Lott," who position Columbine in waning morality and waxing "Goth culture, abortion and godless parenting," Bruce Shapiro (1999:4) argues that "just one salient detail separates the schoolyard shooters of [recent years] from angry and alienated youth of previous generations: greater access to guns and the corporate-marketed culture of firearms."

At first glance, such analyses appear to demonstrate a clear split between those interested in offering subject-centered narratives in a language of personal responsibility and those seeking to avoid it. If this were the case, they would correspond with the historical dichotomy between liberalism and structuralism already discussed and would likely leave us with little more than familiar soliloquies on the relative power of individuals and institutions. But an examination of rhetorics of police brutality and explanations of *state* violence shows how this apparent dichotomy masks an underlying uniformity. While personal responsibility advocates want to hold individuals accountable for their actions, they sing a different tune when officers beat and shoot suspects: working in such a dangerous environment, the story goes, cops cannot afford to step lightly. Similarly, though the structurally minded depersonalize the causes of street crime, this treatment is rarely extended to the perpetrators of police brutality: cops, we hear, are evil and vindictive. Those normally waving the flag of personal responsibility offer systemic explanations, whereas their structural counterparts hold individual cops responsible for their criminal responses to crime (actual, perceived, or presumed).

Each of these paradigmatic positions, in other words, is beholden to a liberal theory of responsibility that roots causality in the actions of unified and autonomous subjects. Because they both thoroughly privatize agency, the options are to concede some form of determinism (biological or social) in which no subject can be responsible for authoring any particular action or to utilize liberal concepts to attribute responsibility to an individual. This means that they must either argue that events are beyond the control of willing subjects or accept methodological individualism. Because the first option effectively proscribes any intervention into the practical arena of electoral politics, even otherwise consistent structuralists ultimately ascribe responsibility to individuals.

The uniformity underlying this apparent dichotomy betrays both the conceptual hegemony and the restricted explanatory potential of liberal responsibility. With its methodological and grammatical commitment to the individual, liberalism compels casting events as the expression of anonymous structures or identifiable individuals; its conceptual blackmail compels either a liberal commitment to individualism or an abandonment of responsibility through the language of structural determinism. Conditions that might not fit into this schema have difficulty finding voice. Indeed, *conditions* are not news; *events* are.

In contrast to both these options, a postliberal theory of agency will focus on the way behaviors both respond to and produce a set of enabling and constraining social conditions—the way subjects and their wills are both producers and products of the conditions of their existence. This is *post*liberal because while it builds upon the liberal insight that agency stems from subjects formed in particular ways, it contests the reifying or essentializing moves of liberal models of the voluntarist subject. As well, it avoids the rival trap of reducing subjects to expressions of structures. A postliberal language allows us to attribute responsibility to agents without presuming the autonomy or coherence of the subject. That is, postliberalism recognizes the porousness of the agent and the inherently metonymic process that is the identification of subjects. Whereas liberalism accepts the causal force of the decisions of individuated subjects, postliberalism examines how these decisions become possible and desired.

Liberalism's hegemony reveals itself in responses to police brutality offered by those seemingly most opposed to the reifying categories of orthodox liberalism. More often than not, those inclined to explain street crime through reference to the disgraceful conditions that pervade low-income neighborhoods and racial ghettos blame officers for events such as the Diallo affair (just as the officers blame the recipients of their rage). While officers and their attorneys argue that Diallo's stop would have been routine if he had not reached for his wallet, we hear the retort that everything would have been fine if the officers were not determined to harass nonwhite males. Responding to the Diallo verdict, New Jersey's (troubled) poet laureate, the activist Amiri Baraka, expresses this view in a statement exceptional perhaps only for its clarity: "The Klan have gone indoors. The Klan wear blue uniforms now" (qtd. in Rashbaum 2000).

Of course, the officers are not the only racists in town. As the civil rights activist, community leader, and minister Calvin O. Butts III states: "I can't say [Mayor] Giuliani pulled the trigger. He was not there. But I can say he has created in this city a divisiveness, a climate that gives a chance for people who are filled with rage, people who are racist, to strike out against the poor or downtrodden" (qtd. in Lipton 2000). Butts's attempt to go beyond the obvious—to admit that there is something notable that underlies officers' behavior—is encouraging. By invoking Giuliani, Butts strategically moves the analysis from the curb to City Hall in order to produce an explanation of the event that exceeds its proximate agents. He troubles orthodox liberalism by implicating a set of established social forces in the ostensibly autonomous will of offending officers. So far, so good. But by ultimately laying the blame in Giuliani's lap—as if the temperament of NYPD officers and the spirit of all New York were fashioned by Giuliani's hands—he demonstrates my thesis. Structural analysis needs a liberal face, and so the new subject produced by Butts concedes to the imperatives of liberalism; Butts's contribution, that is, only appears to challenge liberalism, resting as it is on the attribution of blame to conscious decisions of a single actor. This is a textbook case of vicarious responsibility.

This move becomes pervasive whenever the issue of police misconduct arises.[4] When, also in 1999, LAPD officer Rafael Perez indicted nearly one hundred fellow officers of the Rampart division of the CRASH unit (Los Angeles's version of New York City's SCU) on violations ranging from selling seized narcotics to rape and murder of "suspects," Alexander Cockburn (2000b) used the pages of The Nation to argue that this scandal "traces its specific origin to campaign pledges by Los Angeles Mayor Richard Riordan to hire more police."[5] Bob Herbert (2000), in a New York Times column slightly more sympathetic to conditions of vengeance, describes NYPD officers as "arrogant, tyrannical, poorly trained, often frightened and not infrequently racist" and argues that charging the four assailing officers was misguided in suggesting the problem was one of a few flawed individuals. But he then proceeds to identify Mayor Giuliani (along with Chief Safir) as the problem. While he asks us to recognize Diallo's shooting as an event indicative of wider problems, he says nothing about the causes of these problems beyond pointing to a police chief and mayor who do not discourage this behavior.[6] Given an electoral politics in which individuals are structurally invested with the power and obligation to attend to such events, this move to a representative attribution of responsibility is probably inescapable. This inescapability, however, renders it no less inadequate.

Analyses such as these shift responsibility to executive decisions producing conditions in which police violence is made more likely. Nevertheless, their stock in trade remains a single, identifiable agent upon whom to lay blame. It might be highly advisable to criticize Riordan's or Giuliani's wrongheaded plans to reduce particular types of crime, but suggesting that Riordan and Giuliani are the "specific origin" of these events occludes the fact that both mayors received enormous praise for these positions. Blaming them thus ascribes to them a sovereignty that they only ideologically appear to possess. Indeed, they owe their public support and political careers to the fact that the citizens of their cities supported these policies (see Bai and Beals 1999). Allowing Giuliani to embody the political will of the city—to metonymically stand in for the public sentiment—distracts from a culture of fear and misinformation that rewards such campaign promises with votes. Giuliani is sacrificed for our sins. (At Columbine, it is the parents.) This approach does not attend to Riordan and Giuliani as actors in a set of conditions that precede and exceed them (for politicians are compelled to appease the distorted values of their respective constituencies), and it ignores the inherently inconsistent liberal commandments to Giuliani as both representative of and autonomous from the people.

Critics such as Cockburn and Herbert, then, while usually found in the most structural of postures, are compelled to default to a liberal theory of agency when it comes time to assign responsibility for an event. Typically comfortable invoking structure to link street crime to unemployment and poor education, this approach is not taken to its logical conclusion. Understandably and admirably hesitant to depersonalize tragedies or suggest our impotence to confront overwhelming conditions, these critics offer liberal solutions and attributions of responsibility to particular manifestations of the conditions of our existence (here, the dispositions of officers and elected officials). The resources afforded us by liberalism's concepts and institutions push these critics inexorably toward individualist diagnoses. Responsibility, therefore, falls upon individuals, informing remedies based in punishment and retribution rather than systematic overhauling of institutions and values.

A postliberal approach, however, will complicate this story by characterizing proximate causes and ostensible authors as arbitrary stopping points in retroactive attempts to diagnose events; these metonyms (e.g., "City Hall," "the mayor," or even "Giuliani") are produced by deeper social afflictions. We need not reduce subjects to the unwilling expression of social conditions to attend to the formation of subjects and their wills in such a way as to demonstrate the underlying roots of particular events in a set of social conditions that render events possible and likely. While liberalism is seductive for its ability to isolate remediable causes of events, it does not have a monopoly on coherent notions of agency.

Liberalism's conceptual hegemony, however, also helps explain the public identification of certain types of activity as worthy of consideration. For example, we all know what a candidate's "tough-on-crime" platform means, and it most assuredly does not mean spending collective resources to combat the fraudulent, exploitative, and coercive standard operating procedures of publicly traded corporations. As William Connolly (2000) argues, we tend to consider only those practices that have clear, identifiable, individuated agents; within this "politics of displacement," we focus on the injustice of police brutality (and the specific actors responsible for it) while ignoring the systematic ravages that impersonal forces of capitalism inflict on poor and nonwhite populations. Judith Butler similarly highlights the tendency among American conservatives to localize responsibility for urban violence by focusing on the lyrics of gangsta rappers while ignoring the more intractable issues of race and poverty (1997a:22–3). Public attention falls on predatory serial killers who sensationally murder a handful of victims, whereas profiteering decisions not to produce and distribute medicines to treat malaria and diarrhea lead to millions of unacknowledged deaths. Commuters in suburban assault vehicles are blamed for the shameful quality of our environment, but how much do we hear about the residential landscapes that require long commutes in private vehicles? We vilify parents who risk their children's health by smoking in their presence but not an affluent country that allows nearly 25 percent of its population to live without health insurance. From within the hegemonic codes of liberalism, events that can be ascribed to individuals receive public attention, while situations that do not arise from discrete individuals and decisions persist largely in silence.[7]

The obvious objection here—that serial killers willingly engage in homicidal activities, whereas nobody intends any harm when they produce and distribute Viagra and Botox rather than antimalarials—validates my point. This distinction turns on suspiciously unproblematic notions of authorship and intentionality rooted in a liberal theory of the subject. Returning to the issue of police brutality, our culture's authoritative tales of heroes and villains proscribe as impracticable or apologist any approach other than prosecuting particular offenders. They do not suggest attending to the context of issues or to the formation of desires and abilities. Rather, they propose personal technologies of punishment and containment. Not only does this approach recommend solutions much tidier than their attendant situations, but failures to identify a guilty agent rarely lead to an examination of an event's constituent environment. Instead, as in Los Angeles after the Rodney King verdict, the quest turns impotently to another identifiable and contained racist or classist collection of individuals whom we can blame: jurors.

Since juries serve as proxies for the whole society, the move to hold them responsible might also serve as an indictment of the society at large for sanctioning such behaviors. (As far as I know, this claim has not yet been tested in court.) While the move to the jury remains for the most part couched in the liberal language of individuality, it does mark a productive path toward postliberalism—indicting as it does the general culture. (By the same logic, we should not be surprised at the difficulty in convicting officers of brutality, since we are asking jurors to hold themselves responsible.) Just as radical (or postliberal) democrats argue that political representation rests upon a presumption of individual autonomy and fixity of interests, I propose that punishment and containment are adequate responses to social ills only if we endorse the presumptions of authorship endemic to liberal responsibility. That is, our criminals are as much our representatives as our officials are.[8]

The LAPD officer/apologist (and *noir* novelist) Joseph Wambaugh (2000) inadvertently demonstrates this principle. Wambaugh argues in the *Los Angeles Times* that the abuses of the Rampart division were comparable to the My Lai massacre in Vietnam. Neither was a "tip of the iceberg"; rather, both were isolated events of evil individuals—each was "the whole iceberg." Let's set aside the hotly contested and unsubstantiated claim that My Lai was an aberration, and also the distinction that My Lai was a single event, whereas dozens of officers committed the Rampart division abuses over the course of years. Rather, I want to point out that Wambaugh admits to the liberal presumption of responsibility when he states that the question of military wrongdoing in Vietnam was defused when somebody (here, Lt. William Calley) was legally declared to be the cause of the event. He takes the liberal presumption to remarkable extremes by declaring that even systemic corruption (when and where it exists) is ultimately a single person's fault: "systemic corruption cannot possibly exist . . . unless the chief himself is corrupt." Wambaugh therefore prescribes taking personal and punitive measures and proscribes assessing the structural conditions that lead actors to engage in particular behaviors. Notably, he makes this prescription *even as he implicitly acknowledges that it will not attend to systemic problems.* (Fortunately, Wambaugh can confidently assure us that the LAPD has no systemic problems worthy of our attention.)

By contrast, a postliberal discussion of police brutality would focus not on particular(ly) bad apples but on the conditions that render particular neighborhoods violent and frightening (poverty and lack of education and opportunity), on conditions that render officers of the law violent and frightened as well as frightening (frustration, anxiety, and inadequate training), and on the conditions that lead officers, jurors, and citizens at large to perceive a black man with a piece of leather standing in his own vestibule late at night to be a potential threat (racism, presumptions of black violence, and misinformation as to the origins and frequency of street crime). It would further attend to the practices that compose these conditions; refusing to fetishize structures, it would interrogate the necessity of producing and reproducing subjects who perform their components.

At the risk of suggesting the interchangeability of cases, I look briefly at another highly publicized instance of police brutality to demonstrate this last point. While it seems obvious that the officers who battered Rodney King in 1991 were exonerated because the jurors were able to see King as a threat to the immediate safety of the armed aggressors standing over him, it remains worth asking how this image of King came to be accepted. How, in other words, could an outnumbered and severely beaten King appear "obviously dangerous" and even "controlling the whole show," as one juror put it (qtd. in Serrano and Wilkinson 1992)?

Many have posited that this image was the product of an ingenious defense team who manipulated the sequence of events as portrayed by the videotape and described King's body as a weapon (see Crenshaw and Peller 1993). This is all credible enough, though it seems to neglect a crucial requirement for selling this image of King. Judith Butler (1993b) identifies this neglected component as a paranoiac "white racist episteme" that rendered jurors receptive to interpreting a black man on the ground with one arm raised defensively as a threat to the dozen armed men surrounding him. The Foucaultian term *episteme* signifies a hegemonic complex of ideas that mediates our phenomenal experience.[9] Seen through a racist lens where feral, black bodies are always ready to commit violence, King could be perceived as a threat, justifying the beating he received. The widespread willingness to believe false allegations about false crimes when the reported perpetrators are black—as chronicled in Katheryn Russell's (1999) work on "the racial hoax"—further testifies to this episteme. And if it is this episteme that allows jurors, officers, and citizens to read a prone, beaten black body as a potential assailant, then the "specific origin" of police brutality is not in the will of officers or a sentiment in the mayor's office but in a set of unstated, unrecognized, and unconscious commitments to a racist episteme. Displacing the blame away from a duplicitous defense team and onto an episteme that creates subjects prepared to identify black male bodies as sites of violence and disorder, Butler suggests that responsibility for the event far exceeds the offending officers.[10]

Seductive as this interpretation is, it diminishes a crucial dimension of the affair. King, after all, was clearly *not* seen as a threat to the public when the beating was initially broadcast; Americans at large were overwhelmingly revolted by the brutality on the tape. The initial broadcasts of the videotape were greeted not with a general sigh of relief that our boys in blue were valiantly protecting us from superhuman threats to the public safety but with a collective shriek of disgust. The interpretation of King as a threat marks a dramatic reversal of this sentiment. Not until a dizzying defense mobilized a fear of disorder could a racist episteme take effect and vindicate the officers. The initial reaction indicates a substantial fissure in the white racist episteme; white racism is less totalizing than many critics would have us believe and less stable than critics such as Butler might argue. Subordinate to a pervasive appreciation for the rule of law, Americans seem willing to accept violent police repression *only when it can be sold as a necessary evil*. We do seem distressingly willing to purchase this story, but the King case demonstrates that we do not employ this episteme without aggressive marketing. Here, it was actively mobilized by defense attorneys seeking to legitimate their clients' use of force. More prosaically, it is mobilized by candidates and propagandists courting public support. If this interpretation of King required such promotion, however, if we employ the episteme only when we are actively swayed toward it, then what we are talking about here is politics proper.

The racist episteme that allowed King and Diallo to be seen as potential threats was mobilized through appeal to three norms rooted in the methodological individualism of liberal responsibility. First, we are subject to a xenophobic fear couched in the "thin blue line" argument that less aggressive police enforcement means more crime. This view has been actively promoted by officials seeking to capitalize on public fear and by officers claiming that media scrutiny makes their job more difficult (see Blair 1999; Goldberg 1999; and Wambaugh 2000). Second, we subscribe to a logic of heroism fed by a popular culture that fetishizes the individual and the superhuman. Weaned on movies wherein our representative (be it Arnold Schwarzenegger or some other action hero) single-handedly terminates an entire army of aliens (or robots or Muslims) after enduring multiple gunshot wounds of his own, we have grown willing and able to believe that King was preparing to strike back after receiving his first dozen blows or that Diallo, whose body was momentarily suspended by a barrage of bullets, might have been catching his breath to launch a counterassault. (That Schwarzenegger's gubernatorial campaign would be almost entirely an appeal to this logic of heroism should have come as no surprise. Nor should his victory.) Third, a belief in formal legal equality primes us to presume the innocence of agents of the law.[11] These liberal presumptions—Hobbesian human nature, individual heroism, and formal legal equality—isolate responsibility by locating the root of events in individuals and thus allow us to view instances of police brutality as divorced from conditions that enable them.

If we resist this isolation, however, then we must account for the verdicts in the high-profile police brutality cases, which suggest that we do not, as a society, condemn this behavior.[12] Similarly, we are drawn to acknowledge that our social constitution values and confers votes on promises of aggressive surveillance and containment as means to maintain (appearances of) social and domestic harmony. From within an ideology of self-interest and fear, heroism, and legal equality, the metonymic banner "the police" stands in for a clearly expressed collective preference for aggressive and proactive policing. Privatized agency provides general vindications along with its particular indictments.

Reclaiming Responsibility

Diverging from liberal models of police brutality, Robin D. G. Kelley (2000) offers an analysis (more than slightly indebted to Foucault's *Discipline and Punish*) that invokes the historical spectacle of lynching as disciplining black bodies against the transgression of racial norms. He argues that police brutality today provides the disciplining force that was forfeited with the decline in civilian lynching in the second half of the twentieth century. Attentive to a racist culture among police departments, Kelley delineates the social conditions that facilitate police brutality (in a manner consistent with attempts to explain ghetto crime) yet simultaneously holds officers responsible for their behaviors; that is, he recognizes the inadequacy of the typical explanations for police brutality and searches for a way to overcome the dichotomy.[13]

Kelley attends to the bind in a telling way. Most centrally, he regularly (and typically) conflates officers of the law with the institutions of law enforcement under the ambiguous banner of "the police." For example, he writes, "very few [incidents of Klan terror and violence] led to convictions, in part because in some instances local police were complicit" and "the government-declared 'war on drugs' did more to promote unbridled police repression than to make the streets safer" (2000:44, 48). When he attributes blame to "the police," to whom or what is he really pointing? Particular officers? Police departments? The institution of law enforcement? This ready ambiguity feeds the inconsistency of the more pedestrian analyses. The term allows us to blame both the institution and the actors with a single term—recklessly blaming specific officers while never explicitly locating any blame anywhere.

Attributing blame to "the police" is a particularly facile shortcut through the theoretical complexity of assigning responsibility, appearing to circumvent the inherent restrictions on liberalism's linguistic codes. The semantic slippage offered by the metonym "the police" allows us to ambiguously locate the problem without ever really identifying anything. With this indeterminate marker, we release ourselves from responsibility for the conditions of street violence (that which is used to legitimate police repression and that which *is* police repression): we're not sure exactly where the problem is, but we know it's elsewhere. As Iris Young (2003) argues and as I discussed in previous chapters, one of the central components of liberal responsibility is a general exoneration that accompanies any particular indictment; that is, in finding a particular actor responsible, we render everybody else innocent. Our complicity in constructing a social mood that constructs cops in a certain way—as the only possible solution to many of society's ills—is swept under our cozy individualist rug. Support for punitive and retrospective approaches to social control is removed from the table as one of the enabling conditions of street violence.

Like other subjects, officers of the law exist by virtue of their position in and interaction with social discourses and practices. A postliberal recognition of the power of law to both enable and constrain possibilities for development and action can be powerfully demonstrated in the police. True, to borrow Althusser's (1971) example, we might become subjects of law in acknowledging its interpellating hail, and Foucault's (1977a) work on discipline has extended this analysis to show how we often interpellate *ourselves* as subjects of law even without an actual officer in our presence, yet interpellation *by the law* remains more significant to a cop than to a civilian. In donning a uniform or badge, and in bearing a weapon or weapons, officers are constantly subject to a disciplinary authority that dictates their proper code of conduct.

Adherence to this code, this radical form of subjection, contributes greatly to these individuals' capacities to act (and act with impunity). Returning to an argument from earlier chapters, that responsibility is not something subjects possess so much as something that composes subjects, we might say that investiture as an officer changes one's ability to respond—one's response-ability. By virtue of their capacities for legitimate physical force and their inherent disciplinary force, officers enjoy fewer restrictions on mobility in their day-to-day activities than the average citizen. They also enjoy a presumption of innocence much more pronounced than the subjects they are disciplining. (Note again the reading of King as a threat.) Officers are not individuals in blue clothing or even merely representatives of legitimate institutions of coercion; rather, they are metonymic embodiments of overdetermined social power. This all suggests that police brutality arises not from unbridled police agency but instead from effective interpellation of disciplinary subjects.

This view breaks from traditions of both liberal responsibility and structural determination. Whereas liberalism presumes an inflated level of individual sovereignty, and structuralism (to the extent that it remains structural) denies responsibility, postliberalism focuses on the abilities to respond that are created through overdetermined matrices of power. If police brutality results from the social practices that constitute certain actors so as to discipline working classes and nonwhites (the "dangerous classes," as they were once known [Parks 1970]), then understanding police brutality requires knowing how officers of the law are interpellated in their training and their ongoing police culture—through gender norms that encourage certain types of individuals to pursue careers in law enforcement, a cultural logic of heroism that encourages God complexes among our armed defenders, a division of labor that encourages a certain sector of the working class routinely to risk their lives to ensure the safety of others, and a legal protection of property that encourages the valuation of commodities over human (not to mention nonhuman) life.[14] Officers, in other words, are neither sovereign subjects nor mere tools but overdetermined sites of response.

A postliberal approach such as I suggest does not ignore but announces the metonymy at work here. It challenges the Hobbesian thesis by situating social antagonisms in a historical condition. It troubles the logic of heroism by announcing how events constitute manifestations of enduring and widespread social practices. And it problematizes the ideology of formal legal equality by demonstrating how a limited and ostensibly neutral (i.e., liberal) state masks other sources of social power. Events such as the Diallo shooting are thus in an important sense the self-reflective expression of the world into itself, mediated through an effective agent identified as a liberal self. Both structural and liberal ideologies alienate the conditions that form us and that, in turn, we are responsible for forming. As liberalism reifies the subject, structuralism reifies the object. Both these alienations release us from responsibility for anything we do not directly cause. (Again, this is the logic driving most of Marx's critiques: of Hegel, of Christianity, of Feuerbach, of Proudhon, of Hugo, of bourgeois science, and of capitalism.)

My suggestions for reclaiming responsibility are not unprecedented. Recently some states and municipalities have attempted to hold weapons manufacturers and merchants responsible for violent crime; although these claims have received little sympathy despite federal warnings to manufacturers and marketers that their distribution practices are leading to increased numbers of guns in the hands of criminals, they gesture toward the type of retrieval I suggest. That these attempts have failed should come as no surprise, trading as they do in notions of responsibility not easily reconcilable with the dominant, liberal one.[15]

Yet a number of states have won lawsuits that held cigarette manufacturers responsible for widespread health problems. Indicting the marketing strategies used to produce smokers, these decisions are remarkable for their apparent willingness to break from a strictly liberal model of responsibility, arguing that widespread health issues do not arise from the autonomous decisions of individuals to consume tobacco. This is all the more extraordinary given the degree to which tobacco's health risks are formulated in the lingo of individual choice and personal responsibility. (Smoking's saturation with liberalism's language seems to render this task more difficult than, say, holding the auto industry responsible for air pollution, dependence upon foreign oil, and, therefore, U.S. military aggression.) This is a move toward postliberal responsibility, and the success of this movement evidences substantial fissures in the hegemony of liberal ideology.

Applying this approach to legal and extralegal brutality leads inexorably to recognizing a culture of fetishized violence, ready access to industrial-grade artillery, and rampant alienation—that is, the formation of alienated and violent subjectivities—all of which increase the likelihood and appeal of aggression. At the same time, it avoids the pitfalls of structuralism, which promotes either political resignation or blind faith in progress. Where liberal responsibility indicts a specifiable agent while exonerating others, postliberal responsibility shifts our attention away from culminating events and toward the production and reproduction of social conditions and agents. This suggests that instead of containing and punishing individuals for their violent impulses, we should acknowledge collective responsibility for the conditions of the world and the performance of social relations. That is, postliberalism undermines our ability to release ourselves from responsibility for events that are enabled by conditions embodied in our daily routines.

Examining interpellating practices of the law, we might come to a more sympathetic account of the daily lives of officers and the demands we place upon them for protecting (an image of) social stability and comfort. We might contribute to a dialogue more open and democratic than one that rejects large portions of the population as so many racist cossacks or as unwilling expressions of necessity. Such a discussion of the interpellation of officers (which is contemporaneous with a discussion of the metonymic ambiguity of "the police") remains absent from the overwhelmingly pervasive content of police narratives. Admittedly, there is some discussion that the roots of police brutality run deeper than the racist presumptions of a set of individuals in law enforcement—that police culture itself breeds an antagonistic and hostile disposition toward certain types of civilians. If pressed only slightly, Baraka and Butts would surely admit that their personal attacks quoted earlier represent reductive diagnoses of the situation made indispensable by the structure of representative politics. In other words, the virtual absence of the dialogue I am recommending is not a failure of individual critics but a symptom of a hegemonic theory of agency and its virtual monopoly on the politics of representation.

Unfortunately, recognizing liberalism's inadequacy does not necessarily allow for its overcoming. As I have shown, gestures beyond it remain markedly subject-centered, promoting consonant individual solutions of punishment, containment, and (for the occasional officer) suspension or dismissal. We punish and contain the poor and nonwhite with amazing regularity rather than educate, encourage, and ensure opportunities. Although we prosecute and dismiss abusive officers much less regularly, the difference may arise from our belief that they act in our best interests. This means that though we are largely incapable of holding officers responsible for their brutality, we lack an alternative language with which we can attend to the problem. Once officers are exonerated (as they almost always are), the issue is closed. Because agency is liberal, because *individuals* act, solutions involve addressing the offenders rather than examining how masses and collectives act, how individuals are restricted from acting, and how the alienating and contentious practices in which we daily engage facilitate and even encourage criminal behaviors.

Consider another example: it is easy to blame Osama bin Laden for the horrific tragedies of September 11, just as it is easy to hold George W. Bush responsible for the enduring war on "evil." To do so, however, is to ignore how both these events were made thinkable by a set of historical conditions that we helped to (re)produce. Even more clearly, their possibility emerged from popular support on either side.[16] Unless we are going to argue that bin Laden is a charismatic evil genius who systematically hypnotized thousands of dupes, how can we avoid the fact that he is part of a global network of protesters of Western hegemony? How can we blame Bush for bombing civilian Afghanis when over 80 percent of Americans registered support for the project? How can we blame Bush or Attorney-General John Ashcroft for an enduring assault on U.S. civil liberties when wide and widely discussed abuses seem to inspire relatively little discontent among Americans? And how can we blame officers, chiefs, mayors, or simply "the police" for racial profiling when Americans in large part support decisions to focus enforcement efforts on particular types of crime and believe that nonwhites are the most common perpetrators? Since well before September 11, Americans, generally believing in and taking comfort from the thin blue line, have been open about accepting diminished civil rights (for others) in exchange for (so-called) safer streets. How can we hold bin Laden, Bush, or the police responsible? Only from within a liberal paradigm that demands individuals whom we can identify as the origins of events. Only by presuming liberal responsibility—by believing in the disruptive cognitive shorthand that we are compelled to employ.[17]

The roots of racist and classist practices such as police brutality and punitive approaches to crime lie in a set of material relations that depend upon continued participation (reiteration and performance) for their hegemony and endurance. As Judith Butler (1993a: intro., 1997a:27) suggests, drawing attention to the production and reproduction of conditions of unfreedom has the inciteful (and insightful) effect of enhancing our own responsibility for their perpetuation. In contrast to unidimensional structuralisms or liberalisms, this more dialectical engagement highlights the contestability and inherent instability of sedimented relations of power.

While this position humbles us in forcing us to recognize our own situated existence, it simultaneously demands a responsibility to and for that existence. It contests the liberal paradigm by unseating the priority of the sovereign self while reclaiming the heretofore liberal notion of responsibility by articulating how postliberal subjects remain implicated in the production and reproduction of real life. Humility stems from challenging the liberal myth of individual autonomy; responsibility, from emphasizing how norms and institutions remain dependent on the complicity of imperfectly interpellated subjects (us). This is an ontological challenge to the reports of cause and a political challenge to the liberal range of responses. Responsibility for Diallo's untimely and violent death lies in the overdetermined sentiments toward crime, race, and discipline recommended by liberal ideology and embodied in our daily routines. This diffusion of class power troubles the logic that recommends such retroactive measures as physical containment and deprivation or punishment and suggests attending to enduring conditions rather than addressing particular events.

This logic does not exonerate abusive officers, corporate embezzlers, and international terrorists. Rather, it acknowledges events as arising from overdetermined conditions and refuses to consider issues settled by determinations of individual responsibility. A focus on the formation of subjects suggests that attending to these practices requires seizing them by the root, as Marx reminds us.[18] And the root, clearly, is humanity *in context*—not humanity as such and not autonomous humans but humanity *particularly interpellated*. Seizing the social relations that provide the conditions for particular types of subjects to emerge, it allows us to hold some actors responsible without exonerating all others.

Community Policing

I have argued that the presumptions of liberal responsibility confine us to an impoverished discourse on police brutality. Though liberal responsibility provides a clear and politically expedient picture of individual action, it focuses attention on the proximate and embodied causes of events and thus leaves the conditions that render subjects capable and desirous of violence at best obliquely on the table. These "mitigating" factors remain subordinate to or distracting from the "specific origin" of the problems: the individuated actor with defective preferences. When combined with a theory of self-interest, valorization of individual abilities, and norms of formal legal equality, liberal responsibility's prescriptions become almost entirely punitive and retrospective.

Though a rejection of the liberal subject is commonly supposed to entail an abandonment of the concept of responsibility (and thus our ability to reward or punish actors for their behaviors), visible contours of a postliberal theory of responsibility demonstrate both the inadequacy and the indispensability of individualist approaches to social phenomena such as crime, punishment (both legal and extralegal), and rehabilitation. Highlighting how events are enacted by particularly formed subjects engaging with overdetermined social conditions, postliberal responsibility avoids the historical inclinations to either liberal voluntarism or structural determination. Realigning our approach to subjectivity to account for the social production of desires and abilities, it suggests reexamining the harsh and vindictive punitive measures taken against convicts. If responsibility for crime does not lie solely with the perpetrators of particular acts but extends to the social designation of certain types of violence as deserving legal attention and to the maintenance of social relations that produce particular types of subjects, then isolated remedies can never treat more than symptoms. If these social relations are produced and reproduced through a complex web of social and political interactions, then prescriptions must treat far more than immediate violations.

Diallo was not shot in a social and political vacuum. Rather, he was shot in conditions in which particular types of bodies are violated by other types of bodies with regularity and impunity. These conditions can only simplistically be reduced to the willed acts of particular individuals, although their production can be traced to identifiable practices (such as the ghettoization of nonwhite populations, the armed enforcement of social stratification, a white racist episteme, and a displacing logic of liberal responsibility that releases citizens from the imperative of monitoring police activity). By recognizing the inadequacy of liberal attributions of responsibility and displacing responsibility onto a complex web of social relations, we simultaneously if paradoxically locate that responsibility in our own performative adherence to a set of norms, values, and practices that continues to victimize, exploit, alienate, and brutalize citizens with disfavored demographics.

Thus, we can already see fissures that point toward the articulation of a postliberal form of the oh-so-liberal concept of responsibility. The first informed step toward deciding whether we should continue to believe in liberalism's emancipatory potential is recognizing our complicity in maintaining its hegemony. And who has responsibility for that?

SIX

Conceptions of Responsibility:
On Health as a Choice

Few issues have polarized the U.S. population as effectively as abortion has. Laurence Tribe (1990) famously calls the debate a "clash of absolutes," a seemingly irreconcilable conflict between defenders of two putatively inalienable and contradictory rights: life (of a fetus) and liberty (of a woman). Yet pedestrian evidence demonstrates wide variability within these absolutes: hardly anybody opposes abortion without exception, and few unconditionally support it. In this chapter I argue that intelligible and communicable positions on abortion are limited by the narrow confines of liberal responsibility. These absolutes represent rival applications of liberal responsibility couched in the language of rights. One side argues that pregnant women incur a particular responsibility for ensuring that fetuses receive all the rights and protections of a liberal state, and the other invokes a pregnant woman's right to make responsible choices about the fate of her own body.

From a postliberal perspective, each of these absolutes trades in that dubious territory of individual autonomy. Refusing to fetishize either the fetus or the individual actor, a postliberal approach distributes responsibility to the collective actors capable of responding to the situation of unwanted pregnancy. While liberal autonomy certainly provides women with more agency than did preliberal refusals to acknowledge their full participation in responsible decision making, postliberal subjectivity goes further, highlighting how liberal autonomy places women in the impossible position of being responsible for their condition and thus ultimately legitimates severe restrictions on reproductive freedom.

Private Victories, Public Defeats

Since the 1973 Supreme Court decision in *Roe v. Wade,* access to abortion has been protected by a constitutional right to privacy. But privacy has always been a peculiar and unstable foundation upon which to build the legal edifice of abortion rights, one seemingly antithetical to the familiar feminist pronouncement that the personal is political. This privatization of abortion sits uncomfortably with the relatively successful feminist project of revealing how the logic of privacy conceals and depoliticizes domestic abuse, economic coercion, and other practices of prosaic sexism (Fried 1990; Copelon 1990).

Since the 1970s privacy has been used to establish legal protection for myriad issues related to sexuality, from birth control to abortion to homosexuality to miscegenation and beyond. These privatizations have liberated individual sexual development and expression from the overt control of the state, thus increasing individuals' control over their bodies and their lives. Just as important, the development and distribution of convenient and reliable birth control, the legalization of abortion, and general increases in the social acceptability of nontraditional sexualities have clearly contributed to a decoupling of female sexuality from the immediate concerns of fertility and mothering, offering women greater opportunity for sexual freedom and social identities not forged around reproductive expectations.

Nonetheless, while *Roe* has effectively proscribed state-level bans on abortion, it has done substantially less to stall steady and surreptitious efforts to scale back the procedure's availability via less direct means. The privatization of abortion secured a realm in which the state could not tread but stopped well short of ensuring the resources and opportunities for the exercise of private decisions. *Roe* reduces pregnancy to a personal issue taking place at the level of the individual body; it says nothing about pregnancy's relationship to a sexual division of labor, a gendered state of freedom, the availability of health care, the hegemony of heterosexual desire, or population management.

For advocates of abortion rights, privatization makes strategic political sense, resonating as it does with established elements of an American ideology of individual autonomy and limited government. Nevertheless, this traditional approach to securing abortion rights fails to address—and thus reinscribes—the broader dynamics of sexual politics under patriarchal capitalism. Catherine MacKinnon (1989: ch. 10) expresses anxiety over just this neglect, arguing that while the legal protection of abortion (like the availability of birth control) *appears* to provide greater freedom in sexual activity, this enhanced freedom remains within the confines of largely male-determined sexuality. Sticking closely to Engels's (1978) doctrinal study of the sexual division of labor under capitalism, MacKinnon argues that the sexual liberation apparently afforded by birth control and legalized abortion provides a "false equality"; access to abortion reduces the costs of sexual activity incurred by women, but this masks a continuing context of sexual inequality in which copulation happens. This mirrors her claim that antirape legislation eliminates forced sexual activity but does nothing to address the more invisible forms of force entailed in normalized heterosexual relations.

In one notable articulation of this theoretical and political predicament, Rhonda Copelon (1990) criticizes the political logic of privacy for fetishizing the individual, for suggesting that the woman's body is a private space independent of the social realm in which it operates. Privacy, she argues, removes the choosing individual from a social context and actively ignores the many relations and conditions that facilitate or inhibit choice; it neglects the numerous impersonal obstacles standing between a pregnant woman and a terminated pregnancy. Copelon thus agues that meaningful abortion rights would require not merely the legal security of a private realm but the affirmative promotion of the resources necessary to exercise autonomous choices. This, Copelon argues, means providing economic security (jobs and prenatal health care), the ideological overcoming of sexism, and affirmative legal action on the part of the state (39). In other words, she argues that reproductive freedom cannot be secured through a negative right to privacy but instead requires a positive right to autonomy.

Urging us to supplant privacy with autonomy, Copelon makes a move quite familiar in the history of liberalism—the move from classical, laissez-faire liberalism to environmental or welfare-state liberalism. Advocating a progression from privacy to autonomy, she continues to privilege the individual in a manner that I have argued is both untenable and undesirable. Though sexist cultural and legal institutions and practices continue to privilege opportunities for men over women, Copelon would solve the problem by establishing relations in which women can be held individually responsible for the conditions of their lives. In other words, while postliberals indict the ideal of privacy for bolstering the impossible and frustrating promise of liberal sovereignty, Copelon indicts privacy for not being liberal enough.

Copelon's shift from privacy to autonomy is somewhat deceptive, then, for it continues to privatize responsibility. The goal remains not the recognition that personal life circumstances precede and exceed individual agents but rather the establishment of conditions in which individuals really can be responsible for themselves. Copelon's endorsement of sexual autonomy thus ultimately casts pregnancy as a personal, biological condition, isolated from social and political relations. Abortion remains a question of individual decisions at particular points in history, not one of fertility and procreation in a complicated and overdetermined matrix of gender roles, labor relations, population management, and sexual desire. Copelon's argument, in other words, conforms perfectly to the presumptions of liberal responsibility, focusing on events rather than conditions and ultimately justifying saddling women with the exclusive responsibility for pregnancy and mothering because of their status as autonomous decision makers. Though Copelon seeks to radicalize the movement by moving from privacy to autonomy, autonomy succumbs to the same shortcomings as privacy.

Pointing to this shortcoming of privacy does not deny the real advances in human freedom it has afforded. Copelon has thus remained relatively immune from criticism, even as her endorsement of autonomy receives copious implicit condemnation. As I will show, Alison Jaggar (1998) and Donna Haraway (1997), for example, wage complementary arguments that the prefeminist rhetoric of privacy has failed to address how the burdens of reproduction are disproportionately assigned to women. They turn not to liberal autonomy, however, but to the postliberal vulnerability of pregnant women. Copelon's unsatisfying position reflects, I think, an anxious stab at postliberalism; she appears frustrated with both the solutions of liberalism and the paucity of alternatives. It is, in other words, a symptom of the hegemony and limits of liberal responsibility.

Healthy Choice

Roe's privacy doctrine was never terribly effective at protecting access to abortion. Ironically enough, privatization opened the door for numerous restrictions on the availability of the procedure. The privatization of abortion legitimated the Hyde Amendment (1976), which restricted the use of Medicaid funding for abortions; *Webster v. Reproductive Health Services* (1989), which prohibited public hospitals from performing abortions; and *Hodgson v.*

Minnesota (1990), which validated parental and spousal notification requirements. Though these issues might well have been settled differently if guided by Copelon's argument for autonomy, the reproductive rights movement has never galvanized around autonomy (likely because of the divisive nature of its demand for positive state action). Instead, the movement turned to the now ubiquitous and putatively more demanding rhetoric of women's choice.

In *Bearing Right* (2004) William Saletan chronicles this rhetorical shift from privacy to choice through the 1980s. Beginning with the struggle over Arkansas's Amendment 65 (née "The Unborn Child Amendment") in 1984, abortion-rights advocates found themselves confronting an increasingly conservative population expressing broad opposition to both state power and abortion—especially publicly funded abortion. Saletan demonstrates how the rhetoric of choice proved itself ideal for this constituency, resonating as it did with antigovernment commitments to the sanctity of the family and subsequently yielding unexpected victories against various statewide legislative obstacles to abortion. Nonetheless, this appeal simultaneously legitimated restrictions on funding for pregnant women in need, limitations on the type of services performed or even acknowledged in public facilities, and requirements that women obtain permission of patriarchs before having an abortion. As Saletan puts it elsewhere (1998), the movement, compelled to appeal to a libertarian-leaning audience, "lost control" of the discourse of choice and ended up promoting less government instead of more rights.[1]

Supporters of this transformation would soon come to realize that choice is no less ambivalent than privacy. Laurie Shrage (2003: ch. 3) traces how "choice" was immediately commandeered in the visual and aural propaganda of the pro-life movement. More comprehensively, Rickie Solinger (2001: esp. 20–32) details how the shift ended up casting abortion not as a right but as a consumer freedom, with access depending at least in part on one's ability to pay for it. Solinger shows how the shift facilitated numerous restrictions on women's agency, suggesting not only cuts to public funding of abortions but also welfare reform, since the Aid to Families with Dependent Children program could then be portrayed as state financing of women's "choice" to have more babies. Similarly, though the Supreme Court declared enforced sterilization unconstitutional half a century earlier, the option returned when fertility and procreation were recast as class privileges. Throughout the *Roe* era, women determined to be unfit for mothering have been offered various financial and juridical incentives to submit to sterilization (see Saletan 2004:199–207; Petchesky 1984:178–82).

It also proved, Solinger continues, to be a short step to the commodification of babies and an explosion in international adoption markets encouraging relatively wealthy women to purchase the offspring of relatively poor women on an open market (sometimes via direct payments, but more often by purchasing legal and bureaucratic services). With childbirth as a choice, international adoption is yet another voluntary and thus legitimate transaction. Indeed, social welfare programs interfere with the market's natural ability to balance supply and demand by making it viable to keep babies one could not otherwise afford. The market for babies, like all markets, is organized around satisfying consumers of means and is supported by invoking the adoptee's rights to live a life of relative abundance, but it is almost entirely silent on the rights of those who cannot afford to raise the children they carry to term.[2]

In other words, Shrage and Solinger demonstrate how the rhetorical shift to choice, just like Copelon's endorsement of autonomy, does not address the consequential inadequacies of privacy. Though Copelon recommends a welfare-state notion of autonomy in which subjects are guaranteed the positive rights necessary for the exercise of individual choice, these histories demonstrate what postliberals at least since Marx have been arguing—that the virtues of autonomy and choice cannot be separated from the political institutions of liberalism that issue primacy to individuals' presumed abilities to govern themselves. In her version of the argument, Wendy Brown (1995: chs. 3 and 6) points out that these (and other) rights are emancipatory and empowering for pregnant women *in the abstract,* but they fail to attend to particular bodies in particular predicaments; they insinuate a voluntarist model of the choosing subject whose physical and (perhaps masked) political constraints are actively ignored. This, Brown emphasizes, is where feminists converge with Marx's critique of liberalism.

Though *Roe* appeared to guarantee a right to abortion, new, competing rights weakened it. As Solinger puts it, "by the end of the 1970s, fathers were recognized as having rights, fetuses were granted rights, and 'children's rights' were newly and broadly acknowledged. Women, on the other hand, were accorded only 'choice'" (2001:193). In this transformation from a right to a choice, advocates lost the battle for public funding; other movements that have retained the rhetoric of rights have not met this fate. Civil rights, for example, have never been recast as a choice and so have been relatively immune from public outcry against the use of public resources for their protection. When women *choose* to have either a baby or an abortion, however, they are expected to cover the accompanying costs. The common reduction of abortion rights to such a contract model of individual freedom trades in a notion of autonomous individuals causally responsible for their own situations. As Copelon points out, an emphasis on privacy "obscures the necessity for public responsibility" (1990:39). Even though it places greater emphasis on individual capacities for action, choice clearly has had the same effect.

Birth of an Author

The rhetoric of choice casts individuals as the autonomous authors of their situations. The standard pro-choice argument thus offers a powerful democratic corrective to preliberal patriarchal bias, establishing women on the liberal political stage as full human agents rather than mere vessels for unborn children. Nevertheless, this advance remains mired in the myth of autonomous decision making and possessive individualism that postliberals have revealed as the philosophical expression of capitalist markets. Choice takes us back to the problematic assumptions of liberal responsibility: continuity in personhood, subjective autonomy, and the causal force of individual will. It conjures a notion of pregnancy as the product of willed sexual activity, casting individuals as morally responsible for their own pregnancies.

This dilemma plays out not only in the policy disputes over abortion but in the cultural and legislative battles over women's health more generally. Ann Oakley (1984, 1992, 1993) has repeatedly demonstrated how women's health—especially pregnant women's health—is increasingly portrayed as the product of autonomous women's choices about diet and exercise; "the argument that health is about individual choice," Oakley declares, ignores "the *material*, or *social*, basis of health—the social factors and conditions that make health possible, or militate against it" (1993:104–5).

The ideology of health as a choice finds its paradigmatic icon in the smoker, especially the pregnant smoker (see Oaks 2000). More than most other health-related practices, smoking is largely seen as yet another consumer choice; despite class concentrations in both consumption and marketing, tobacco is rarely depicted as a medical addiction and even more rarely as yet another self-administered mechanism for dealing with stress. Smoking, that is, is immediately and ubiquitously reduced to the categories of liberal responsibility, where individuals are sovereign over their desires and their abilities. With reference to pregnancy, the public disfavor toward smoking informs an inordinate amount of attention on this activity and the threat it poses to the fetus, displacing the complicated conditions of industrial life that pose equal or greater threats but cannot be explained with the rhetoric of individual choice—malnutrition, water pollution, lack of health care, domestic violence, and anxiety, to name just a few. Despite evidence that smoking rates among pregnant women have decreased since the U.S. surgeon-general's first warnings about smoking in 1964, the figure of the pregnant smoker continues to consolidate the numerous threats to fetal health endemic to an industrialized society (Oaks 2000:10). We take what we *think* we can control and then we call that a choice.

So, for example, the declaration by the U.S. Department of Health and Human Services (HHS) that smoking by pregnant women is "probably the most important *modifiable* cause of poor pregnancy outcome among women in the United States" (ctd. in Oaks 2000:7; emphasis added) reflects unstated biases about appropriate or possible domains of human intervention. Economic and environmental threats to individual health and safety are taken as unchangeable—fetishized—conditions that will not be challenged in the quest to ensure healthy births. Indeed, the supposition that pollution and the availability of health care are not "modifiable" conditions reflects a severely limited understanding of politics and possibilities, an understanding rooted in the ontopolitical commitments of liberal responsibility. Smoking stands as the primary threat to fetal development only from within an ideology of liberal responsibility that isolates and judges individual behaviors while ignoring impersonal and enduring conditions. Because these conditions do not conform to the familiar and comforting rhetoric of liberal responsibility, they will almost assuredly not receive attention commensurate with their effects. According to HHS, they are officially not relevant.

The obvious social and political determinants of reproduction, however, interrupt any attempt to reduce sexual activity, fetal development, and infant health to issues of individual choice. Economically and medically motivated population-management campaigns have, at least through modernity, consistently encouraged or discouraged reproduction through contraception and abortion, incentives to marriage, public assistance to fight malnutrition, enforced sterilization, and monogamous morality tales. Efforts to regulate pregnancy are plainly not exclusive to totalitarian societies and dystopian fantasies. Successful civilizations of recent centuries have realized that population growth and maintenance is far too important to leave to the vagaries of spontaneous sexual and domestic desire (see Diamond 2005). Indeed, state policies on reproduction have been explicitly guided by Malthusian theory in recent centuries, either through channels of moralism (Petchesky 1984:34–42; Stevens 1999: ch. 5) or eugenics (Black 2004;

Hardt and Negri 2004:165–66). Debora Spar (2006), with a case at once both shocking and totally unsurprising, argues that the large and heavily regulated consumer markets in babies and their constituent parts (eggs, sperm, wombs) recommend understanding pregnancy as an economic, rather than merely biological, condition. In another illuminating case, Ann Stoler (1991) demonstrates how the British government boosted reproductive activity by increasing economic assistance and mobilizing nationalistic sentiment when disease and malnutrition were interfering with women's abilities to produce the quality and quantity of bodies needed to staff the expanding imperial army. Clearly, though pregnancy is a lived, bodily experience that touches individual women specifically and incomparably, its determinants and significance are no less social and political than are the economic and criminal liabilities discussed in the previous two chapters.

Even the most immediately biological processes of pregnancy do not avoid social and political mediation. Take the issue of fetal viability, the point at which a fetus can be expected to survive outside the private space of the womb. The notion that states have a compelling interest in restricting nontherapeutic abortions after the point of viability, introduced in *Roe* and reaffirmed two decades later in *Planned Parenthood v. Casey* (1992), currently enjoys widespread popular support. This is surely because of the ease with which a so-called viable fetus can be seen as an autonomous being; indeed, viability is the point in fetal development at which it could be expected to realize the liberal ideal of independent existence (see Zaitchik 1981). But this viability—not merely its determination, but its actuality—intimately depends on available medical technologies. Indeed, premature yet (now) viable fetuses survive only by being transplanted into life-supporting incubators, a dependence that significantly troubles the myth of autonomy.

Significantly, all evidence indicates that Justice Blackmun wrote viability into the *Roe* decision (at Justice Brennan's and especially Justice Marshall's urging) not because it has pretensions to the purely biological but precisely because viability depends upon economic and geographic position (see Garrow 1994:580–86; Shrage 2003:13). Since viability of a fetus depends upon the type of care available both before and after its removal from the womb, viability differed from the strict twelve-week cutoff also considered for the *Roe* decision by affording greater protection to rural and poor women, who might have greater difficulty in finding abortion facilities. Ironically, this socioeconomic understanding of viability has been largely eclipsed by the ready (and deceptive) consonance of viability and autonomy.

The social and political nature of fertility and reproduction is on display not only in government offices and medical facilities, however. Marketing and distribution of such commodities as infant formula seriously affect social fertility and the viability of infant life. Donna Haraway (1997) further points to the impact of "labor patterns, land use, capital accumulation, and current kinds of class reformation" on reproductive habits and possibilities; indeed, "agribusiness seed technologies, which come with packages of labor and resource use, or marketing systems for national and international customers are at least as much reproductive technologies as are sonograph machines, cesarean surgical operations, or *in vitro* fertilization techniques" (208). Against the fetishization of the female body and the reduction of sexual and breeding practices to individual choice, Haraway points instead to social, political, technological, and economic determinants of breeding: "computers in financial centers in Geneva, New York, or Brasília are reproductive technologies that have their bite in the breasts of marginalized women and the guts of their babies" (208).

In other words, though pregnancy remains a condition biologically locatable in specific bodies, and though the material organization of those bodies may be less historically variable than, say, economic systems or criminal codes, the condition of pregnancy always and immediately transcends the body of the pregnant woman. Pregnant women, like all other subjects, are metonymic productions, consolidations of a multiplicity of forces under a single banner who appear as autonomous actors because of liberal ideology and its preferences for individualized treatment, punishment, and reward. Indeed, political battles over the proper signifier for a pregnant woman (interested parties insisting on calling her a "mother") amount to struggles over the determination and severity of the metonym; *woman* reduces the agent to particular social roles, whereas *mother* reduces her to but one.

For Haraway, the fetus itself is yet another metonym that consolidates a multiplicity of relations and understandings of (at least) sexuality, kinship, motherhood, labor, and capital. She describes the fetus not as a creature for or to whom a pregnant woman is exclusively responsible, or as a possession of a pregnant woman, but as a signifier given meaning by the demands and preferences of a given division of labor and resources. Haraway thus deconstructs the iconography of the pro-life movement and popular culture more generally, exploring the production of this metonym through the visual representation of an autonomous fetus. This ubiquitous image—inevitably lacking placenta, umbilical cord, blood, and amniotic fluid; always depicting a fetus in the final stage of development; and often manipulated to enhance the fetus's appearance as a fully formed human baby—is the paradigmatic representation of the "Teflon subject" of liberal autonomy.

Valerie Hartouni (1997) points to this iconographic development as evidence of the social and technological mediation of pregnancy, for these images have created a new social actor by giving shape and tangible existence to the fetus, issuing primacy and moral authority to the supposed individual victim of the procedure.[3] Clearly, this representation has contributed significantly to the ideology of the fetus as a person with legal rights (see Condit 1990:79–92; Newman 1996; and Shrage 2003: ch. 3). As Rosalind Petchesky (1987) declares in her study of visual culture in the abortion debates, "the fetus rose to instant stardom" (264) with the 1985 network broadcast of the now infamous pro-life film *The Silent Scream*. This stardom, and the distressing trend toward the fetus as the central character in the debate over women's health, is perhaps but one particularly egregious outcome of the ideology of heroism I discussed in chapter 2. Perhaps the most discernible impact of this visual mediation culture is the recent Partial Birth Abortion Act of 2003. This act criminalized a particular abortion procedure (dilation and extraction, or D&X), a target chosen less from a principled opposition to the procedure than from its ability to provide propagandists a particularly gripping and exploitable set of visuals—visuals that could overwhelm the widely accepted but utterly unheroic evidence that this is the safest means to perform an abortion at this point in pregnancy (see Gorney 2004).

In contrast to the heroic narratives of individual pregnancy, an approach like Haraway's, which focuses on the economic, political, social, and technological determinants of reproduction, highlights the material relations that induce menstruation, pregnancy, and lactation and thus renders less taboo the conventionally hidden operations of women's bodies. It removes pregnancy from a discourse of divine creation and presents it instead as a corporeal and potentially democratic mode of reproduction. In other words, while situating pregnancy beyond the realm of the choosing individual might appear to lead to a paralyzing condition in which nobody can be held responsible for his or her situation, Haraway suggests that reducing reproduction to a series of discrete events provides an unrealizable model of agency in which individuals are called upon to heroically overcome the constraining material relations that precede and exceed them. By focusing on these relations instead of denying them, however, she introduces a form of subjected agency where the performative adherence to patriarchal and capitalist institutions creates the very possibility of reproduction and, indeed, reproductive freedom.

While liberals feminists present choice as the bearer and protectors of women's agency (see, e.g., Condit 1990: chs. 5–6), postliberals emphasize how this inevitably reduces conditions of life—procreation and fertility, sickness and health—to the operations of individual will, thus masking the varied determinants of a subject's behaviors. Patricia Mann (1994: ch. 3), for example, argues that in denying the social mediation of pregnancy, the promise of liberal autonomy actually limits women's agency; in denying the political, economic, and technological determinants of reproduction, liberals end up reducing it to a biological process and ultimately insinuate conventional gendered narratives of sexuality and fertility wherein women are essentially mothers. Focusing not on ostensibly autonomous bodies but instead on the overdetermination of pregnancy, Mann points to what she calls "cyborgean reproduction": procreation not as an unmediated biological process but as a social dynamic, children not as pure expressions of human biology but as the products of numerous dimensions of social exchange, including normalized heterosexual desire, technologies of birth control and prenatal care, and the political economy of the family.

Mann thus invokes "interpersonal agency," which asserts not the autonomy of women but instead the socially produced opportunities for action and inaction. Whereas the pro-life movement promotes the fetus to the status of hero, Mann explores how the pro-choice movement does the same for the woman. Her move from a rhetoric of biological reproduction to one of social reproduction, from individual agency to interpersonal agency, challenges this logic of heroism and exemplifies the move from a liberal to a postliberal understanding of procreation.

In forwarding this claim, Mann argues that the rhetoric of responsibility limits women's agency in precisely the familiar ways, by trivializing the conditions in which women find themselves and asserting their duty to take care of themselves despite these conditions. But this is clearly an indictment of *liberal* responsibility, hegemonically sutured to putatively autonomous wills and demanding heroism from a population no less inundated than any other. Just as the replacement of fetal autonomy with women's autonomy reflects the hegemony of liberal responsibility, Mann's critique of responsibility accepts liberalism's monopolistic claim that responsibility is a function of autonomous, willed actions.

Of course, women's autonomy remains a vibrant political cause because of the visibility of preliberal threats to reproductive freedom. This is why Brown (1995: ch. 5) argues that the virtues identified by liberalism (e.g., rights and autonomy) operate in "diverse, inconstant, even contradictory ways . . . across various histories, cultures, and social strata" (97). For Brown, and for postliberals generally, the question is not whether autonomy is an emancipatory virtue in the abstract but how it functions in any concrete instance. While such principles "may operate as an indisputable force of emancipation at one moment in history . . . , they may become at another time a regulatory discourse, a means of co-opting or obstructing more radical political demands, or simply the most hollow of empty promises" (98). Petchesky (1984) demonstrates the hollowness of this particular promise, showing how the juridical right to abortion coincided with rapid increases in other disciplinary apparatuses, namely, the medical management and family-planning industries. Even relatively little investigation shows the difficulty of equating rights with freedom.

While the liberalization of pregnancy has undoubtedly contributed to greater agency for individual women, the myth of individual authorship and the rhetoric of liberal responsibility have saddled women with the heroic task of overcoming conditions they could neither cause nor hope to control. Indeed, the basic rights and privileges of even liberal autonomy have yet to be realized for many women, and the postliberal challenge to this myth of heroism certainly does not justify increasing the professional management of pregnancy and paternalistic regulation of abortion. Rather, it admits that situations are overdetermined by social and political circumstances, and simplistically characterizing pregnancy as the product of women's autonomous choices threatens to put women in the impossible situation of having to care for themselves, diverting attention from the real causes of pregnancy and fertility.

Exceptional Responses

Steeped in the logic of will and causality, liberal responsibility reduces the complicated origins and perils of pregnancy to isolated acts, individual events, and personal choices. It thus suggests a way to talk about pregnant women as being responsible for the fetuses they have conceived or as capable of making responsible consumer choices regarding their own health, but it offers few if any resources for understanding the unwilled and impersonal causes and costs of unwanted pregnancy, population growth, or the scarcity of pre- and postnatal health care. For that, we need a postliberal theory of responsibility.

Liberalism's hegemony over rhetorics of responsibility in abortion is demonstrated perhaps most clearly in Judith Jarvis Thomson's (1971) now famous analogy of abortion to medical Samaritanism. Thomson argues that the condition of unwanted pregnancy can be analogous to that of a woman awakening to find that she has been surgically connected to a violinist with failing kidneys and that this violinist will recover from the ailment only if the connection is maintained for nine months. Not only does Thomson tellingly rely upon a narrative of heroism to make her point, but she ultimately argues that few would hold the unwilling participant in this relationship to bear responsibility for the violinist. Her point is that *even if we grant that life begins at conception* (the ostensible trump card so coveted by the pro-life movement), the argument that women have a prima facie responsibility to carry the fetus to term is indefensible. Thomson's argument conforms precisely to the tenets of liberal responsibility. It deals with events rather than conditions (she offers no discussion of responsibility for the violinist's illness or the availability of health care), and it rests fundamentally on the integrity of individual will and intentionality (the Samaritan has no responsibility because she did not consent to the procedure). Thomson expects widespread support for her reasoning because it is rooted in commonplace notions of what makes for responsibility.

That a woman's responsibility to a fetus is linked to her willed causality—the price she pays for her freely chosen sexual activity—is attested by the near universal willingness to admit abortions in the cases of rape or incest. Yet it remains unclear how the conditions of a fetus's conception could affect the sanctity of its right to live. The all but universal willingness to admit these excusing conditions suggests that opposition to abortion is not fundamentally about saving lives but about holding people responsible for their actions. The pregnancy that arises from nonconsensual sex is distinct from the garden variety unwanted pregnancy only in the role a woman plays in causing the pregnancy. The sexual agent is responsible for her pregnancy; the rape victim is not.[4]

Causality also justifies the increasingly acceptable distinction between abortions undertaken because of a woman's choice not to carry a fetus to term and those motivated by the detection of a fetal "defect" such as Down Syndrome.[5] Press and Cole (1999) show how these latter cases are subject to significantly less social stigma than the former, a fact that Barbara Ehrenreich

(2004) thinks explains why data show more U.S. women benefiting from legalized abortion than supporting it. Ehrenreich points to studies indicating that women who have abortions because their standard, insurance-funded prenatal screening revealed a fetal imperfection see themselves as qualitatively different from women who have abortions out of inconvenience or undesirability of giving birth. In this class-biased resignification of abortion, women of means avoid being classified as having had abortions, while others bear the enduring scrutiny of failed individual responsibility. Echoing Butler, Ehrenreich courageously indicts women who contribute to this resignification by positing a moral exceptionalism of their own abortions.

This particular resignification is wholly consistent with the understanding of childbirth as a matter of consumer freedom, with women of means afforded the opportunities and options for more uncomplicated births by preselecting against troublesome fetuses. The increased agency afforded women of means here is nonetheless probably less substantial than the general threat to women's agency that stems from the increased social and political management of pregnancy through the rhetoric of risk and the disciplinary force of what Oaks (2000) calls the "pregnancy police." It also raises significant questions about the disciplinary authority of insurance companies that fund extensive prenatal screenings to predict the costs of birth and postnatal care more accurately. Screening technologies complicate a woman's choices, in other words, by introducing into reproductive decisions the insurance provider's calculations of economic risks and liabilities (see Peters 1997:50–56).

As in cases of rape and incest, fetal defect is generally admitted as a condition that excuses women from carrying a pregnancy to term because of the absence of causal responsibility. This excuse trades in those familiar and dubious categories of independent action, autonomous will, and the fetishization of the individual body. It points to inquiries into who is responsible for any particular pregnancy but provides scant resources for asking who is responsible for pregnancy rates, the (un)availability of effective birth control, sexual education, and pre- and postnatal care. The presumptions of liberal responsibility do not lend themselves to examining these broader issues.

To redeploy the concept of responsibility toward these issues requires decoupling responsibility from individual will. The literature on pregnancy and abortion does explore this postliberal approach, but not nearly enough. When Haraway situates pregnancy in a set of political and technological strategies for population management and capital concentration, she belies the fiction of pregnancy as an isolated event contained in a single body. She thus diverts attention from the liberal concerns with individual morality and choice and points instead at broad and enduring social trends that have no single cause. Like Butler's move to postliberal responsibility discussed in chapter 3, situating pregnancy in a matrix of overdetermined relations does not, contra voluntarist critiques, jettison the notion of responsibility. Rather, it expands and disperses responsibility to the subjects who actively produce and reproduce the relevant cultural history. Breaking from the heroic and fetishistic notion of an individual author does not eliminate—but transforms—the possibility and the potential site of response.

A story such as Haraway's, then, inevitably lacks the malicious or heroic characters populating contemporary abortion debates: the selfless mother who kicks an addiction for the sake of a fetus; the sexual miscreant who uses abortion as birth control; the deadbeat dad and the "back-alley butcher," who victimize women in times of need; the recently criminalized physician willing to perform D&X; and the assailant now liable under the Unborn Victims of Violence Act. Reliance on these characters puts a face on particular obstacles to a healthy birth, reducing pregnancy to a Manichean battle between heroes and villains, a series of nefarious events rather than a continuous process of discipline and deprivation.[6] These characters are seductive for their resonance with conventional liberal categories, whereas the general unavailability of adequate health care, education, birth control, and ethical confidence do not have these touchstones and so go relatively unmentioned. While character-driven politics has clearly prevented particular violations of women's safety by fostering legislation to sanitize and regulate the abortion industry, it has done little if anything to protect against the generalized violation of women in need. As Solinger puts it, "despite the overwhelming power of anti-abortion laws to create a world where women were in danger, we continue to remember and name inept, perverse mercenaries as the source of women's danger" (2001:46).

Similarly, Nancy Hirschmann (1992:102–25) argues that such a refigured notion of responsibility, in which actors are responsible not *despite* their being composed and compromised by their relations but rather because of this, is part of a feminist critique of the presumptions of social contract theory. Certainly, this refusal to isolate and reify the individual, focusing instead on the relationships that compose subjects, is the postliberal sensibility that unites marxists, postmodernists, and (many) feminists. Alison Jaggar (1975, 1998), for instance, defends abortion rights with reference not to individual autonomy but to the distribution of responsibilities that accompanies cultural conceptions of pregnancy. Assigning to women the primary responsibility for infants' care, she argues, bestows upon women the "moral authority to decide whether to carry their pregnancies to term" (1998:340). This is a strong claim, steeped in a recognition that what justifies a right to abortion is not the political or ontological autonomy of women or inherently contentious claims about the morality of the practice but rather the established expectations and opportunities for response to reproduction. Another way of saying this is that in relinquishing responsibility for the care of children, society has also sacrificed the authority to control reproduction. By privatizing responsibility, Hirschmann suggests, liberals have created a situation in which individuals try to avoid responsibility. By contrast, she argues that a feminist ethos encourages agents to consider the general needs of society and individuals in a manner that mitigates the liberal evasion of responsibility (1992:110–11).

Jaggar offers an exemplary postliberal response to the myopic liberalism that has so far dominated pregnancy legislation. She both implicitly (1975) and explicitly (1998) bypasses the stagnated moral and medical controversies surrounding abortion, revealing instead how morality and medicality interact to create capacities for action. While admitting that her view of abortion as a question about the distribution of obligations and responsibilities will inevitably face opposition in a pluralistic society such as the United States, she nevertheless argues that the permissibility of abortion cannot be settled by any abstract and disengaged theory of morality or science but must turn on the distribution of responsibilities to care for an infant and the established norms of motherhood and family. Abortion is fundamentally a question of motherhood, and since motherhood is socially variable, so must be approaches to abortion.[7] So when Jaggar claims that abortion is an issue of private rather than public morality—a question of the good life rather than one of justice (1998:342–44)—she does so with the recognition that this is so by virtue of convention; abortion's status as private arises specifically from the liberal framework of the family.

Postliberal defenses of a woman's right to choose, in other words, are rooted not in the sanctity of individual choice but in the economics of motherhood and the general disavowal of social responsibility for the costs of social reproduction. Hirschmann, Haraway, Jaggar, and Mann all defend an uncompromising right to terminate a pregnancy *not* by invoking a right to privacy or individual autonomy and *not* by employing any notion of causal responsibility, however mitigated, but instead by emphasizing the social relations that render particular populations capable of responding to particular situations. Legalized abortion still affords only a limited range of individualized responses, failing to address the general causes of unwanted pregnancy and health crises, but this rights-based approach readily conforms to the hegemony of individual responsibility, making it the most viable program for protecting reproductive freedom in U.S. electoral politics. Indeed, given the hegemony of liberal responsibility and preference for event-based diagnoses, legalized abortion seems an easier sell than would be the provision of universal health care, living wages, education, day care, birth control, and less formal modes of social support. This more responsive program seems realizable only after a transformation in conventional understandings of responsibility.

CONCLUSION

Forgetting to Forgive

i want to leave a lasting impression on the world. and god damnit do not blame anyone else besides me and V [Klebold] for this. don't blame my family, they had no clue and there is nothing they could have done, they brought me up just fucking fine. don't blame toy stores or any other stores for selling us ammo, bomb materials, or anything like that because it's not their fault. . . . don't blame the school, don't fucking put cops all over the place. . . . the admin is doing a fine job as it is. i don't know who will be left after we kill but damnit don't change any policies just because of us. it would be stupid, and if there is any way in this fucked up universe we can come back as ghosts or what the fuck ever we will haunt the life out of anyone who blames anyone besides me and V.

—From the journal of Eric Harris, before he and Dylan Klebold
  killed thirteen people and themselves at Columbine High School
  in April 1999

Like most, I'm sure, I find this passage chilling. Not only because it reminds me of what happened that horrible day at Columbine High School. Not only because it compels me to recognize the anomic and alienating conditions of contemporary children, adolescents, and adults at the home, school, and workplace. And not only because it forces me to think about the capacities for violence available to citizens of an industrialized state (to say nothing of the exponentially greater capacities afforded to the state itself). The passage chills me also for what it suggests about notions of responsibility that permeate our culture.

I do not mean to suggest that Eric Harris is a representative figure for public thought and opinion in our nation. But the claim to responsibility that this teenager offered just before attempting to kill nearly everybody he knew remains telling. Despite preparing to express his rage against (some of the) figures he identified as the source of his agonies, he adamantly claims complete responsibility for the affair. Perhaps seduced by the backlash against "political correctness" and namby-pamby, bleeding-heart structural apologias, Harris refuses to assign responsibility for the coming horrors to anybody but his accomplice and himself. Despite his recognition that the conditions that made his life unlivable arose from the practices of others, he insists that we see in the event the pure expression of his individual will. He not only accepts full responsibility for his actions, he demands it, invoking a heroic individual who conjures a momentous historical event out of thin air.

Harris locates himself in liberalism's alienating logic of heroism, neatly divorcing himself from the social forces through which he was formed. In this process, he accepts full responsibility for who he is and how he feels. He accepts full responsibility for a complicated web of social relations that formed and tormented him. He insists that responsibility not be distributed among the various forces and actors whose existence made the event thinkable; all responsibility must be heroically concentrated on himself and Klebold. As a pure expression of his individual initiative, the event will not be contextualized, not historicized, not mediated by circumstance. Within the ideological constraints of a liberal humanism, Harris implicitly rejects the thesis that his being does not emerge fully formed but is itself a product of social relations of production beyond his control. In fact, it may well be just this alienation and solipsism that rendered such an act of destruction possible.

But even in death and after achieving a horrifying level of success, Harris cannot attain the autonomy he demands. Harris today continues to be formed by these forces, now standing as an emotionally charged cultural landmark signifying suburban alienation, predatory youth, a culture of violence, or the decline in the family. Though he demands that we see him as the author of the event and that he be allowed to determine its meaning, mass mediation, the democracy of interpretation, and the violence of punditry ensure that this will be only the final frustration of his short, tragic life.

Frustrated Responses

From a postliberal perspective, Harris's frustration (if not his reaction) is somewhat predictable. As individuals inevitably fail to live up to the liberal model of individual sovereignty, consistently frustrated by the weight and scarring of history, anxious and desperate resentments are to be expected. Resentment born in an individual's inability to become the heroic and autonomous figure ubiquitously (if usually only implicitly) promised by a liberal society is a familiar enough theme in popular culture today; such Hollywood films as *Fight Club, The Eternal Sunshine of the Spotless Mind,* and *The Assassination of Richard Nixon* jump out as recent articulations of this frustration.

From a liberal perspective, however, obviously uninterested in rooting such tragedies as Columbine in the inevitable shortcoming of liberal ideals themselves, such events are coded as ruptures from baseline social harmony, cleavages in an organic whole that must be rectified so as to facilitate a return to the normal routine.[1] This rectification is typically offered through one of three channels: compensation, or payment for injuries suffered; revenge, or payback for same; or forgiveness, wherein victims voluntarily forgo payment or payback. Each of these responses owes its possibility to a liberal ontopolitics that isolates actors and blames causal agents. Each of these approaches promises to repair a rupture in an established social order. They thus say little if anything about the condition of the order before the rupture, reducing questions of justice to ones of healing distinct violations. Events are tears in the social fabric, or wounds of the corporeal or political body—violations of autonomy through penetrations of either one's body (as in physical violence) or one's consciousness (through coercion or manipulation). Whereas liberals theorize such ruptures as injuries, positing a healthy individual that owes its existence of an unrealizable model of autonomy, postliberals theorize such violations of autonomy not as aberrations but as the unavoidable condition of human life.[2]

From a liberal understanding of events, the most common response to injury is compensation. Offering restitution (usually, though not necessarily, financial) to the victims of injury is a ready application of the logic of contract and most evident in tort law. If I cause you harm, I must compensate you for that violation.[3] This logic is visible in both local, pedestrian incidents (such as car accidents and libel suits) and more momentous situations (such as acts of terrorism and international war). A family member seeking compensation for 9/11 offers the typical statement: "I want to know exactly what happened. . . . Tell me, why is my son dead? I want whoever did it to be held accountable" (qtd. in Glaberson 2003). We need not belittle this grief to see the limitations on such a line of inquiry. Though this parent demands to know "exactly what happened" to end her son's life, the question itself reveals her presumption that some particular party bears responsibility. Reminiscent of

Condoleeza Rice's infamous statement to the 9/11 commission that there was "no silver bullet" that could have prevented the event, such attempts to hold individual actors responsible, to decontextualize and dehistoricize the event, clearly conforms to the desire to exact compensation.

This compensatory response seemed unquestioned throughout the formal inquiry into 9/11. The 9/11 commission did not examine how to curtail international terrorism or even how to safeguard institutions or populations; rather, it sought to determine the specific liability of particular individuals and agencies of the U.S. government. Indeed, the committee almost explicitly focused on establishing a precedent that could guide negligence lawsuits against the FBI, the CIA, or President Bush. It did not investigate appropriate responses or capacities for response but asked only whose actions rendered them causally responsible for the affair. More specifically, the committee seemed organized around investigating whether any U.S. official or agency was so negligent as to have broken a contract with the American people, who might thus deserve compensation.

When compensation is deemed inadequate, victims might instead pursue revenge, through either institutional or illicit channels. "Criminal justice" typically serves as code for a retributive model of law enforcement, with institutionalized punishment promising to heal a social wound by removing the offending element (usually via imprisonment) or at least allowing the victims to purge their grief. The popularity of equating vengeance with justice is readily visible in the passionate objections that victims' families made to Illinois governor George Ryan's commutation of his state's capital sentences in 2003 (see Sadovi 2003).

Further, the figure of the vigilante confidently equates revenge with justice. Embodying the liberal tension between heroism and institutionalism, the vigilante has played a prominent role in the American consciousness, from early American lynch mobs through "Dirty" Harry Callahan. Offering heroic justice when stable judicial institutions prove themselves inadequately responsive to a situation, the vigilante is the archetypal American hero, though an unnervingly celebrated one. As evidenced by the protests of victims' families in Illinois, liberal societies formally transfer the burden of response from victims and their families to impartial judges and juries *not* out of any disenchantment with revenge but out of a recognition of the dangers of vigilantism.[4]

A third response to injury is forgiveness. Here, the social rift is healed not by repayment or retribution for injury but by the injured party's voluntarily surrender of a claim to injury. At times, this response can be strikingly illib-

eral, abandoning a model of contractual obligation for a promise of a universal reconciliation. This, for example, is how Hegel talks about forgiveness, as
the dialectical move toward community that overcomes the alienation of the
individual from the universal. Through forgiveness, Hegel posits, individuated beings overcome this primal injury such that "the wounds of the Spirit
heal and leave no scars behind" (1977: §669; see also Meyler 2002; Friedland
2004). As I discussed in chapter 3, Hegel's approach to subjectivity does not
conform to the dictates of orthodox liberalism, leading to the conventional
criticisms of his illiberalism or totalitarianism. And the sort of reconciliation
he seems to advocate here certainly nourishes such interpretations. It also
informs the oft repeated position that forgiveness is somewhat antithetical
to more appropriately liberal responses of compensation and vengeance. As
Jacques Derrida (2001) points out, this promise of total reconciliation is the
promise of the end of politics, a universal harmony that evokes the primal
unity ostensibly overcome with the decline in metaphysical certainty and
religious consensus. Liberals and postliberals alike, in other words, emphasize that the body politic is *always* scarred and that this scarring is not a
regrettable failure to heal but instead the mark of enduring difference and
the continuing possibility of democracy (Derrida 2001:58–59).

But not everybody forgives like Hegel. Indeed, Derrida also points out
how practical forgiveness resonates with liberal ontopolitics when he argues
that it depends on a presumed sovereignty of a subject able to forgive. This
subject might be the victim of a particular injury or a state exercising representative legitimacy. In either case, the forgiver is afforded the legitimacy
to absolve the guilty party for an event (Derrida 2001:59). As we know from
religious conventions, this not only burdens victims with a moral imperative
to forgive their violators (see Minnow 1998:14–21), but it also consolidates
the innumerable conditions and forces that contribute to a violation into a
single perpetrator that can be forgiven and a distinct victim that can forgive.
Forgiveness thus neatly packages history into a series of discrete events with
identifiable causes.

For Derrida, this is where forgiveness meets its ontopolitical limits. When
forgiveness is offered on the condition that the guilty party admit guilt
and request it, forgiveness ceases to be forgiveness and becomes instead a
form of exchange (Derrida 2001:32–35). In exchange for the wrongdoer's
repentance, the injured party agrees to overlook the injury, and both agree
to "re-establish a normality" (32) determined by a liberal ontopolitics of
autonomy. Such forgiveness requires people to ignore the untenability of
liberal ontology, to consciously ignore the persistence of violation (on the

condition that violators admit their errors). And in demanding a sovereign agent authorized to forgive, it reinscribes individual sovereignty right at the moment when it is least evident. As one commentator puts it, "there exists the very real possibility that forgiveness serves as a catchword for suturing, or closing the necessary space of political discourse about accountability and recognition that ought *not* be excised prematurely from broader debates about history and political memory" (Verdeja 2004:26). In other words, the ethical drive to forgiveness threatens to undermine the political drive toward democracy by reducing encounters to individual exchanges rather than parts of an inevitable condition of interpersonal vulnerability. Hastily closing "the necessary space of political discourse" entails isolating the violation from the history of violations and the liberal fetish of injury, promising a reconciliation that vastly exceeds the ethical powers of the supposedly sovereign participants. Victims are unfairly burdened with the imperative to forgive, releasing the community from the responsibility to attend to the conditions under which violations are recognized, conceptualized, and addressed.

Forgiveness, compensation, and vengeance depend upon a presumption of individual sovereignty such that actors can be considered the authors of events and can be justifiably fined, punished, or absolved. They each operate with a decontextualized and ahistorical theory of responsibility for events that is at best indifferent to responses to enduring conditions that do not fit this sovereign conceit. These responses to discrete injuries would be untenable within a postliberal ontopolitics that emphasizes the permanence of injury; they are mitigated by—but cannot themselves account for and are therefore rendered suspect by—the excitability of actions and the fact that all actions admit to uncountable causes. These responses correspond to a liberal responsibility in which life is a series of discrete encounters for which I, as a sovereign agent, am to request compensation, exact vengeance, or offer forgiveness as a means to close the transaction and return to a state of autonomy, only to await the next discrete injury and repeat the episodic, ahistorical nature of social life.

Exceptions Are the Rule

Throughout this book, I have argued that liberal responsibility has an episodic prejudice more attuned to events than to conditions. In addition to casting justice as something inherent to particular transactions rather than enduring conditions, this prejudice also more subtly directs discourses of responsibility toward particular types of events. Indeed, the ethical move in the political philosophy of responsibility—away from macrolevel questions of justice and toward microlevel questions of forgiveness, for example—arises from the colonization of responsibility by studies of mass violence such as the Holocaust, My Lai, and 9/11. Again, I do not mean to trivialize these atrocities, but their political, ethical, and rhetorical weight continues to distract from the impersonal conditions of injustice that are irreducible to specific instances of injury or violation but nevertheless command responsibility.

Martha Minnow's *Between Vengeance and Forgiveness* (1998) offers a telling demonstration of this colonization. Minnow scrutinizes three familiar responses to mass violence: criminal prosecution of violators, truth commissions that offer violators some amnesty in exchange for testimony, and reparations that afford victims resources to aid their recovery.[5] Ultimately, she finds some value in each of these approaches, but because she thinks they all fall short in at least one crucial area, she ends up on the familiar terrain of recommending that none be pursued to the exclusion of the others. Trials, she argues, are inadequate not only because they draw on limited prosecutorial resources (we cannot possibly prosecute all participants in such atrocities) but also because they focus on exclusive blame (a focus that she attributes to an adversarial legal process but that I have earlier rooted in liberal ontopolitics). While truth commissions promise collective healing through therapeutic discourse, Minnow is unconvinced that the logic of individual therapy translates faithfully to a social level. Finally, she argues that while reparations offer a kind of restorative justice, not actually compensating for a loss but offering symbolic restitution that promotes repentance and forgiveness, such payments are really useful only in instances where the victims are coming to achieve democratic representation (1998:92). Minnow thus focuses on the "incompleteness and inescapable inadequacy of each possible response to collective atrocities" (5) and advocates a "resistance to tidiness" (4), since justice rarely involves the sort of closure that these available responses promise.

This resistance to tidiness leads Minnow to endorse memorialization, an institutionalized attempt to retain the scars of history that rejects the sort of healing Hegel promotes. This institutionalized memory ensures that, despite comforting grasps at such closure, history remains with us. For Minnow, compensation, vengeance, and forgiveness are each predicated on tidy, Hegelian, forgetful healing. They each endeavor to close the issue and return to a state of harmony before the event. Trials complemented by truth commissions and reparations, by contrast, endeavor to keep the issue open, to force the retention of the event in the public memory, to ensure that scars remain to remind us of our historical mistakes.

While this desire to retain history is certainly more compatible with postliberal ontopolitics than with the episodic and ahistorical presentism discussed earlier, its focus on memorialization continues to purify and isolate events. Memorialization thus promotes precisely the sort of reconciliation that Minnow herself eschews. Constructing memorials, monuments to collective injuries, suggests that injury is exceptional. Certainly, the genocides and enslavements that Minnow discusses are exceptional, but by isolating and compartmentalizing them, memorials suggest that injury itself is exceptional. The monument glut in Washington, D.C., the product of a vibrant competition to canonize particular injuries, testifies to the general exceptionalism of widespread injury (see Reston 1995). I do not mean to belittle the severity of these violations when I suggest that physical violence is simply the most visible and bloody type of the vulnerability that individuals experience daily in some form. For postliberals, however, the project is not so much to heal the rift that was opened by a particular violation, or to establish a harmonious order that avoids violation, but rather to recognize the unavoidability of rifts and vulnerabilities so as to render us less anxious over our failed endeavors to autonomy and more generous toward our interdependent Other.

Mass violence's colonization of discourses of political responsibility is not only limiting, however; it is also illustrative. The scenario ubiquitous in philosophical, legal, and popular discourses of responsibility is clearly the soldier who is "just following orders." We can see this situation in cases of what Minnow calls "administrative massacres," from the Holocaust to My Lai to Rwanda, as well as in military dramas such as *A Few Good Men* (1992) and *Casualties of War* (1989), in which soldiers are caught between the imperative to follow orders and the pursuit of individual conscience. The question in this recurring scenario is whether their subordinate positions exonerate soldiers from the illegal acts they perpetrate. This has proven a recalcitrant and fascinating question, despite its ostensibly being decided in the negative at Nuremberg.[6] The enduring fascination, I argue, lies not in its being peculiar to military hierarchy but in its being an amplified instance of the excitability of actions that compose our daily lives. If, as Foucault (1977a) illustrates, military discipline is only quantitatively (not qualitatively) different from the daily discipline of political subjects, then the situation of committing acts under duress is universal, not idiosyncratic to soldiers on distant fields of battle. Indeed, the situation of military wrongdoing intensifies and highlights the sort of excitable actions that populate our daily lives, and these cases strike right to the heart of the pedestrian questions of causality and responsibility that we navigate every day. Surely, it is its familiarity rather than its exceptionalism that renders the scenario so appealing as a narrative.

Postliberal Alternatives

The colonization of responsibility by mass violence threatens to reduce politics to a series of isolated encounters rather than an unavoidable social condition of interdependence and vulnerability. This move corresponds to the tenets of liberal responsibility that I have rehearsed throughout this book. Tying responsibility to causal force and individual (or collective) will draws our attention toward specific disturbances and massacres. And without question, liberal ontopolitics offers definitive and gratifying responses to these events. This, again, is why challenges that upset liberalism's definitive and satisfying prescriptions are received with such anxiety and even hostility. How, liberals demand, can we punish war criminals and human rights violators without recourse to the liberal foundation of an autonomous will? A pressing question indeed.

Nonetheless, I have demonstrated how this demand threatens to reduce questions of distributive justice to a procedural contractualism, state violence to episodic brutalities, and health to a series of individual choices. Such episodes are characterized by the features and roles requisite to liberal responsibility and the responses of compensation, vengeance, and forgiveness. Postliberal responsibility does not deny the value of compensation, vengeance, and forgiveness, as a dogmatic marxist might deny the value of privacy or a libertarian, the value of public schools; the postliberal critique is not that these responses are wrongheaded but that they are appropriate to particular historical circumstances and inappropriate to others. Specifically, postliberal responsibility roots compensation, vengeance, and forgiveness in a particular understanding of the subject as an autonomous agent in possession of its own body and capacities, an understanding that itself sits snugly in the demands of a market economy. The critique of these liberal responses is not that they are mistaken but that they prove themselves inadequate and, today, increasingly unsatisfying.

Judith Butler expresses and exploits this dissatisfaction with liberal response in her recent reflections on political violence (2004, 2005). Though she does not address Minnow specifically, she does address the futility and political peril involved in responding to such violence with attempts to safeguard or reestablish autonomy. Writing after 9/11, Butler admits a political imperative to protect bodies from violent assault. As she puts it, in a perhaps unintentional nod to MacPherson, "It is important to claim our bodies are in a sense *our own* and that we are entitled to claim right of autonomy over bodies. . . . I am not suggesting that we cease to make these claims. We have to, we must" (2004:25). At the same time, Butler warns that responding to political violence with reactive and legalistic assertions of individual or national autonomy tends to be militaristic, a tendency that she thinks might be avoided by supplanting a liberal ontopolitics of autonomy with a postliberal ontopolitics of vulnerability (2004:39–40). For though physical violence demonstrates individual vulnerability most unmistakably, postliberals emphasize the myriad vulnerabilities of the liberal self. Again, one need not belittle the horrors of mass political violence to admit that vulnerability is not episodic but an unavoidable component of human experience.

Butler argues that collective grief, such as that experienced in the wake of 9/11, brings this vulnerability to the fore and opens the possibility of non-militaristic responses to political crises. Such grief, she argues, displays "the thrall in which our relations with others hold us, in ways that we cannot always recount or explain, in ways that often interrupt the self-conscious account of ourselves we try to provide, in ways that challenge the very notion of ourselves as autonomous and in control" (2004:23). Recognition of these attachments is unavoidable in the context of mass, collective grief, but they are no less evident in the case of individual grief. At the risk of allegorizing an event too recent to allegorize, Butler suggests that the unexpected breech of the U.S. national border on that dreadful September morning mirrors the breech of individual autonomy in instances of physical or emotional injury. For example, she declares that "we now see the national border was more permeable than we thought. Our general response is anxiety, rage; a radical desire for security, a shoring up of borders against what is perceived as alien" (2004:39). Although she speaks of national borders, her analysis is clear that this reaction is appropriate to both national invasions and individual violations.[7] The violation of 9/11 was particularly acute for its visible refutation of U.S. national autonomy, and the ongoing military response is intent on reasserting that frustrated autonomy. By contrast, a mindfulness of vulnerability, Butler suggests, opens the door for a recognition of the mutual and eradicable interdependence of agents: "Is this not another way of imagining community, one in which we are alike only in having this condition separately and so having in common a condition that cannot be thought without difference?" (2004:27).[8]

Let's return to Eric Harris. The frustrations of Harris's life are accentuated by a failure to attain the sort of autonomy he had been promised. His violent reaction reflects a desperate attempt to take control of his situation. By contrast, an ethic of vulnerability rather than autonomy would not merely have rendered Harris more tolerant of the harassments and violations he experienced daily but might perhaps have rendered those harassments less likely. To be sure, I do not wish to condemn Harris or exonerate him. I seek only to situate his actions in a political condition that renders them slightly more comprehensible than the superficial condemnations and exonerations that are, I assume, familiar enough.

Though Minnow attempts to avoid the poles of vengeance and forgiveness because the former focuses exclusively on the perpetrator and the latter, exclusively on the victim, she remains mired in the same old dualism in which events are either caused by agents (in which case vengeance) or just happen to victims (who might be called upon to forgive). As her title indicates, Minnow does not attempt to get "beyond" this dualism but only tries to find a comfortable position "between" them, promoting a recognizably liberal compromise. Butler, by contrast, does not recommend all things in moderation, because she argues that both these alternatives—as well as the compromise between them—remain beholden to the conceit of individual sovereignty. Instead of accepting this conceit, Butler recommends acknowledging "an inevitable interdependency . . . as the basis for global political community." She continues: "I confess to not knowing how to theorize that interdependency. I would suggest, however, that both our political and ethical responsibilities are rooted in the recognition that radical forms of self-sufficiency and unbridled sovereignty are, by definition, disrupted by the larger global processes of which they are a part, that no final control can be secured, and that final control is not, cannot be, an ultimate value" (Butler 2004:xiii). This refusal of sovereignty upsets the ontopolitical foundation for both vengeance and forgiveness, though it simultaneously admits to their present indispensability ("I confess to not knowing how . . ."). With this focus on vulnerability, Butler does not isolate events and actors that can give or receive forgiveness or vengeance. Instead, she places these events and actors in historical circumstance without which neither is thinkable. This move does not abandon responsibility, as liberals maintain, but rather casts actors in a persistent position of dependence in which their every desire and action is a response to both the conditions and agents they encounter.

This vulnerability is similarly on display in Iris Young's refusal to reduce economic justice to the play of discrete contracts (see chapter 4), in the extension of Althusser to account for the interpellation *of* (not merely *by*) the police (chapter 5), and in Donna Haraway's refusal to isolate particular pregnancies from the political economy of reproduction (see chapter 6).

The project of postliberalism is not so much to heal the rift that particular violations open but to recognize the unavoidability of rifts and vulnerabilities so as to render us less anxious over our failed endeavors to autonomy and more generous toward the Other on whom our existence is finally recognized as dependent. While this might not be a concrete response, it does expand the sorts of situations we can view as calling for response and democratizes the capacities for response by locating them not in the institutional control of forces but in the performative capacities for transformative agency endemic to our daily lives. The project, in other words, is not to conclude the transaction and heal the wound via compensation, vengeance, or forgiveness, or even to compartmentalize the wound via memorialization, but instead to challenge the very notion that the holes in the body might heal. Indeed, it is only through holes in the body that nutrients can be absorbed.

A Horizon of Responsibility

Throughout this book, I have tried to show how liberal responsibility, based in a so-called commonsense account of individual agency, operates with dubious ontological assumptions and informs deeply problematic political positions. The liberal, procedural imperative to isolate causal agents and ascribe to them authority over their desires and intents fetishizes moments and actors by removing them from their constituent environments, arbitrarily consolidating a host of effective political inputs into actors that can be blamed for causing events. While I have argued that this metonymic isolation is indispensable to any attempt to conceptualize political life, liberal political thought and practice tend to deny the metonymy, to assign the metonym undue ontological weight.

The phenomenological and performative move, highlighted in this book through the concept of *Bildung,* suggests that responding with compensation, revenge, and forgiveness requires a presumption of individuals' sovereignty over their constituent forces. These responses also limit political attention to situations with identifiable subjects who can offer and receive them. Postliberal responsibility, by contrast, paints such reconciliatory mechanisms as nostalgic attempts to restore a state of autonomy and equilibrium that never existed in the first place. It rejects the sovereign conceit that underlies the fetishistic approach to injury, and by highlighting the political and economic circumstances that interpellate, it reveals how the political virtue of choice ironically impoverishes responsibility in attempts to save it. I have argued that the postliberal subject remains a responsible subject. Indeed, polemics aside, it is more responsible than the liberal subject, since it is able to respond to more (and more types of) situations and is afforded a greater range of responses. By resisting the liberal seduction to privatize responsibility, postliberals are able to theorize responsibility for a greater range of political affairs and reveal how the liberal drive to salvage responsibility actually impoverishes it.

Unfortunately, this means that postliberals promote a different understanding of what makes for an agent. Though it rejects the conventional, quantitative debate wherein agency increases in inverse relationship to the influence of structures, postliberalism is typically reduced to one of the familiar alternatives: radical liberalism or radical antiliberalism. Despite vitriolic critiques to the contrary, postliberalism is not—never has been—about the death of the subject per se but about the death of a particular subject. In contrast to the liberal subject, who is characterized by coherence and sovereignty, the postliberal subject is characterized by vulnerability and dependence. Postliberalism does not eliminate but rather heightens the ability to respond, since response becomes an ever-present possibility rather than an ethical and episodic charge relevant to particular situations. In short, the postliberal subject is, ontopolitically, a responsible subject.

The second part of this book has explored how postliberal responsibility speaks to some of the more central debates in political life. Economically, it provides an approach to distributive justice that is unavailable from within the liberal focus on contracts. Legally, it speaks to a host of social circumstances that are irreducible to the criminal focus on intent and causality but are no less pernicious. Ethically, it promotes a responsibility to others that a liberal protection of individual choice neglects. In each of these realms, the ontopolitical commitments of liberalism release actors from responsibility for the production and maintenance of brutal and brutalizing conditions of existence. In its attempt to salvage responsibility while the integrity of the choosing subject comes under heavy theoretical and political fire, liberalism limits the concept to apply to particular types of events (e.g., broken contracts, isolated assaults, particular choices) but not to situations that render these events likely (e.g., market imperatives, intensive surveillance, and the unavailability of basic health care).

These domains—economic, criminal, and medical justice—are illustrative for covering three principal areas of political life. But they are far from comprehensive. Postliberal analyses are visible in numerous other realms as well. Recent approaches to American obesity, for example, have struggled to avoid casting the problem as either the product of individual gluttony or consumer manipulation, trying instead to situate the problem in a complex convergence of the economics of agribusiness, shifting work and pay schedules, financial strains on public schools, new styles and modes of leisure, and transformed expectations of gratification.[9] Postliberal arguments are also visible both in the surprisingly successful attempts to get cigarette companies to respond to the ease with which cigarettes find their way into the hands of teens and in the predictably unsuccessful attempts to force weapons manufacturers to do the same for guns. (Though the imperatives of marketing often compel these claims to be pitched in the language of causality, the absurdity of holding handgun manufacturers casually responsible for street crime demonstrates the looseness of this rhetorical move.)

Such approaches may continue to slowly proliferate, but they are still anything but conventional in the United States today. In 2004 the U.S. Congress passed the defiantly named Personal Responsibility in Food Consumption Act, which unambiguously shuns the previously mentioned attempts to locate a public health crisis anywhere but in the dietary choices of sovereign consumers. Similarly, the 1996 welfare-reform bill, officially named the Personal Responsibility and Work Opportunity Reconciliation Act, casts poverty and unemployment as private issues. This act all but denies outright the central importance that several significant factors bear to the household economy: the availability of well-paying jobs; the structure of private-sector wages; and the real costs of housing, food, transportation and health care. Widely praised for its reduction of the number of people on welfare rolls, the act recasts welfare recipients as workers, rhetorically displacing them beyond the immediate concern of the state into a private sphere (the labor market) where individual responsibility reigns. This act, in other words, officially declares that individuals are responsible for earning a living, since nobody could be said to be responsible for structural requirements of a market economy or the unequal bargaining power of the economically disfranchised.

These two acts, however, are merely codified expressions of a more general social hegemony. Every day, liberal responsibility draws attention to serial killers who may sensationally murder a handful of victims, whereas the millions of individual deaths that ensue from a market compulsion to produce Viagra instead of antimalarials go unnoticed. It vilifies the soccer mom in an SUV for polluting the environment or increasing U.S. dependence on foreign oil but ignores the aggressive marketing of fuel-inefficient practices and products. It condemns parents for neglecting children but says nothing about the accessibility of affordable, quality day care. It blames the sick for lousy diets and lifestyles but overlooks the general unavailability of health insurance, preventative care, nourishing meals, and nutritional information.

These personalized narratives do little to solve widespread problems of public health and safety, but they do shore up shared the notions of autonomy and personal responsibility so threatened in an industrialized society. Indeed, the acts just mentioned were made urgent precisely because of the rise in challenges to liberal responsibility in economic and public health debates. Studious attention to such intractable phenomena as epidemics, environmental degradation, social unrest, and economic inequality always point well beyond the facile narratives of willed causal actions, and solutions are rarely available to heroic individuals. Rather, responsibility more reasonably lies with the kind of prosaic and unheroic performances that culminate in social situations: civil rights violations can be traced back to electoral support for increased surveillance and containment of suspect populations; investigations into environmental degradation, national weight gain, and declining job security all point, in part, to the growth of particular food industries; poverty is made possible and probable by shifting interactions in market regulation, taxes, technological developments, and social trends of consumption and management. As Iris Young (2004) puts it, attempts to assign responsibility for such phenomena make little sense from within the liberal conception of responsibility. The liberal focus on supposedly discrete contractual encounters neither encourages nor rewards such investigations.

While some might therefore attempt to address these situations without reference to responsibility, I have tried to show how such complex narratives evoke a reworked notion of responsibility. This reworked concept depends not on identifying a sovereign actor that can be seen as the cause of an event but instead on recognizing interpellated actors capable of responding to situations by virtue of their interpellations. This responsibility is much more elastic than the liberal variety, since assigning responsibility for an affair to certain actors does not deplete the general stock of responsibility. In this way, responsibility becomes not an episodic feature of our lives but the very condition of our existence.

Though the liberal subject has achieved something of a monopoly over discourses of responsibility, responsibility is essentially a historical question. Historical changes in the conception and constitution of the subject determine the appropriate ascriptions of responsibility, and different historical situations admit differing capacities of subjects to respond. Today, liberal ideology and institutions (e.g., representative government, competitive markets, and belief in individual efficacy) provide particular possibilities for agency. As markets and states become less responsible to the demands of consumers and citizens, however, the limits of liberal responsibility become increasingly difficult to deny. As global markets reveal the conceit entailed in the liberal vision of sovereign states, liberal responsibility itself suffers devastating collateral damage. As the ontopolitical inadequacy of the liberal model of exclusive responsibility becomes increasingly visible, possibilities for democracy become intimately tied to the creation of a more capacious theory of responsibility. This book has been an attempt to contribute to the emergence of postliberal ideology and thus to the emergence of postliberal democracy.

Clearly, this book cannot cause such a change in public consciousness. Public consciousness and ideology get their force from continued iteration of conventions and presumptions. Nonetheless, it does identify an emergent trend in reconstructing an indispensable political resource, a trend that is bound to continue as the conditions giving rise to it intensify.

Notes

Preface: Responsibility after Liberalism

1. Iris Young unfortunately passed away soon after I drafted this book. As much of her work on responsibility remains to be published, I continue to discuss it as ongoing.

Chapter One: Responsible Subjects

1. "In an Animal the fitness of the Organization, and the Motion wherein Life consists, begin together, the Motion coming from within; but in Machines the force, coming sensibly from without, is often away, when the Organ is in order, and well fitted to receive it" (Locke 1975:331).

2. "Is it not remarkable that the key philosophical notions which are still in use today when dealing with individual rights and personality were actually invented or systematized by Locke?" (Balibar 1996:233).

3. To be sure, in his most famous work, *Individuals* (1959), Strawson roots this individualist metaphysics in a "massive central core of human thinking which has no history" (10). This clear separation of subject and object contrasts directly with Hegelian dialectics and Foucaultian genealogy, as I will show in coming chapters.

4. In vicarious responsibility, responsibility lies not with the actor ("the agent") but with the one who orders or otherwise instigates the action ("the principal"). In strict liability, somebody is held responsible for something he or she did not cause, via vicarious responsibility or, more often, an agreement to bear this responsibility (as with a consumer warranty, for example).

5. Elsewhere, Feinberg (1970: ch. 6) discusses the "accordion effect" to illustrate how causal responsibility is ascribed to singular or multiple sites, depending on both conventions of grammar (presaging Scheffler's dominant "phenomenology of agency") and capricious preferences (resonating with Ripstein's focus on political prejudice).

6. See, for example, Berlin 1969 (essay 2), where Berlin condemns various rejections of the model of a free, choosing subject not primarily for their conceptual absurdity but for abandoning any notion of responsibility that might help organize social life. Making only a slight qualification, Scheffler (2001) argues that attempts to produce "a more expansive conception of responsibility" that is not rooted in the willing subject will probably fail, leading to an abandonment

rather than an expansion of the concept. For rejections of particular alternatives, see Adkins 1960 and 1970 (on the ancients); Ripstein 1999 (on marxists); and Nussbaum 1999 (on postmoderns).

7. Williams acknowledges that this focus on intent is more evident in criminal than in tort law, but he claims that this reflects not a qualitatively different conception of responsibility but a different conception of law; because liberals harbor greater anxiety about the state's power over the individual, the conditions for responsibility (blame) are more stringent in cases between the state and the individual than in cases between individuals (1993:63–6).

8. Notably, recent approaches to American obesity, such as Greg Critser's *Fat Land* (2003) and Morgan Spurlock's self-immolating documentary film *Super Size Me* (2004), have for the most part avoided questions of responsibility, perhaps because its dominant (liberal) understandings are inappropriate to the situation. Indeed, though the bulk of the often vitriolic debate about *Super Size Me* surrounded its contentious ascriptions of responsibility, the terms *responsible* and *responsibility* appear in the film a mere three times, in an opening voiceover (asking "Where does personal responsibility stop and corporate responsibility begin?") and in two pitches from a lawyer pursuing a lawsuit against the fast food industry. Such an approach stands in direct contrast to recent legislation such as the Personal Responsibility in Food Consumption Act of 2003 (a.k.a. "the Cheeseburger Bill"), which officially diagnoses dramatic rises in obesity and type 2 diabetes as products of personal deficiency rather than the convenience and ubiquity of fattening foods.

9. Scheffler (2001: ch. 2) similarly argues that global transformations threaten the individual and national sovereignty upon which liberal responsibility rests. He is, however, much more wary of attempts to formulate an alternative. Though he identifies these incipient alternatives as symptoms of a decline in these liberal categories, he argues that the stakes are simply too high to pursue them. Hardt and Negri (2000, 2004) also discuss the relationship between globalization and individual sovereignty, though with markedly different predictions.

Chapter Two: Making Marx Effective

1. This phrasing is drawn from Judith Butler (1997b:15), who defines agency as the "assumption of a purpose *unintended* by power."

2. This dichotomy is not exclusive to explicitly *political* philosophy. Describing Foucault's approach to the social sciences and the history of epistemology, Dreyfus and Rabinow (1983) encounter the same dilemma. Ultimately, they declare that because Foucault refuses both the structural theory of autonomous discourse and the reifying presumptions of individual production of meaning, he is "beyond structuralism and hermeneutics."

3. Marx does this in numerous writings, but most clearly in his critique of the public/private split in *On the Jewish Question*.

4. The supposed centrality of this metaphor for Marx depends upon a single use in the 1859 preface to *A Contribution to the Critique of Political Economy* (1970b:20). Marx does gesture toward its terms in a few other writings, but this is the only

time he issues it with any particular significance. Compare Cohen's (1978:136–42) use of this passage to argue for the metaphor's theoretical primacy in Marx.

5. Foucault's use of the term *effective* is somewhat idiomatic, as neither the French *effective* nor the German *wirkliche* translates literally into English as "effective"; they are, rather, both better translated as "real" or "actual." But Foucault seems to use the French and English terms interchangeably, perhaps playfully hinting that to be real is to be effective. Similarly, the etymological link between Nietzsche's *wirkliche* (real) and *wirksame* (effective) lies in their common root, *wirk-* (work).

6. Ultimately, this approach to completion could be the most significant contribution of the movement often called postmarxism (see Laclau 1990).

7. The surrounding essays of this trilogy are *The Class Struggles in France, 1848–1850* (written in 1851) and *The Civil War in France* (written in 1871).

8. "Brumaire" was a month in the French Republican calendar.

9. This argument that events are always experienced through a mediating body of ideas is anything but new. For examples, see Bowles and Gintis 1986; Jameson 1981; Foucault 1977c; H. White 1973; and Carr 1961. For a compelling argument that this is what Marx means by "ideology" (rather than the brazenly reductive "false consciousness"), see Althusser 1970.

10. Indeed, displacement is *always* half of Marx's story. The contradictions of *Capital,* for example, are always displaced (never reconciled) and continue to operate in their displacement (Harvey 1999).

11. Marx points to the threat that cooperative labor poses for notions of individuality in chapter 13 of *Capital.* But if the technologies of industrial manufacture disrupt the ideology of the individual, the technologies of modern celebrity intensify it. On a related note, see the fascinating discussion by Jacqueline Stevens (1999) of the way ostensibly discrete dimensions of identity such as family, race, nationality, religion, and ethnicity form "metonymic chains" impossible to untangle.

12. This complements Avineri's (1968) claim that Marx does not so much reject mechanistic materialisms as read them as expressions of an alienated existence. Marx problematizes the reductions of liberalism, but given existing society, we could only ideologically claim to abandon them.

13. For more on the historical cargo carried in an author's name, see Foucault 1977c (122–23).

14. Again, the criticism here is not that this ideology is wrong but that it is appropriate only to a particular historical stage. Of course, this ideology of the sovereign individual does not necessarily inform a conventionally liberal politics. Liberal ideology, after all, is not unilaterally determinate, and the *Brumaire* is concerned with the mobilization of this ideology in the service of a classically authoritarian power grab.

15. My phrasing here self-consciously echoes Judith Butler's theory of performativity.

16. This parallels Markus (1986) on Hegel's "double bind."

17. Lenin will receive more sustained attention in chapter 4. For now, note that Lenin takes *Bildung* to be closer to construction than to cultivation, an in-

terpretation that not only conveniently places him in an unambiguous position of architect in the base/superstructure metaphor but also provides a model of sovereign authorship that, Marx already suggests, has some profound links to authoritarian politics.

18. "Division of labour only becomes truly such from the moment when a division of material and mental labour appears. From this moment onwards consciousness *can* really flatter itself that it is something other than consciousness of existing practice . . . ; from now on consciousness is in a position to emancipate itself from the world and to proceed to the formation [*Bildung*] of 'pure' theory" (Marx and Engels 1947:20).

Chapter Three: Judith Butler's Responsible Performance

1. I had already drafted this chapter when Butler released a collection of lectures under the title *Giving an Account of Oneself* (2005). I therefore make scarce use of this book, though it clearly bolsters my argument. In fact, the final lecture in the collection is called "Responsibility."

2. This is admittedly a contentious claim. Stephen White (1991) gives the honor to Heidegger, while Foucault (1977b) clearly gets most of his sustenance from Nietzsche. Fred Dallmayr (1981), perhaps sagely, divides the contribution among Heidegger, Merleau-Ponty, and Adorno (the latter two being Dallmayr's own mentors and obvious legacies of Hegel and Marx). I focus on Hegel largely because his obvious links to both Marx and Butler help chart a trajectory. (Also, each thinker's first major work—if we count Butler's dissertation but not Marx's, which seems fair—focuses on Hegel). Ironically, by the looks of avowed debts among democratic theorists today, Nietzsche's appropriation by and Heidegger's flirtation with Nazism seem much more forgivable (or forgiven) than Hegel's own brushes with authoritarianism.

3. Berlin's critique of determinism (1969: essay 2) and Popper's of totalitarianism (1945: vol. 2) are aimed directly at Hegel.

4. The best example of this tension is probably John Stuart Mill's (1978:9–10) coupled demand for individual liberty as well as civic participation, for freedom of consciousness as well as compulsory education of barbaric individuals and cultures.

5. Lenin can be seen to make this same mistake, reducing *Bildung* to instruction in revolutionary theory by a trained group of professional revolutionaries. Ironically, this idea that the failure of the dialectic is its very success has come to be the defining feature of so-called postmarxism (see Žižek 1989; Laclau 1990), but one might note that Žižek identifies the first postmarxist as . . . Hegel (1989:5). Relatedly, Sheldon Wolin (1996) endorses a "fugitive" democracy that admits the necessity of institutionalizing the results of contestations in law but claims that democracy inheres in recognizing that reconciliations are always "partial and provisional."

6. One also sees this dilemma playing out in the rise of cultural studies as an academic discipline. In response to Frankfurt School claims about the totalitarian power of the culture industry, cultural studies emerged to herald the democratic

power of critical reading. The former privileged the text; the latter, the reader (see Frank 2001a: ch. 8).

7. Seyla Benhabib, for example, charges Butler with a "complete debunking of any concepts of selfhood, agency, and autonomy" (1995:21). Martha Nussbaum, more abrasively, opens with a statement that Butler's political thought "looks very much like quietism and retreat" and closes with a claim that it "collaborates with evil" (1999:38, 45). In her latest book, Butler explains that though critics "worry that [her work] means there is no concept of the subject that can serve as the ground for moral agency and moral accountability," she aims to show "how a theory of subject formation that acknowledges the limits of self-knowledge can serve a conception of ethics and, indeed, responsibility" (2005:8, 19).

8. One more reason that Butler is helpful in this debate is that she has made a virtual career out of responding to her critics. Perhaps more than other philosophers, she allows (mis)readings of her work to guide her future projects, such that the introduction to *Bodies That Matter* (1993a) is a response to criticisms of *Gender Trouble* (1990), and the introduction to *Excitable Speech* (1997a) is largely a response to concerns raised about *Bodies That Matter*.

9. Cf. "Men make their own history . . . under the given and inherited circumstances with which they are directly confronted" (Marx 1973:146).

10. Again, this claim runs through the entirety of her work, from her earliest work on Hegel (Butler 1987) to her most recent work on political violence (2004, 2005).

11. This accounts for unequal distributions of responsibility across subjects. Some (such as elected officials) might have a greater ability to respond because they inhabit a position of authority.

12. Again, Nussbaum (1999) manages to indict Butler on both these counts. It is surely no coincidence that Butler's discussion of French appropriations of Hegel is organized around this same conundrum: Kojève, Hyppolite, and Sartre promote Hegel for championing agency, whereas Foucault, Derrida, and Lacan indict him for determinism (1987: chs. 2 and 4).

13. Butler uses this theory as she discusses the gendering of infants through the such routine hailings as "It's a girl!" (1993a:7–8); the assignation of names (1993a:122); and her friends' practice of addressing her as "Judy" rather than "Judith" to dislocate her from her pedestal of academic posturing toward a more ordinary realm of the everyday lived body (1993a:ix).

14. Butler expresses this same ambivalence with regard to Foucault. Though she defends Foucault against simplistic readings that have him dissolving the subject into a morass of "power," she also suggests that his relative silence on the matter leaves himself open to this criticism (1993a:8–9, 1997b: ch. 3, 2000a:151).

15. This notion of being a "bad subject" has always been central in Butler's work; her title *Gender Trouble* refers to the disruptive politics of making trouble, of being bad (1990:vii–ix).

16. In "A Plea for Excuses" (1961:27), Austin admits to a "complicated internal machinery" that must operate flawlessly to create a distinct, blameworthy act. We have excuses, he argues, for cases in which this machinery—the normally harmonious and complementary relationship among will, intent, and body—

breaks down, as when our bodies do something other than what we intended. For Butler, however, we are never in control of this complicated internal machinery, nor should we presume any organic agreement among its components.

17. Though Butler does not pursue this possibility explicitly, Althusser's story does implicitly offer this account, since it suggests not only interpellations *by* the officer but also interpellations *of* the officer who, by virtue of an extraordinary set of physical and psychological practices, becomes capable of any number of novel moments of agency. Absent a claim that cops are not agents, it seems difficult to see Althusser's model as providing no space for agency. I pursue this issue at length in chapter 5.

18. William Connolly's recent interest in neurology reflects a similar concern. As he puts it, "in their laudable attempt to ward off one type of reductionism too many cultural theorists fall into another: they lapse into a reductionism that ignores how biology is mixed into thinking and culture and how other aspects of nature are folded into both" (2002:3).

19. Butler provides the example of a preoperative transsexual prostitute who was murdered when a client discovered that she was not what she seemed. For further testimony to this danger, consider the cases of Emmett Till (lynched for ostensibly flirting with a white woman) and Teena Brandon (whose violent death was dramatized in the 1999 film *Boys Don't Cry*). On the anxieties and fears stirred by such subversions, see "Fear, Radical Democracy, and Ontological Methadone" (Lavin 2006).

20. See, for example, the exchange between Butler and Nancy Fraser, in which Butler highlights how supposedly "cultural" institutions (e.g., heterosexual monogamy) are profoundly economic, whereas Fraser argues that Butler's focus risks suggesting that homosexuality itself poses a threat to capital (Butler 1997c; Fraser 1997). Fraser's point might be validated by the consumerist cant of the television show *Queer Eye for the Straight Guy*, but it is certainly undermined by the capitalist accommodation to (and manifest sexism and racism in) labor unions. For her part, Butler claims only that the type of resignification she proposes *can* threaten capital, not that it *does* (1995:41).

21. For other attempts to think of poststructuralism along with—instead of against—marxism, see Read 2003; Gibson-Graham, Resnick, and Wolff 2000 and 2001; Hardt and Negri 2000; and Laclau and Mouffe 1985. I will return to this literature in chapter 4.

22. Note that Gramsci broke with Croce for the same reason (Boggs 1976:34).

23. "Of course, the political task is not to refuse representational politics—as if we could" (Butler 1990:5).

Chapter Four: Who Responds to Global Capital?

1. The point is not merely that individual will pales in the face of corporate will. Corporate autonomy is no less compromised by demands for profits and efficiency.

2. Slavoj Žižek similarly claims that while identity politics has "repoliticized" myriad dimensions of identity, it has depoliticized capitalism (2000:98)—a claim

that might find evidence in John Rawls's (1993) identification of capitalism as part of the "overlapping consensus" among decent peoples. For a rebuttal to this critique of identity politics, see Nancy Fraser's (1996) argument that one need not abandon anticapitalism to pursue such a politics of recognition, since heightened recognition often brings with it demands for redistribution. But I read Brown's (and Žižek's) point to be that recognition itself must be refigured if it is to correspond with a critique of capital, since capital has its own mode of recognition (i.e., contract).

3. I discussed many of these condemnations in previous chapters. To wit: Popper, Berlin, Scheffler, and Nussbaum.

4. For another example, see Cohen's (1978) functionalism and his reconsideration of same (2001).

5. I rehearsed most of these critiques in chapter 2. For the fetish, see Marx 1977 (ch. 1, sect. 4).

6. In its annual reports issued since 2001, the State Department has estimated the number of sex slaves in the United States as low as 14,000 or as high as 50,000. The higher estimates have received, of course, the most publicity and the most criticism, though the lowest estimate (which Attorney-General Alberto Gonzales has argued might itself be inflated) is still an appalling possibility. On these numbers and their controversy, see Landesman 2004 and Shafer 2005. On the political economy of prison labor, see Christian Parenti's otherwise polemical *Lockdown America* (2000: ch. 11). On the political economy of domestic, cooperative, and slave labor, see Gibson-Graham's *Postcapitalist Politics* (2007: ch. 3). On the endurance of slave labor globally, see Bales's *Disposable People* (1999).

7. See also Hardt and Negri 1994 (chs. 1–2) and Read 2003.

8. Perhaps the best demonstration of this dilemma comes from Fredric Jameson. Though he criticizes Foucault for "constructing an increasingly closed and terrifying machine" that renders resistance unthinkable (1991:5), he seems to do the same thing in rejecting the pluralization and fragmentation of capital: "without a conception of the social totality . . . no properly socialist politics is possible" (1988:355).

9. Though Reich announced that the 1990s would be the age of the "knowledge worker" or the "symbolic analyst," the internet's devaluation of knowledge, symbolism, and analysis led him to modify this into the "creative worker" in 2001. Hardt and Negri have also made revisions. They claim in *Empire* that the "computerization of production" may homogenize formerly quite distinct activities (such as weaving and tailoring) so that they "involve exactly the same concrete practices" (2000:292). In *Multitude,* however, they argue merely that the requirements of "immaterial labor" (flexibility, contingency, and dependence upon intellectual property) set the terms by which even traditional jobs will be performed. In other words, agricultural work remains material but becomes more temporary and flexible as seed technologies are introduced to better manage the landscape and harvesting patterns (2004:108–14).

10. Perhaps our era's greatest novelty hawker, Thomas Friedman heralded the "second era of globalization" in 2000 (though he could never seem to decide if that era began before or after the cold war). He has since grown tired of this

label, announcing in 2005 the arrival of "Globalization 3.0" and moving the opening of the second era back a century and a half to around 1800.

11. Žižek (2001, 2004) is one of his—and Hegel's—few remaining defenders.

12. Unfortunately, this rejection of economics often blinds their analysis, as when they dismiss Lenin with a claim that all of his "terminological innovations . . . belong to military vocabulary (tactical alliance, strategic line, so many steps forward so many steps back); none refers to the very structuring of social relations" (Laclau and Mouffe 1985:57). This statement is possible only with the unforgivable neglect of Lenin's principal terminological innovation: imperialism. Cf. Hardt and Negri (2000:231–33).

13. Alan Keenan's (1997) review of two books sharing the title *Radical Democracy* suggests that the term does not mark a specific political or philosophical movement so much as it allows individual theorists to announce their revolutionary credibility.

14. See also Mouffe's (1992) disclosure that radical democracy is actually the realization of liberalism. With such concessions, the hostility with which many marxists receive Laclau and Mouffe provokes little wonder. For example, pointing explicitly to *Hegemony and Socialist Strategy,* Hardt and Negri write: "Poor Gramsci, communist and militant before all else, tortured and killed by fascism and ultimately by the bosses who financed fascism—poor Gramsci was given the gift of being considered the founder of a strange notion of hegemony that leaves no place for a Marxian politics . . . We have to defend ourselves against such generous gifts!" (2000:451 n. 26).

15. As Aronowitz (1986–87) puts this, Laclau and Mouffe confuse authority with authoritarianism. In a particularly telling demonstration of the politics of "radical democracy," Arroyo-Vázquez (2004) argues that liberalism and constitutionalism are not merely inadequate to democracy but fundamentally incompatible with it. He describes institutionalization not as the codification of democratic contestation but as its failure. Yet a world without institutions seems not just impractical but inconceivable.

16. The sovereignty of "the people," at least since Hobbes, is itself predicated on the sovereignty of "the individual" and its authority to voluntarily enter into the social contract. Hardt and Negri challenge this conceit of sovereignty through Foucault's conception of governmentality (2000:88).

17. In a parallel to Butler's claim that the hegemony of identity politics suggests that there is no *political* opposition to its tenets (1995:36), Hardt and Negri seek to debunk the presumption that there is no politics without sovereignty (2004:329).

18. Heroism's declining resonance in politics, however, has an immediate complement in nostalgia. Witness the comic book revivalism in Hollywood (Spiderman, Batman, Superman, X-Men, the Fantastic Four, the Incredible Hulk, Daredevil, Elektra, Hellboy, Ghost Rider, and The Incredibles), television shows such as *Heroes* (NBC), *Smallville* (WB and CW), and *Who Wants to Be a Superhero?* (Sci-Fi), and books by Jonathan Lethem (2003, 2004) and Michael Chabon (2000, 2004).

19. As they themselves have grown fond of pointing out, their relationship to

the events in Seattle mirrors Marx's to the Paris Commune of 1871: after being challenged for an inability to point to a demonstration of their concept, the example presents itself (Hardt and Negri 2004:380 n. 44).

20. Young uses the terms "responsibility as blame" or "the liability model" for what I'm calling "liberal responsibility" and offers an alternative that she calls "political responsibility." Though her explanation of this alternative maps fairly well onto my own work, I find the term "political responsibility" both redundant and deceptive, since blame and liability remain quite political. For these reasons and those covered in chapter 1, I prefer the term "postliberal responsibility" to "political responsibility."

21. On shame and guilt, see Williams 1993 and chapter 1 of this book.

22. For more extensive discussion of the way these approaches play out, see Deen Chatterjee's recent edited volume *The Ethics of Assistance* (2004) and my essay "Who Responds to Global Poverty?" (Lavin 2005).

23. For the relationship between generosity and postliberal ontology, see Coles 1997; Connolly 1995; and S. White 2000.

Chapter Five: Postliberal Responsibility and the Death of Amadou Diallo

1. These narratives are my own concoctions, drawn (but not quoted) from various accounts and sources. The NYPD officer Edward Conlon (2004:313–22) rehearses each of these basic approaches in his discussion of Diallo. Regina Lawrence (2000) identifies them as *the* alternatives to discussing police brutality in general.

2. I draw this term from Bauman 1999 (72–78).

3. Podhoretz seems somewhat unaware that this comparison puts common civilians in the enemy's place. At least, I hope he is unaware of this.

4. In an extensive analysis of media coverage of police brutality, Regina Lawrence (2000: ch. 3) demonstrates that most coverage is individualized. She ultimately understates her case, however, since even most of the coverage that she labels "systemic" is focused on individuals in the manner I am suggesting here (see esp. 40–49). She also suggests that this occurs because Americans see the world through an individualist lens (60).

5. For criticisms of the 1997 SCU expansion, see Barry 2000 and Toobin 2002.

6. Herbert is an illustrative example. In another column discussing Abu Ghraib, Herbert (2004) conspicuously avoids the question of responsibility, suggesting that this inquiry would presume these events to be exceptional, whereas he reads them as yet another instance of the routine brutalities of domestic prisoners. Because responsibility—that is, liberal responsibility—does not help to explain the results of standard operating procedures, the concept does not help him discuss this case. Taken together, I think, these disparate analyses indicate Herbert's discomfort with the available explanatory concepts and his lack of viable alternatives.

7. For an exception to this tendency, consider Thomas Frank's (2001b) claim

that Madison Avenue's ideology of the extreme in everything from potato chips to sneakers should be noted in any attempt to understand why a seemingly normal, suburban, American teenager (John Walker Lindh) might have been attracted to radical Islam.

8. Mark Warren (1996) argues that as a political philosophy, liberalism is essentially tied to the logic of representation. My claim here is a direct complement: we select representatives not only for our future (in elections and legislation) but also for our past (in prosecution and punishment). With regard to cases of police brutality, Lawrence (2000:204 n. 11) argues that this is the only viable option in the existing legal structure.

9. Foucault (1970:xxi–xxii) describes an episteme as "the epistemological field" that allows something like presumptions to knowledge to arise—"the historical *a priori*." My discussion of the design and marketing of epistemes draws heavily on Louis Althusser (1971), whose pioneering essay on the production and reproduction of ideological subjects invites a comparison of the Foucaultian "episteme" with a strictly marxist "ideology."

10. I am being more charitable to the officers than Butler is. Her work is a reading of the way the jury and the public experienced the King videotape. Because she does go on to analyze how the officers experienced King's outstretched hand, she leaves us with the implicit claim that they were merely venting racist hostility. She further personalizes the argument by suggesting that the officers beat King not only because he was black but because his position on his knees further enraged them by invoking the homosexual fantasies that plague cops— apparently both homophobic and latently homosexual (1993b:21).

11. Crenshaw and Peller (1993) argue that this appeal to the rule of law facilitated widespread condemnation of both the King beating and the uprising following the verdict. Lawrence (2000:5–9, 43–49) further attributes the presumption of innocence to the fact that news accounts of police activity are dominated by accounts provided by police officials (rather than what she calls "critical nonofficials").

12. The case of Abner Louima, beaten and sodomized by NYPD officers in 1997, might seem to offer a counterexample. King's and Diallo's cases, however, represent the complications of law enforcement, whereas Louima's torture in the stationhouse was completely divorced from legitimate policing activity. It is difficult to imagine how one might justify sodomizing a prisoner. Similarly, the fact that King eventually won $3.8 million in a civil suit against the city of Los Angeles did nothing to invalidate the *legal* vindication of our representatives' violent behavior. In fact, the two King verdicts together suggest a receptivity to the notion that civil rights violations are a normal cost of law enforcement. In an age of increasingly privatized police forces, this is a distressing precedent.

13. Contrast this with straightforward structuralist accounts that explain increases in police brutality and prison populations purely as symptoms of an economic crisis (e.g., Parenti 2000; Marable 1983).

14. For social and psychological backgrounds of police officers, see Wrightsman 1987. Regarding recruitment, trends suggest a preference for quantity over quality when it comes to putting police on the street: though the NYPD budget

increased by 17.7 percent between 1990 and 2000, this facilitated a 29.4 percent increase in the size of the force (from 31,236 to 40,435) and a 9.1 percent *decrease* in money spent per officer for pay, training, equipment, and so on. Nationwide, the trend is similar, if less dramatic (see Reaves and Hickman 2002).

15. Most of the nearly three dozen lawsuits were dismissed outright, and thirty state legislatures passed laws banning them before President Bush signed the Protection of Lawful Commerce in Arms Act (2005). Weapons manufacturers and dealers are now immune from civil or criminal liability for crimes committed with their products, though the constitutionality of this law has yet to be tested in court.

16. This is to say that both bin Laden and Bush have wide networks of followers who support, encourage, and make possible the decisions and actions we uncomplicatedly attribute to these individuals. This should not be confused with Baudrillard's (2002) claim that we all secretly wanted to destroy the World Trade Center, even though it does share something with his claim that this act of terrorism was a response to the triumph of neoliberal globalization, for which we do bear some responsibility. It also suggests examining the origins of global terrorism, including the formation of organizations such as al Qaeda and leaders such as bin Laden—examinations that tend to point uncomfortably toward U.S. efforts to win the cold war (see Clarke 2004; Cooley 1999).

17. Note also the so-called atonement trials in the South, in which a handful of exceptional racists are being tried to atone for rampant and systemic injustices of Jim Crow.

18. "To be radical is to grasp things by the root. But for man the root is man himself" (Marx 1970a:137).

Chapter Six: Conceptions of Responsibility

1. Rickie Solinger (2001:132) places the shift from privacy to choice a decade earlier, when Governor Ronald Reagan was attempting to limit welfare payments made to mothers, President Jimmy Carter was proposing economic incentives to carry babies to term, and Representative Henry Hyde was (successfully) arguing that the state need not fund private decisions. I see no need to arbitrate these rival start dates, though Saletan's attention to Planned Parenthood's internal documents suggests that the transformation was not terribly well theorized until the 1980s. Celeste Condit (1990: chs. 5–6, esp. pp. 67–8), however, tells a strikingly different story in which "choice" was a spontaneous outgrowth of a feminist movement concerned with increasing women's agency. Claiming that choice is "concretely indigenous to women's experiences" and endemic to the struggles for birth control and employment opportunities, Condit implicitly denies its emergence as reaction to *Roe*'s declining capabilities. Condit's story is less grounded in cases, though to be fair, hers is a work of rhetorical theory rather than political history.

2. For a completely unsentimental look at the business of international adoption, including the going rate for particular types of babies and the impact of *Roe* on the domestic adoption market, see Spar 2006 (ch. 6).

3. Hartouni also discusses how visual technology and the ability to freeze and isolate images played the same role in constructing an image of Rodney King as a threat (1997:14–17). Note also Barbara Duden's (1993) argument about the "disembodiment" of pregnancy pursuant to these new visual technologies.

4. Of course, many feminists (e.g., Catherine MacKinnon [1989]) take issue with the presumed distinction of rape, since condemnations of the physical force of conventional rape implicitly legitimize the less overt coercions in heterosexual monogamy. This model of ubiquitous victimhood, however, continues to prioritize the individual will. Like Copelon, MacKinnon holds out the possibility of a more equitable distribution of power so that women's actions really are autonomous.

5. Often branded a kinder and gentler form of eugenics, the movement to allow parents to select the traits of their offspring is clearly gaining momentum. Julian Savulesco (2001), currently the head of Oxford University's Uehiro Centre for Practical Ethics, has championed what he calls a principle of "procreative beneficence," allowing parents to use available technologies to select not only traits affecting their children's health but also such traits as hair and eye color.

6. For a discussion of these villains and their production, see Condit 1990 (ch. 2).

7. Petschesky (1984:13) frets that this emphasis on social roles neglects how pregnancy affects women's *bodies;* she is concerned that a transformed division of labor that releases women from their role as primary caregivers might also, from Jaggar's position, legitimate state control over their bodies. Jaggar, in reflections on her earlier article, addresses this concern by stressing that she *does* recognize that the unique involvement of women's bodies in pregnancy ensures that women will always bear greater responsibility for reproduction and that her earlier endorsement of possible collective restrictions on abortion was colored by a youthful, utopian vision of a truly harmonious society (1998:340, 344–46). In other words, Jaggar claims that she has rethought the unmitigated rejection of rights she espoused in the 1970s, recognizing the often emancipatory potential of rights as identified by Marx, Brown, and other postliberals.

Conclusion

1. To be sure, that day in Littleton, Colorado, remains one of the more awful days in U.S. history. My goal here is not to deny this but to use this notable, punctuating moment to illustrate something about history and responsibility in the United States.

2. For such liberals as Richard Rorty (1989) and Judith Shklar (1984, 1989), the philosophy of liberalism is grounded in a fear of such injury. Sheldon Wolin (1960: ch. 9) similarly roots liberalism in a pervasive anxiety over individual safety. For a fascinating alternative approach to injury, see Abbas 2005.

3. As I argued in chapter 1, the fact that such plaints do not require the elevated demand of intent suggests how these determinations of responsibility are rooted more in political preferences than in any deeper sense of actual responsibility.

4. Some have read the career of Dirty Harry himself (Clint Eastwood) as dem-

onstrating this danger, with Eastwood's recent films (especially *Mystic River* and *Unforgiven*) serving as atonement for the street justice he exemplified in his earlier career—an atonement that has been rewarded with two Academy Awards for Best Picture.

5. These responses correspond to the three I discussed in the previous section: criminal punishment as vengeance, truth commissions as forgiveness, and reparations as compensation. This last correspondence is less direct than the others are, as Minnow (1998:92) points out, since reparations seek not to financially compensate for particular injuries but rather to rework distributions in service of democratic progress. This divergence stems from the exceptional nature of the injuries being discussed—the immeasurable severity of the injuries and the fact that many victims are dead.

6. "The fact that a person acted pursuant to order of his Government or of a superior does not relieve him from responsibility under international law, provided a moral choice was in fact possible to him" (principle 4 of the Nuremberg Tribunal).

7. For more on this at the individual level, see Connolly 1995 and Lavin 2006.

8. Such statements betray Butler's recent use of Emmanuel Lévinas, most explicit in the titular essay of this collection of post-9/11 essays, *Precarious Life*.

9. Critser (2003) is probably most explicit in exploring the intractability of the obesity issue, looking at trends in agriculture, work, leisure, fashion, technology, and religion, among other things. But see also Pollan's (2002a, 2002b, 2006) crusade against corn and Morgan Spurlock's career-making stunt in *Super Size Me*.

Bibliography

Abbas, Asma. 2005. "Suffering Liberalism: A Critique of the Political Economy of Injury." Ph.D. diss., Penn State University.

Adkins, A. W. H. 1960. *Merit and Responsibility.* Oxford: Clarendon.

———. 1970. *From the Many to the One.* Ithaca, N.Y.: Cornell University Press.

Althusser, Louis. 1970. *For Marx.* Translated by B. Brewster. New York: Vintage.

———. 1971. "Ideology and Ideological State Apparatuses." In *Lenin and Philosophy and Other Essays.* Translated by B. Brewster. New York: Monthly Review Press.

Arendt, Hannah. 1963. *Eichmann In Jerusalem.* New York: Penguin.

Aristotle. 1962. *Nicomachean Ethics.* New York: Macmillan.

Aronowitz, Stanley. 1986–87. "Theory and Socialist Strategy." *Social Text* 16 (Winter).

Arrighi, Giovanni. 1994. *The Long Twentieth Century.* New York: Verso.

Arroyo-Vázquez, Antonio Y. 2004. "Agonized Liberalism: The Liberal Theory of William E. Connolly." *Radical Philosophy* 127 (Sept.–Oct.).

Austin, J. L. 1961. "A Plea for Excuses." In *Philosophical Papers,* edited by J. O. Urmson and G. J. Warnock. Oxford University Press.

———. 1975. *How to Do Things with Words.* Cambridge, Mass.: Harvard University Press.

Avineri, Shlomo. 1968. *The Social and Political Thought of Karl Marx.* Cambridge: Cambridge University Press.

Bai, Matt, and Gregory Beals. 1999. "A Mayor under Siege." *Newsweek,* April 5.

Bales, Kevin. 1999. *Disposable People: New Slavery in the Global Economy.* Berkeley: University of California Press.

Balibar, Etienne. 1996. "What Is 'Man' in Seventeenth-Century Philosophy? Subject, Individual, Citizen." In *The Individual in Political Theory and Practice,* edited by Janet Coleman. Oxford: Clarendon.

Barry, Dan. 2000. "One Legacy of a 41-Bullet Barrage Is a Hard Look at Aggressive Tactics on the Street." *New York Times,* February 27.

Barthes, Roland. 1977. "The Death of the Author." In *Image, Music, Text.* Translated by S. Heath. New York: Hill and Wang.

Baudrillard, Jean. 2002. "L'Esprit du Terrorisme." Translated by D. Hohn. *Harper's Magazine,* February.

Bauman, Zygmunt. 1999. *In Search of Politics.* Stanford, Calif.: Stanford University Press.

Benhabib, Seyla, Judith Butler, Drucilla Cornell, and Nancy Fraser. 1995. "Feminism and Postmodernism." *Feminist Contentions: A Philosophical Exchange.* New York: Routledge.

Berlin, Isaiah. 1969. *Four Essays on Liberty.* Oxford University Press.

Black, Edwin. 2004. *War against the Weak.* New York: Four Walls Eight Windows.

Blair, Jayson. 1999. "Police Official Blames News Coverage for Murder Increase." *New York Times,* October 9.

Boggs, Carl. 1976. *Gramsci's Marxism.* London: Pluto.

Bové, Paul. 1992. *Mastering Discourse.* Durham, N.C.: Duke University Press.

Bowles, Samuel, and Herbert Gintis. 1986. *Democracy and Capitalism.* New York: Basic Books.

Brown, Wendy. 1995. *States of Injury.* Princeton, N.J.: Princeton University Press.

Bruford, W. H. 1975. *The German Tradition of Self-Cultivation.* Cambridge: Cambridge University Press.

Butler, Judith. 1987. *Subjects of Desire.* New York: Columbia University Press.

———. 1990. *Gender Trouble.* New York: Routledge.

———. 1993a. *Bodies That Matter.* New York: Routledge.

———. 1993b. "Endangered/Endangering: Schematic Racism and White Paranoia." In *Reading Rodney King/Reading Urban Uprising,* edited by R. Gooding-Williams. New York: Routledge.

———. 1995. "Contingent Foundations."In Seyla Benhabib, Judith Butler, Drucilla Cornell, and Nancy Fraser, *Feminist Contentions.* New York: Routledge.

———. 1996. "Universality in Culture." In *For Love of Country—Debating the Limits of Patriotism,* edited by M. Nussbaum. Boston: Beacon.

———. 1997a. *Excitable Speech.* New York: Routledge.

———. 1997b. *The Psychic Life of Power.* Stanford, Calif.: Stanford University Press.

———. 1997c. "Merely Cultural." *Social Text* 52–53 (Fall–Winter).

———. 2000a. "Competing Universalities." In Judith Butler, Ernesto Laclau, and Slavoj Žižek, *Contingency, Hegemony, Universality.* New York: Verso.

———. 2000b. "Restaging the Universal." In Judith Butler, Ernesto Laclau, and Slavoj Žižek, *Contingency, Hegemony, Universality.* New York: Verso.

———. 2000c. "Dynamic Conclusions." In Judith Butler, Ernesto Laclau, and Slavoj Žižek, *Contingency, Hegemony, Universality.* New York: Verso.

———. 2004. *Precarious Life.* New York: Verso.

———. 2005. *Giving an Account of Oneself.* New York: Fordham University Press.

Butler, Judith, and William Connolly. 2000. "Politics, Power and Ethics." *Theory & Event* 4.2.

Carr, Edward Hallett. 1961. *What Is History?* New York: Knopf.

Chabon, Michael. 2000. *The Amazing Adventures of Kavalier and Clay.* New York: Random House.

———. 2004. *The Amazing Adventures of the Escapist.* New York: Dark Horse.

Chatterjee, Deen, ed. 2004. *The Ethics of Assistance.* Cambridge: Cambridge University Press.

Cheever, Ben. 2001. *Selling Ben Cheever.* New York: Bloomsbury.

Clarke, Richard. 2004. *Against All Enemies.* New York: Free Press.

Cockburn, Alexander. 2000a. "Crazed Cops, 'Fallen Heroes.'" *The Nation,* February 14.

————. 2000b. "Cops and Dogs." *The Nation,* March 27.

Cohen, G. A. 1978. *Karl Marx's Theory of History: A Defence.* Princeton, N.J.: Princeton University Press.

————. 2001. *If You're an Egalitarian, How Come You're So Rich?* Cambridge, Mass.: Harvard University Press.

Coles, Romand. 1997. *Rethinking Generosity.* Ithaca, N.Y.: Cornell University Press.

Condit, Celeste Michelle. 1990. *Decoding Abortion Rhetoric.* Urbana: University of Illinois Press.

Conlon, Edward. 2004. *Blue Blood.* New York: Riverhead Books.

Connolly, William. 1993. *The Terms of Political Discourse.* 3d ed. Princeton, N.J.: Princeton University Press.

————. 1995. *The Ethos of Pluralization.* Minneapolis: University of Minnesota Press.

————. 2000. *Why I Am Not a Secularist.* Minneapolis: University of Minnesota Press.

————. 2002. *Neuropolitics.* Minneapolis: University of Minnesota Press.

Cooley, John. 1999. *Unholy Wars.* London: Pluto.

Coombes, John. 1978. "The Political Aesthetics of *The 18th Brumaire of Louis Bonaparte.*" In *1848: The Sociology of Literature,* edited by Francis Barker, John Coombes, Peter Hulme, Colin Mercer, and David Musselwhite. Colchester: University of Essex.

Copelon, Rhonda. 1990. "From Privacy to Autonomy: The Conditions for Sexual and Reproductive Freedom." In *From Abortion to Reproductive Freedom: Transforming a Movement,* edited by M. Gerber Fried. Boston: South End.

Crenshaw, Kimberlé, and Gary Peller. 1993. "Reel Time/Real Justice." In *Reading Rodney King/Reading Urban Uprising,* edited by R. Gooding-Williams. New York: Routledge.

Critser, Greg. 2003. *Fat Land.* New York: Houghton Mifflin.

Dallmayr, Fred. 1981. *Twilight of Subjectivity.* Amherst: University of Massachusetts Press.

Debord, Guy. 1977. *Society of the Spectacle.* Detroit: Black and Red.

Derrida, Jacques. 2001. *On Cosmopolitanism and Forgiveness.* Translated by Mark Dooley and Michael Hughes. New York: Routledge.

Diamond, Jared. 2005. *Collapse.* New York: Viking.

Disch, Lisa. 1999. "Judith Butler and the Politics of the Performative." *Political Theory* 27.4 (Aug.).

Douglas, Mary. 1992. *Risk and Blame.* New York: Routledge.

Dreyfus, Hubert, and Paul Rabinow. 1983. *Michel Foucault: Beyond Structuralism and Hermeneutics.* Chicago: University of Chicago Press.

Duden, Barbara. 1993. *Disembodying Women.* Translated by Lee Hoinacki. Cambridge, Mass.: Harvard University Press.

Dumm, Thomas. 1993. "The New Enclosures: Racism in the Normalized Community." In *Reading Rodney King/Reading Urban Uprising,* edited by R. Gooding-Williams. New York: Routledge.

Ehrenreich, Barbara. 2001. *Nickel and Dimed.* New York: Metropolitan Books.

————. 2004. "Owning Up to Abortion." *New York Times,* July 22.

Engels, Friedrich. 1978. "The Origin of the Family, Private Property, and the State." In *The Marx-Engels Reader.* 2d ed. Edited by R. Tucker. New York: Norton.

Feinberg, Joel. 1968. "Collective Responsibility." *Journal of Philosophy* 65.7. (Rpr. in French 1984).

———. 1970. *Doing and Deserving.* Princeton, N.J.: Princeton University Press.

Fischer, John Martin, and Mark Ravizza. 1993. *Perspectives on Moral Responsibility.* Ithaca, N.Y.: Cornell University Press.

———. 1998. *Responsibility and Control.* Cambridge: Cambridge University Press.

Flathman, Richard. 1992. *Willful Liberalism.* Ithaca, N.Y.: Cornell University Press.

Foucault, Michel. 1970. *The Order of Things.* New York: Vintage.

———. 1977a. *Discipline and Punish.* Translated by A. Sheridan. New York: Vintage.

———. 1977b. "Nietzsche, Genealogy, History." *Language, Counter-Memory, Practice.* Edited by D. Bouchard. Ithaca, N.Y.: Cornell University Press.

———. 1977c. "What Is an Author?" *Language, Counter-Memory, Practice.* Edited by D. Bouchard. Ithaca, N.Y.: Cornell University Press.

Frank, Thomas. 2001a. *One Market Under God.* New York: Random House.

———. 2001b. "Totally Extreme Taliban." *New York Times,* December 22.

Fraser, Jill Andresky. 2001. *White-Collar Sweatshop.* New York: Norton.

Fraser, Nancy. 1996. *Justice Interruptus.* New York: Routledge.

———. 1997. "Heterosexism, Misrecognition, and Capitalism: A Response to Judith Butler." *Social Text* 52–53 (Fall–Winter).

French, Peter, ed. 1984. *Individual and Collective Responsibility.* Rochester, Vt.: Schenkman Books.

———. 1998. *Collective and Corporate Responsibility.* New York: Columbia University Press.

Fried, Marlene Gerber. 1990. "Transforming the Reproductive Rights Movement: The Post-Webster Agenda." In *From Abortion to Reproductive Freedom: Transforming a Movement,* edited by M. Gerber Fried. Boston: South End.

Friedland, Amos. 2004. "Evil and Forgiveness: Transitions." *Perspectives on Evil and Human Wickedness* 1.4. Internet journal, www.wickedness.net/ejv1n4.htm, accessed 31 Oct. 2007.

Friedman, Thomas. 2000. *The Lexus and the Olive Tree.* New York: Anchor Books.

———. 2005. *The World Is Flat.* New York: Farrar, Strauss, and Giroux.

Fukuyama, Francis. 1992. *The End of History and the Last Man.* New York: New Press.

Gadamer, Hans-Georg. 1995. *Truth and Method,* 2d, rev. ed. Translated by J. Weinsheimer and D. Marshall. New York: Continuum.

Garrow, David. 1994. *Liberty and Sexuality.* New York: Macmillan.

Gibson-Graham, J. K. 1993. "Waiting for the Revolution, or How to Smash Capitalism While Working at Home in Your Spare Time." *Rethinking Marxism* 6.2.

———. 2007. *A Postcapitalist Politics.* Minneapolis: University of Minnesota Press.

Gibson-Graham, J. K., Stephen Resnick, and Richard Wolff, eds. 2000. *Class and Its Others.* Minneapolis: University of Minnesota Press.

———, eds. 2001. *Re/Presenting Class: Essays in Postmodern Marxism.* Durham, N.C.: Duke University Press.

Glaberson, William. 2003. "Turning to a Judge's Gavel to Strike a Blow at Terror." *New York Times,* September 14.

Goldberg, Jeffrey. 1999. "The Color of Suspicion." *New York Times Magazine,* June 20.

Gorney, Cynthia. 2004. "Gambling with Abortion." *Harper's Magazine,* November.

Haraway, Donna. 1997. *Modest_Witness@Second_Millennium.FemaleMan©_Meets_OncoMouse™.* New York: Routledge.

Hardt, Michael, and Antonio Negri. 1994. *Labor of Dionysus.* Minneapolis: University of Minnesota Press.

———. 2000. *Empire.* Cambridge, Mass.: Harvard University Press.

———. 2004. *Multitude.* New York: Penguin.

Hart, H. L. A. 1968. *Punishment and Responsibility.* Oxford: Clarendon.

Hartouni, Valerie. 1997. *Cultural Conceptions.* Minneapolis: University of Minnesota Press.

Harvey, David. 1999. *Limits to Capital.* New York: Verso.

Hegel, G. W. F. 1952. *Philosophy of Right.* Translated by T. M. Knox. Oxford: Oxford University Press.

———. 1977. *Phenomenology of Spirit.* Translated by A. V. Miller. Oxford: Oxford University Press.

Herbert, Bob. 2000. "At the Heart of the Diallo Case." *New York Times,* February 28.

———. 2004. "America's Abu Ghraibs." *New York Times,* May 31.

Hirschmann, Nancy. 1992. *Rethinking Obligation.* Ithaca, N.Y.: Cornell University Press.

Human Rights Watch. 1998. "Shielded From Justice: Police Brutality and Accountability in the United States." www.hrw.org/reports98/police, accessed 30 Oct. 2007.

Humboldt, Wilhelm von. 1969. *The Limits of State Action.* Edited by J. W. Burrow. Cambridge: University of Cambridge Press.

Jaggar, Alison. 1975. "Abortion and a Woman's Right to Decide." *Philosophical Forum* 5.1–2 (Winter).

———. 1998. "Regendering the U.S. Abortion Debate." In *Abortion Wars,* edited by R. Solinger. Berkeley: University of California Press.

Jameson, Fredric. 1981. *The Political Unconscious.* Ithaca, N.Y.: Cornell University Press.

———. 1988. "Cognitive Mapping." In *Marxism and the Interpretation of Culture,* edited by C. Nelson and L. Grossberg. Urbana: University of Illinois Press.

———. 1991. *Postmodernism, or, the Cultural Logic of Late Capitalism.* Durham, N.C.: Duke University Press.

Keenan, Alan. 1997. "The Beautiful Enigma of Radical Democracy." *Theory & Event* 1.3.

Kelley, Robin D. G. 2000. "'Slangin' Rocks. Palestinian Style' Dispatches from the Occupied Zones of North America." In *Police Brutality,* ed. J. Nelson. New York: Norton.

Kojève, Alexandre. 1969. *Introduction to the Reading of Hegel.* Translated by H. J. Nichols. Edited by A. Bloom. Ithaca, N.Y.: Cornell University Press.

Kymlicka, Will. 1991. *Liberalism, Community, and Culture.* Oxford: Oxford University Press.

LaCapra, Dominick. 1983. *Rethinking Intellectual History.* Ithaca, N.Y.: Cornell University Press.

Laclau, Ernesto. 1990. "The Impossibility of Society." *New Reflections on the Revolution of Our Time.* New York: Verso.

———. 2000a. "Structure, History, and the Political." In *Contingency, Hegemony, Universality,* by Judith Butler, Ernesto Laclau, and Slavoj Žižek. New York: Verso.

———. 2000b. "Identity and Hegemony." In *Contingency, Hegemony, Universality,* by Judith Butler, Ernesto Laclau, and Slavoj Žižek. New York: Verso.

Laclau, Ernesto, and Chantal Mouffe. 1985. *Hegemony and Socialist Strategy.* New York: Verso.

Landesman, Peter. 2004. "The Girls Next Door." *New York Times Magazine,* January 25.

Lavin, Chad. 2005. "Who Responds to Global Poverty?" *Social Theory and Practice* 31.1 (Jan.).

———. 2006. "Fear, Radical Democracy, and Theoretical Methadone." *Polity* 38.2 (Apr.).

Lawrence, Regina. 2000. *The Politics of Force.* Berkeley: University of California Press.

Lethem, Jonathan. 2003. *The Fortress of Solitude.* New York: Doubleday.

———. 2004. *Men and Cartoons.* New York: Doubleday.

Levison, Iain. 2002. *A Working Stiff's Manifesto.* New York: Soho.

Lewis, H. D. 1984. "The Non-Moral Notion of Collective Responsibility." In *Individual and Collective Responsibility,* edited by P. French. Rochester, Vt.: Schenkman Books.

Lipton, Eric. 2000. "From Pulpits to Politics, Angry Voices on Diallo." *New York Times,* February 28.

Locke, John. 1975. *An Essay Concerning Human Understanding.* Oxford: Clarendon.

MacKinnon, Catherine. 1989. *Toward a Feminist Theory of the State.* Cambridge, Mass.: Harvard University Press.

MacPherson, C. B. 1962. *The Political Philosophy of Possessive Individualism: Hobbes to Locke.* Oxford: Oxford University Press.

Mandel, Ernest. 1978. *Late Capitalism.* New York: Verso.

Mann, Patricia. 1994. *Micro-Politics.* Minneapolis: University of Minnesota Press.

Marable, Manning. 1983. *How Capitalism Underdeveloped Black America.* Boston: South End.

Markus, Gyorgy. 1986. "The Hegelian Concept of Culture." *Praxis International* 6.

Marx, Karl. 1970a. *Critique of Hegel's "Philosophy of Right."* Translated by A. Jolin and J. O'Malley. Cambridge: Cambridge University Press.

———. 1970b. *A Contribution to the Critique of Political Economy.* Edited by M. Dobb. New York: International.

———. 1973. *The Eighteenth Brumaire of Louis Bonaparte.* In *Surveys in Exile: Political Writings, Vol. 2,* edited by D. Fernbach. New York: Penguin.

———. 1977. *Capital.* Vol. 1, translated by B. Fowkes. New York: Vintage.

Marx, Karl, and Friedrich Engels. 1947. *The German Ideology.* Edited by R. Pascal. New York: International.

———. 1973. *Manifesto of the Communist Party.* In *The Revolutions of 1848: Political Writings, Vol. 1,* edited by D. Fernbach. New York: Penguin.

McClintock, Anne. 1995. *Imperial Leather.* New York: Routledge.

Meyler, Bernadette. 2002. "Does Forgiveness Have a Place? Hegel, Arendt, and Revolution." *Theory & Event* 6.1.

Mill, John Stuart. 1978. *On Liberty.* Indianapolis: Hackett.

Minnow, Martha. 1998. *Between Vengeance and Forgiveness.* Boston: Beacon.

Mouffe, Chantal. 1992. "Democratic Politics Today." In *Dimensions of Radical Democracy,* edited by Chantal Mouffe. New York: Verso.

Nealon, Jeffrey. 1998. *Alterity Politics.* Durham, N.C.: Duke University Press.

Negri, Antonio. 1991. *Marx Beyond Marx.* Translated by H. Cleaver, M. Ryan, and M. Viano. New York: Autonomedia.

Newman, Karen. 1996. *Fetal Positions.* Stanford, Calif.: Stanford University Press.

Nussbaum, Martha. 1999. "The Professor of Parody." *New Republic* 220.8 (Feb. 22).

Oakley, Ann. 1984. *The Captured Womb.* Oxford: Blackwell.

———. 1992. *Social Support and Motherhood.* Oxford: Blackwell.

———. 1993. *Women, Medicine, and Health.* Edinburgh: Edinburgh University Press.

Oaks, Laury. 2000. *Smoking and Pregnancy.* New Brunswick, N.J.: Rutgers University Press.

O'Neill, Onora. 1985. *Faces of Hunger.* London: Allen and Unwin.

———. 1996. *Towards Justice and Virtue.* Cambridge: Cambridge University Press.

Parenti, Christian. 2000. *Lockdown America.* New York: Verso.

Parks, Evelyn. 1970. "From Constabulary to Police Society: Implications for Social Control." *Catalyst* 5 (Summer).

Petchesky, Rosalind Pollack. 1984. *Abortion and Woman's Choice: The State, Sexuality, and Reproductive Freedom.* New York: Longman.

———. 1987. "Fetal Images: The Power of Visual Culture in the Politics of Reproduction." *Feminist Studies* 13.2 (Summer).

Peters, Ted. 1997. *Playing God: Genetic Determinism and Human Freedom.* New York: Routledge.

Podhoretz, John. 1999. "The War on Rudy Giuliani." *Weekly Standard,* April 5.

———. 2000. "Racing to Indict Rudy's Cops." *Weekly Standard,* March 6.

Pogge, Thomas. 2002. *World Poverty and Human Rights.* Cambridge: Polity Press.

————. 2004. "'Assisting' the Global Poor." In *The Ethics of Assistance*, edited by Deen Chatterjee. Cambridge: Cambridge University Press.

Pollan, Michael. 2002a. "Power Steer." *New York Times Magazine*, March 31.

————. 2002b. "When a Crop Becomes King." *New York Times*, July 19.

————. 2006. *The Omnivore's Dilemma*. New York: Penguin.

Popper, Karl. 1945. *The Open Society and Its Enemies*. 2 vols. New York: Harper and Row.

Press, Andrea, and Elizabeth Cole. 1999. *Speaking of Abortion*. Chicago: University of Chicago Press.

Rashbaum, William. 2000. "Marchers Protest Diallo Verdict, Taunting Police along the Way." *New York Times*, February 27.

Rawls, John. 1993. *Political Liberalism*. New York: Columbia University Press.

————. 1999. *The Law of Peoples*. Cambridge, Mass.: Harvard University Press.

Read, Jason. 2003. *The Micro-Politics of Capital*. Albany, N.Y.: SUNY Press.

Reaves, Brian, and Matthew Hickman. 2002. "Police Departments in Large Cities, 1990–2000." Washington: U.S. Department of Justice.

Reich, Robert. 1991. *The Work of Nations*. New York: Knopf.

————. 2001. *The Future of Success*. New York: Knopf.

Reston, James, Jr. 1995. "The Monument Glut." *New York Times Magazine*, September 10.

Ripstein, Arthur. 1999. *Equality, Responsibility, and the Law*. Cambridge: Cambridge University Press.

Rorty, Richard. 1989. *Contingency, Irony, and Solidarity*. Cambridge: Cambridge University Press.

Ross, Andrew. 2002. *No Collar*. New York: Basic Books.

Russell, Katheryn. 1999. *The Color of Crime*. New York: New York University Press.

Sadovi, Carlos. 2003. "Families of the Dead: For Inmate, a Second Chance; for Victims' Families, More Grief." *Chicago Sun-Times*, January 12.

Saletan, William. 1998. "Electoral Politics and Abortion." In *Abortion Wars*, edited by R. Solinger. Berkeley: University of California Press.

————. 2004. *Bearing Right*. Berkeley: University of California Press.

Savulesco, Julian. 2001. "Procreative Beneficence: Why We Should Select the Best Children." *Bioethics* 15.5–6.

Scheffler, Samuel. 2001. *Boundaries and Allegiances*. Oxford: Oxford University Press.

Schlosser, Eric. 2001. *Fast Food Nation*. Boston: Houghton Mifflin.

Schmidt, James. 1981. "A Paideia for the 'Bürger als Bourgeois': The Concept of 'Civil Society' in Hegel's Political Thought." *History of Political Thought* 2.3 (Winter).

Seery, John. 1988. "Deviations: On the Difference between Marx and Marxist Theorists." *History of Political Thought* 9.2 (Summer).

Serrano, Richard, and Tracy Wilkinson. 1992. "All Four in King Beating Acquitted." *Los Angeles Times*, April 30.

Shafer, Jack. 2005. "Sex Slaves, Revisited." *Slate* (June 7). www.slate.com/id/2120331/, accessed 30 Oct. 2007.

Shapiro, Bruce. 1999. "The Guns of Littleton." *The Nation,* May 17.

Shklar, Judith. 1984. *Ordinary Vices.* Cambridge, Mass.: Harvard University Press.

———. 1989. "The Liberalism of Fear." In *Liberalism and the Moral Life,* edited by N. Rosenblum. Cambridge, Mass.: Harvard University Press.

———. 1990. *The Faces of Injustice.* New Haven, Conn.: Yale University Press.

Shrage, Laurie. 2003. *Abortion and Social Responsibility.* Oxford: Oxford University Press.

Singer, Peter. 1972. "Famine, Affluence, and Morality." *Philosophy and Public Affairs* 1:2.

——— 2004. "Outsiders: Our Obligations to Those beyond Our Borders." In *The Ethics of Assistance,* edited by Deen Chatterjee. Cambridge: Cambridge University Press.

Solinger, Rickie, ed. 2001. *Beggars and Choosers.* New York: Hill and Wang.

Sontag, Susan. 2004. "Regarding the Torture of Others." *New York Times Magazine,* May 23.

Spar, Debora. 2006. *The Baby Business.* Boston, Mass.: Harvard Business School Press.

Sparks, Holloway. 1997. "Dissident Citizenship: Democratic Theory, Political Courage, and Activist Women." *Hypatia* 12.4 (Fall)

Stevens, Jacqueline. 1999. *Reproducing the State.* Princeton, N.J.: Princeton University Press.

Stoler, Ann Laura. 1991. "Carnal Knowledge and Imperial Power." In *Gender at the Crossroads of Knowledge: Feminist Anthropology in the Postmodern Era,* edited by M. di Leonardo. Berkeley: University of California Press.

Strawson, Peter. 1959. *Individuals: An Essay in Descriptive Metaphysics.* London: Methuen.

———. 1974. *Freedom and Resentment, and Other Essays.* London: Methuen.

Taylor, Charles. 1975. *Hegel.* Cambridge: Cambridge University Press.

Thomson, Judith Jarvis. 1971. "A Defense of Abortion." *Philosophy and Public Affairs* 1.1.

Toobin, Jeffrey. 2002. "The Unasked Question." *The New Yorker,* March 6.

Tribe, Laurence. 1990. *Abortion: The Clash of Absolutes.* New York: Norton.

Verdeja, Ernesto. 2004. "Derrida and the Impossibility of Forgiveness." *Contemporary Political Theory* 3.

Vološinov, V. N. 1973. *Marxism and the Philosophy of Language.* Translated by L. Matejka and I. R. Titunik. Cambridge, Mass.: Harvard University Press.

Vondung, Klaus. 1988. "Unity through *Bildung*: A German Dream of Perfection." *Journal of Independent Philosophy* 5–6.

Wambaugh, Joseph. 2000. "A Few—Only a Few—CRASH Cowboys Took an Outlaw Path." *Los Angeles Times,* March 8.

Warren, Mark. 1996. "What Should We Expect from More Democracy? Radically Democratic Responses to Politics." *Political Theory* 24.2.

White, Hayden. 1973. *Metahistory.* Baltimore, Md.: Johns Hopkins University Press.

White, Stephen. 1991. *Political Theory and Postmodernism.* Cambridge: Cambridge University Press.

———. 2000. *Sustaining Affirmation.* Princeton, N.J.: Princeton University Press.

Williams, Bernard. 1973. *Problems of the Self.* Cambridge: Cambridge University Press.

———. 1981. *Moral Luck.* Cambridge: Cambridge University Press.

———. 1993. *Shame and Necessity.* Berkeley: University of California Press.

———. 1995. *Making Sense of Humanity.* Cambridge: Cambridge University Press.

Williams, Raymond. 1977. *Marxism and Literature.* Oxford: Oxford University Press.

Wilson, James Q. 1992. "Crime, Race, and Values." *Society* 30.1

Wilson, James Q., and Richard Herrnstein. 1985. *Crime and Human Nature.* New York: Simon and Schuster.

Wolin, Sheldon. 1960. *Politics and Vision.* Boston: Little, Brown.

———. 1996. "Fugitive Democracy." In *Democracy and Difference,* edited by Seyla Benhabib. Princeton, N.J.: Princeton University Press.

Wood, Ellen Meiksins. 2003. "A Manifesto for Global Capital?" In *Debating Empire,* edited by Gopal Balakrishnan and Stanley Aronowitz. New York: Verso.

Wrightsman, Lawrence. 1987. *Psychology and the Legal System.* Monterey, Calif.: Brooks/Cove.

Young, Iris. 2003. "From Guilt to Solidarity: Sweatshops and Political Responsibility." *Dissent* (Spring).

———. 2004. "Responsibility and Global Labor Justice." *Journal of Political Philosophy* 12.4 (Dec.).

———. N.d. "Political Responsibility and Structural Injustice." Unpublished manuscript.

Zaitchik, Alan. 1981. "Viability and the Morality of Abortion." *Philosophy and Public Affairs* 10.1.

Zakaria, Fareed. 2003. *The Future of Freedom.* New York: Norton.

Žižek, Slavoj. 1989. *The Sublime Object of Ideology.* New York: Verso.

———. 2000. "Class Struggle or Postmodernism? Yes, Please!" In *Contingency, Hegemony, Universality,* by Judith Butler, Ernesto Laclau, and Slavoj Žižek. New York: Verso.

———. 2001. "What Can Lenin Tell Us about Freedom Today?" *Rethinking Marxism* 13.2 (Summer).

———. 2004. *Revolution at the Gates: Žižek on Lenin, the 1917 Writings.* New York: Verso.

Index

abortion: autonomy provision and, 104–5; causality, individual will and, 115–16, 148n4; as choice, 105–7; competing rights impacting, 107, 112; as consumer freedom, 116; heroism ethos and, 112, 115; liberal feminists v. postliberal feminists and, 113–14; liberalism limitations regarding, 115–18; metonymy and, 111–12; overview of, xix; postliberal viewpoint about, 113–14, 116–19; privacy v. choice shift in, 106–8, 147n1; privatization of, 103–4; pro-choice argument and, 108–16; social variability and, 118–19
Abu Ghraib military torture, ix–x
administrative massacres, 128–29
agency, 83–87
Althusser, Louis, 21, 47–48, 132
antisweatshop movement, 75–78, 145n20
Arendt, Hannah, xii, 53
Aristotle, 6, 7
Arrighi, Giovanni, 65, 67
Ashcroft, John, 99
Austin, J. L., 48
authoritarianism, 72, 144n15

Balibar, Étienne, 7
Baraka, Amiri, 87, 98
Barthes, Roland, 41
Bearing Right (Saletan), 106
Berlin, Isaiah, 16, 38
Between Vengeance and Forgiveness (Minnow), 127
Bildung concept, 23–25, 38–41, 70, 132, 140n5, 140–41n6
bin Laden, Osama, 98–99
biological determinism, 85
Brown, Wendy, 107, 114
Bush, George W., 98–99
Butler, Judith: Althusser influence on,

47–49; condition v. event recognition in theories of, 99; on Hegel, 42; Hegel v., 43; on identity politics, 64; liberalism v., 46–47, 54–56; Marxism relationship to, xviii; Marx v., 37–38, 43, 54; overview, xiv, xv, 37–38; postliberal tradition and, 50–53; psychoanalysis in, 49–50; on sovereignty, 131; urban violence responsibility viewpoints of, 90, 93, 146n10; on vulnerability, 129–32. *See also* performativity theory
Butts, Calvin O. III, 88, 98

capitalism: globalization and, 67–70; historical varieties of, 65; as metonym, 66, 68, 143n8; multiplicity of current forms of, 65–66, 143n6; overview, xviii–xix; totalizing theories of, 66–68
class politics, 70, 72, 144n12
Cockburn, Alexander, 88
Cole, Elizabeth, 115
Columbine High School massacre, 86, 121–23, 131
compensation, 123–24
Connolly, William, xiii, 5, 6, 16, 18, 90
Copelon, Rhonda, 104–5, 107–8
criminal justice. See police brutality

Dallmayr, Fred, 20–21, 22, 53
Debord, Guy, 28–29
Derrida, Jacques, 125–26
determinism, 85, 86
Diallo, Amadou, xix, 14, 82–84, 85, 87–90
Disch, Lisa, 29
Douglas, Mary, xiv

Ehrenreich, Barbara, 115–16
The Eighteenth Brumaire of Louis Bonaparte (Marx). *See* Marx, Karl
Empire (Hardt and Negri), 68–70, 72–75

CHAD LAVIN is an assistant professor of political science at Virginia Tech. He has published articles in *New Political Science, Polity, Rethinking Marxism,* and *Social Theory and Practice.*

The University of Illinois Press
is a founding member of the
Association of American University Presses.

———————————————————

Composed in 9/13 ITC Stone Serif
with ITC Stone Sans display
at the University of Illinois Press
Manufactured by Thomson-Shore, Inc.

University of Illinois Press
1325 South Oak Street
Champaign, IL 61820-6903
www.press.uillinois.edu